"Today, we lack metrics to know if we are winning or losing the global war on terror. Are we capturing, killing or deterring and dissuading more terrorists every day than the madrassas and the radical clerics are recruiting, training and deploying against us? ... Is our current situation such that 'the harder we work, the behinder we get'? ... The cost-benefit ratio is against us! Our cost is billions against the terrorists' costs of millions." **U.S. Defense Secretary Donald Rumsfeld, in an e-mail to his four closest advisors, on October 16th, 2003, seven months after the start of the invasion of Iraq, and two years after the 9/11 attacks. This e-mail was leaked to *USA Today*, which published it on their front page October 22nd.** The questions the e-mail raised hadn't been discussed, debated, and analyzed, at the top levels of the Bush Administration, prior to planning the invasion of Iraq, nor even prior to invading the country. This e-mail started that questioning/debate.

"What is our purpose here? Was this invasion because of weapons of mass destruction, as we have so often heard? If so, where are they? ... I once believed that I was serving for a cause – 'to uphold and defend the constitution of the United States'. Now I no longer believe that; I have lost my conviction, as well as my determination." **Tim Predmore, U.S. soldier fighting in Iraq, in a commentary published in the *Guardian*, September 19, 2003, and *Peoria* (Illinois) *Journal Star*, August 24, 2003.**

"I am very concerned in the coming days we will find we killed many civilians as well as Iraqi irregular fighters. I would feel great if all the people we killed were all enemy guerrillas, but I can't say that. We are probably turning many Iraqis against us." **Signed, "A COMBAT LEADER" in Iraq; message posted at www.sftt.org, on December 1, 2003**

Arabs Blame United States for Baghdad Bloodbath

By Edmund Blair, Tue. Oct. 28, 2003

CAIRO (Reuters) – Arabs Tuesday saw the latest bombings in Baghdad as an unholy bloodbath. But ... most agreed Washington had only itself to blame for the chaos.

They said the United States had failed to provide Iraqis with enough security to prevent the devastating suicide attacks in the capital that killed 35 people ...

"America is responsible for all deaths in Iraq. It is responsible for the emergence of gangs and thieves because the absence of leadership like Saddam's was filled with chaos and anarchy," said [one typical Arab interviewed]. ...

New Iraq 'well on way to becoming Islamic state'

The *Telegraph* (London)
By David Rennie in Washington *(Filed: 29/10/2003)*

The United States is failing in its mission to create a secular, overtly pro-Western Iraq, a leading adviser to the American administrator Paul Bremer said yesterday.

Instead, ... Noah Feldman, a leading American expert in Islamic law, told The Daily Telegraph ... the new, democratic Iraq appears bound to be an Islamic state. ...

Dr Feldman served as senior constitutional adviser to the Coalition Provisional Authority, working closely with Mr Bremer. ...

IRAQ WAR:
THE TRUTH

Eric Zuesse

DELPHIC PRESS
Whiting, Vermont

Delphic Press
P.O. Box 66
Whiting, VT 05778
delphicpress@yahoo.com

Special and appreciative acknowledgment is made to the following, as sources credited in this book, for rights (including "fair use" rights) to reprint here excerpts/quotations from works they have previously published: *USA Today, Peoria Journal Star,* Reuters, *Telegraph, Denver Post,* NPR, CNN, alternet.org, Creators Syndicate, *Newsweek, Guardian, Observer, Los Angeles Times, Financial Times, The Herald, Sydney Morning Herald, The New York Times, Christian Science Monitor, New York, New Yorker,* CBS, *Washington Post, Mercury News,* Knight Ridder, *Independent, Daily Express, Frankfurter Algemeine Zeitung,* bodyandsoul .blogspot.com, *U.S. News & World Report,* thehill.com, PBS, Lehrer NewsHour, Fox News, *New Statesman,* NBC, findlaw.com, *Times* of London, Agence France Presse, Pew Research Center, *Extra!, Editor & Publisher,* BBC, *Register Star, The Age, Sunday Herald, Time, Wall Street Journal, Business Week, American Journalism Review,* Associated Press, ABC, KRON-TV, *Journal Sentinel,* United Press International, *Economist, Toronto Star,* WNTA-AM, Scripps Howard, CNBC, *San Francisco Chronicle,* riverbend.blogspot.com, christian-aid.org, Boston *Globe,* maketh emaccountable.com, *St. Petersburg Times, The Star, Le Monde, St. Louis Business Journal,* pipa.org, *Nation,* slate.com, *Washingtonian, New York Post,* pointer.org, *Newsday,* buzzflash.org, *Village Voice,* salon.com, *N.Y. Review of Books, Philadelphia Inquirer,* Project Censored, *Irish Times,* Walker & Co., jayware.com, Hillsdale College, Penguin Putnam Inc., CBN, workingforchange.com, Inter Press Service, Word Publishing, 4religious-right.info, Livin gston.net, *Christianity and Civilization, New American,* fpif.org, beliefnet.com, *Stern,* Gallup Organization, *Readers Digest, Toronto Globe and Mail,* eurolegal.org, *CounterPunch,* iraq-today.com, Beirut *Daily Star, Washington Times,* Human Rights Watch, *Seattle Post-Intelligencer, Chicago Tribune, San Diego Union Tribune.*

This book is, to a large extent, a critical commentary upon press coverage of the invasion of Iraq. Thus, these quotations are essential to the work. Any reader who wishes to find out more about a subject covered here is encouraged to consult the original referenced document in print or on the internet; and all of these sources are available on the internet.

Publishers Cataloging-in-Publication Data:
Zuesse, Eric, 1943-
Iraq war: the truth / Eric Zuesse; foreword by Emad Aysha. — 1st ed.
p.   cm.
Includes bibliographical references and index.
ISBN 0-9628103-1-2 (cloth: alk. paper)
1. Iraq War, 2003. 2. Journalism—Objectivity.
3. Weapons of mass destruction—Iraq.
DS79.76.Z84 2004
956.7044/3 22

CONTENTS

Foreword

Eric Zuesse is one of those rarities in American journalism in the post-9/11 era of media conformity, an independent investigative journalist, winner of the 1982 Mencken Award for the Year's Best Investigative News Report, and a historian to boot. Journalists tend to lack historical depth, an affliction almost as bad as not being independent, treating everything as new and not rooted in the cataclysms of the past. This makes them incapable of connecting the dots of the here and now with what has gone on before. Zuesse does more than expose the lies that the Bush administration and its allies in the mass media propagated to go to war with Iraq. He exposes the fact that the current phase of world history is very similar to that of the inter-war period that gave birth to the new breed of ideologically motivated, mass-driven, popular imperialism, commonly known as Fascism and Nazism.

Many have already called Bush a Fascist and compared him to Hitler because of his callous disregard for international law in the run-up to the war. Many have also made comparisons between the Bush propaganda machine and the Nazi propaganda machine. But Zuesse goes further, seeing a parallel between the ideological mania that drove Hitler, and the motives behind Bush's attack on Iraq. He documents it well. My comments here do not repeat that documentation, but will, I hope, round it out.

Hitler's conquests were not driven just by the vested interests of the arms manufacturers and media moguls who funded his party, seeing in military Keynesianism a solution to Germany's economic woes and to their own financial crisis. Hitler and the whole Nazi movement existed long before these cartelists took them up and helped popularize their agenda. Nazism was driven by the maniacal dream of world domination and white supremacy that had been made possible by the example of British imperialism and its ideological rationale, the "White Man's Burden." Nazism was part of the whole imperial project of post-Columbian Europe, where the white race had finally taken over the world, with ascendancy shifting from the Spaniards to the Portuguese, to the Dutch, to British, and then finally to the Germans. In this current phase of history, the torch has been handed to a group in America who believe it is their country's destiny to rule the world, to set up a "Fourth Reich."

Zuesse does an excellent job cataloguing and analyzing the role of the Christian right in pushing Bush towards the objective of world domination, so I'd merely like to supplement his account here by focusing a little more on the neo-conservatives, which he mentions but views as being less central. The neo-con agenda and their motives behind the policies they advocate are far more complex than the Christian right. Ideologically, the neo-cons used to be Marxist leaning left-wingers from the Democratic Party who deserted and went to the opposite ideological extreme during the Vietnam War for a variety of reasons. They believed the Democrats couldn't fathom the resilience and inherent evil of Communism, while they abhorred the cultural and moral relativism of the 1960's. This set the neo-cons on a dual path of advocating an American empire abroad and conservative cultural renewal at home, through such myths as the frontier ethic and the manifest destiny of the American people. There is a fair amount of profiteering from war in neo-con circles, as the examples of Richard Perle and James Woolsey demonstrate, but the consensus among researchers – especially those that know neo-cons directly – is that they genuinely believe that Pax Americana is a good thing. The American peace perpetuated through an American empire will be a good thing for the world because the world is an inherently evil place, while America is inherently benign. As for their domestic agenda, they hope to use warfare and foreign enemies as rallying cries to transform the American public culturally and morally in line with their ideological preferences. That means no to multiculturalism, abortion, homosexuality, and secularism, things they have in common with the Christian right.

Neo-conservatives hold many important posts in the Bush Administration. The original neo-con is generally considered to have been the anti-modernist philosopher Leo Strauss, who advocated a Platonic version of theocracy, even though theocracy directly contradicts the U.S. constitutional doctrine of separation of church and state. Thomas Jefferson made this point about the First Amendment, saying it had erected a "wall of separation between church and state." The neo-cons argue that the First Amendment's religion clause was intended only to prevent politics interfering in religion, such as the establishment of a national church. But no such reservations exist, they claim, when it comes to religion interfering in politics. Shadia Drury has noted that Irving Kristol, among other neo-conservatives, argued that separating church and state was the biggest mistake made by the founders of the U.S. Republic. Bernard Lewis, one of the favored Middle East experts of the neo-cons, goes even farther and describes the separation of church and state as a "Western Disease" (see Henry C K Liu, "From Cold War to Holy War," *Asia Times*, May 13, 2003).

The neo-cons also seem to be the main agents behind the Bush administration's deception of the public, sparing Christian fanatics the moral dilemma of having to perpetrate that lie. Strauss, on their interpretation, believed in the right of leaders to deceive those that are led, because normal people couldn't handle the truth that Socrates discovered so many years ago: that there is no truth, that all gods are false, and that all customs and laws are relative. So much for the neo-con disdain of relativism! According to Shadia Drury, author of 1999's *Leo Strauss and the American Right*, Strauss believed that "some are fit to lead, and others to be led," while "those who are fit to rule are those who realize there is no morality and that there is only one natural right, the right of the superior to rule over the inferior" (quoted in Jim Lobe, "Neocons Dance a Strauss Waltz," *Asia Times*, May 9, 2003). He also believed that political elites had every right to deceive their citizens, because the average person is not intelligent enough to realize the good that would come from decisions made by their government.

Sadly, I'm too much of a passive observer and social scientist to do more than give you a brief account of the forces responsible for the madness we're all suffering from since Bush came to power and several passenger planes hit the World Trade Center and the Pentagon. I'll have to leave combating this madness to Eric Zuesse. He's fighting the good fight, telling the world about the mass deceptions that stand behind the invasion of Iraq.

Emad El-Din Aysha, PhD
Cairo, Egypt.

Prologue

"No one believes that U.S. intelligence got it so wrong that Saddam Hussein actually had none of the weapons or manufacturing capabilities the Bush administration claimed. Some of the stocks may have been destroyed or taken out of the country. Others may still be hidden in the dark corners of Hussein's former regime." **Michael Riley in the *Denver Post*, in his April 18, 2003, news article: "Stakes High for White House in Arms Search."**

"They will certainly find a stack of rockets filled with chemical and biological weapons." **Terry Taylor, a U.N. weapons inspector during the mid-1990's, interviewed on American National Public Radio's Weekend Edition, April 19th.**

"There's not any doubt that he had weapons of mass destruction. The question is, where are they?" **U.S. Senator Orrin Hatch, on CNN's Late Edition, May 25th.**

* * *

Supposedly, we invaded Iraq on account of that country's weapons of mass destruction (WMD). Was this just a smokescreen – an elaborate lie? Was it, to the contrary, a monumental failure of intelligence? Or was it simply true?

Despite the official investigations into the Iraq war, millions of people throughout the world are still asking themselves, "Whatever happened to 'Saddam's weapons of mass destruction'?" And decreasing numbers seem to be answering this question confidently on such assumptions as were here quoted from Michael Riley, Terry Taylor, and Orrin Hatch.

Perhaps British Prime Minister Tony Blair was just following the lead of American President George W. Bush, but clearly Mr. Bush was determined, for his own reasons, to overthrow Iraqi leader Saddam Hussein (he eagerly called it "regime change"). In order to do so, Mr. Bush had to persuade the American people that Iraq retained massive quantities of WMD. Like the three quoted individuals, the majority of Americans were persuaded by President Bush, by Secretary of State Colin Powell, and by others in the U.S. Administration, to think that Saddam Hussein still possessed these banned weapons. This book will document that the WMD rationale behind the invasion was, in fact, merely a pretext, and will further document what the real reason was behind the invasion of Iraq.

About half of the American people, according to polls, mistakenly also believed that Saddam was behind the 9/11 terrorist attacks. The source of this widespread false belief was likewise, as will be shown, the Bush Administration. It will be documented here that polls right after the 9/11 attacks indicated that only 3% of Americans believed that Saddam's regime was connected to the terrorist assaults. No evidence has been presented since that time, to indicate that Saddam, or any of his people, were in any way involved in those attacks against the United States. It will be shown that the sole basis for the spread of this false belief to half of the American people was the same Bush Administration disinformation campaign that deceived the U.S. Congress, and public, into believing in the continued existence of huge quantities of Iraqi WMD.

The reason behind this disinformation campaign will be made clear. To boil this down right at the start: President Bush, knowing that none of the above allegations about Saddam were true, nonetheless needed a pretext with a color of international law for his invasion, which was actually driven by ulterior motives, as we will soon see. He needed such a pretext because an invasion in obvious violation of international law wouldn't win so much as a single "coalition" partner, and because American opinion polls at the time showed that Mr. Bush's electorate was opposed to going it alone in Iraq. President Bush, in other words, needed to pick up at least one invasion partner (he tried, but failed, to win many others); and, in order to do that, he felt compelled to lie about Saddam's weapons of mass destruction (WMD), and to say that he possessed conclusive proof that massive quantities of these banned weapons still existed in Iraq, even though his Administration actually possessed no such evidence at all – none whatsoever, it will be shown.

Some Americans, right after the invasion, were persuaded to ignore this issue by the Administration's ostentatious celebrations of "victory," such as by dressing up the President in all the regalia of a bomber pilot (although he himself had avoided combat duty and even went AWOL from the National Guard for an entire year during the Vietnam War, as has been well documented; e.g., see www.awolbush .com or http://democrats.com/display.cfm?id=154). This invasion of

Iraq was portrayed as a repeat of World War II, with Saddam Hussein standing in for Adolf Hitler. Mr. Bush was presented in the role of a modern-day Winston Churchill.

However, on December 28, 1998, Anthony H. Cordesman, at the Center for Strategic and International Studies, had estimated that Iraq's entire annual military budget was only $1.3 billion, an amount equivalent to about one two-hundredth of what the U.S. was then spending. Pitting a 200-pound fighter against a one-pound opponent can give no authentic cause for national military pride, when such an opponent ends up being squashed. That's why heavyweight fighters are never pitted against bantamweights.

Obviously, if this war was a cynical political stunt aimed to appeal to macho fools, in order to jack back up the poll-ratings of a President whose poll-numbers had sunk back down to his pre-9/11 political doldrums, when a miserable U.S. economy was the dominant national issue, then the invasion was hardly an honorable undertaking, much less any authentic cause for military strutting. But, as we shall see, President Bush had other and, unfortunately, even less savory, reasons for this invasion, besides its being politically highly opportune, given America's ailing economy and macho culture.

In order to understand why Mr. Bush lied, and why he invaded Iraq, it's essential to understand the historical background, the actual framework for the invasion. These are facts that the U.S. Administration would rather that the American public not think about in the present context – or, better yet, not even know at all. And many Americans don't know these facts, because the country's surging political right wing makes certain they're not taught to the country's children in high school history, civics, and social studies courses.

For example, one teacher who merely assigned his students to debate both the pro-war and the anti-war arguments, Tom Treece, at Spaulding High School in Barre, Vermont, attracted so much negative attention from the Republican national talk-show host Rush Limbaugh, that the unfortunate fellow almost lost his job after the local school superintendent received hate mail from across the country. Many news stories were published about this incident; one can be found at www.commondreams.org/views03/0510-06.htm.

Americans are raised to be political naïfs. Then we vote. A prospective American dictator would be delighted.

An old adage, which is often falsely attributed to Thomas Jefferson, says, "Eternal vigilance is the price of liberty." Conservatives like Mr. Limbaugh – and Mr. Bush – thrive by its being ignored. But the public-at-large suffer. It is for them that this book is written.

Chapter 1
Bush's Nemesis: International Law

"We must make clear to the Germans that the wrong for which their fallen leaders are on trial is not that they lost the war, but that they started it. And we must not allow ourselves to be drawn into a trial of the causes of the war, for our position is that no grievances or policies will justify resort to aggressive war. It is utterly renounced and condemned as an instrument of policy." **U.S. Supreme Court Justice Robert Jackson, Chief Prosecutor at the Nuremberg International Military Tribunal, Aug. 12, 1945, explaining the reason for the trials.**

* * *

George W. Bush has asserted numerous times that the United States should not be subject to international law at the International Criminal Court or World Court. He has said numerous times that the U.S. should not have to meet the legal demands of the Kyoto Protocol on Global Warming, nor of a number of other international agreements that his Administration resolutely refuses to sign. The Bush Administration has also been judged by the World Trade Organization to be acting in violation of agreements that the United States, under earlier presidents, joined. This President has also unilaterally abrogated and declared null and void the Antiballistic Missile Treaty and other international agreements that previous U.S. administrations signed. These acts in opposition to international law by the Bush Administration make clear the low priority this American President places upon the demands of international law.

President Bush's hostility toward international law has not gone unnoticed. For example, Princeton University's Richard Falk, a world-famous authority on international law, and the author of numerous standard books on the subject, was so disturbed at the phenomenon, that on December 20, 2001, he posted, at www.alternet.org/

story.html?StoryID=12134, a blistering commentary titled "Bush's International Charade," citing a litany of this President's historically unprecedented actions virtually trashing international law. Dr. Falk especially condemned George W. Bush's unilateral and "blithe dismissal of the 1972 Antiballistic Missile Treaty," to which the U.S. had been a prime signatory, and he observed that this Administration's hostility toward international law "has been evident ever since they set up shop."

However, regardless of what any particular President might or might not happen to think, international law inevitably imposes certain diplomatic constraints upon even a hostile national leader. The U.S., powerful though it is, still has to work with other countries. Furthermore, few Americans are willing to become international pariahs. President Bush recognizes that international relations have domestic political consequences, which can affect his chances of re-election. Thus, he must at least appear to adhere to certain basic international norms, even if he doesn't agree with them.

One of the most widespread international norms is a deep-rooted principle from international law: invading a nation that is not invading your own, and that's not invading any other nation, is prohibited. In civil wars such as Kosovo, there has been debate about how this principle ought to be applied. However, Iraq was not engaged in any civil war. Consequently, the only legal pretext that was available for Mr. Bush to launch an attack against Iraq was another basic principle from international law: national self-defense. This self-defense principle raised the issue of Iraq's possible continuing possession of weapons of mass destruction (WMD), because every nation is permitted to possess regular weapons for its own defense, but Iraq (on account of its having invaded Kuwait in 1991) had been prohibited by the U.N. to hold WMD. Furthermore, in the wake of the 9/11 attacks against the United States, any Iraqi WMD would have constituted an especially grave issue for American self-defense.

Mr. Bush took advantage of these facts, and in doing so, he was heeding some lessons of recent history. One of these lessons concerned Adolf Hitler. Another pertained to the Chilean dictator Augusto Pinochet.

The German people in 1939 were no different from people in other countries, in that they wanted no part in attacking a country that was not attacking them. However, Hitler very much wanted to attack Poland. He therefore hoodwinked his people into supporting a German invasion of Poland – the invasion that started World War II. Hitler fabricated "evidence" to make Germans fear they were being attacked by Poland. His method was to dress some of his S.S. troops in Polish uniforms and to have these men fake an attack on the German radio station at Gleiwitz on August 31, 1939. Paul Craig Roberts astutely noted the historical parallel, in his American syndicated column on March 19th of 2003, while American and British troops were in the process of invading Iraq. He said that, "Following the faked attack, Hitler announced: 'This night for the first time Polish regular soldiers fired on our territory.' ... The German High Command called the German invasion of Poland a 'counterattack.'" The duped German people supported the invasion of Poland, because they had been deceived into believing that it was in Germany's self-defense. Similarly, on account of Saddam's alleged WMD, Americans supported the invasion of Iraq, falsely believing this to be in America's self-defense.

As has been mentioned earlier, the post-9/11 question in America, of whether Saddam Hussein still retained huge stores from his former stockpiles of chemical and biological weapons, presented a convenient pretext, if a pretext were wanted, for the U.S. President to launch an invasion of Iraq; and so, President Bush made it the pretext – he talked up that issue constantly, in speech after speech. And not only did he raise the question of whether Saddam still retained these huge weapons stockpiles, but he insisted that he had seen conclusive evidence that Saddam did.

"Saddam Hussein is a threat to the American people. ... He has weapons of mass destruction. ... He has trained and financed al Qaeda-type organizations before, al Qaeda and other terrorist organizations." **George W. Bush, Press Conference, March 6, 2003.**

"Intelligence gathered by this and other governments leaves no doubt that the Iraq regime continues to possess and conceal some of the most lethal weapons ever devised." **Bush, March 17th, announcing the invasion of Iraq.**

These repeated emphatic assertions by the Bush Administration are the reason why, even in the midst of the attack against Iraq, on April 12th, a *Newsweek* poll showed that 67% of Americans felt that, "It is very important to find convincing evidence of banned chemical or biological weapons" there. That very same day, the (British) *Guardian* was discordantly reporting under the headline, "Weapons Teams Scour Iraq: Secret units in desperate hunt for banned arsenal," that, "No banned weapons have so far been found." This story noted, moreover, that United Nations officials were "infuriated" that the United States, which had actually aborted the U.N.'s weapons-search in order to invade Iraq, was now leading its own "search."

Several commentators were cynically predicting that the U.S., desperate to manufacture "evidence" to provide legal justification for its invasion, might actually plant banned weapons in Iraq, aiming to expose these weapons as "Saddam's stockpile." This is the reason the international community wanted to send U.N. inspectors back into Iraq, and to keep away American "inspectors," who would be answering to Mr. Bush instead of to the U.N. The people of the world were skeptical of George W. Bush, even if the people of America were not.

Indeed, an online poll of readers (which ended when the war started) at www.time.com/time/europe/gdml/peace2003.html (the European edition of *Time* magazine) showed that, of the 706,842 respondents, 87% thought that President Bush's United States was "the greatest danger to world peace in 2003," and Iraq and North Korea were each voted only a 6.5% threat; many other polls likewise showed that George W. Bush was overwhelmingly the most hated and despised head of state in the entire world. Even a broadly representative and scientific March 11th poll by ITV Channel 4 in Britain showed that, by a margin of 45% to 38%, the people in America's ally, the U.K., believed that George W. Bush was a greater threat to world peace than was Saddam Hussein, the official "enemy."

Still, President Bush won his war against Saddam Hussein, and no conqueror has ever been convicted, or even prosecuted, for violating international law. However, the recent prosecution, decades after the fact, of the retired Chilean dictator Augusto Pinochet, for war crimes that he was alleged to have committed while in office, greatly increased the international liability of national leaders, so Mr. Bush is not entirely safe. President Bush claimed that Saddam's weapons of mass destruction justified, under international law, invasion of Iraq by the "coalition." And so, we are now coming to the American President's moment of truth, which is likewise a challenge for his British follower, Prime Minister Tony Blair.

President Bush would perhaps not have wished it to work out this way; but, occasionally, even an American President doesn't have the choices he would prefer. Even an American President has to play the hand that he's dealt.

The big problem for Mr. Bush lay with his great nemesis, international law. Unfortunately for the President, the only basis in international law that was available to the United States as supposedly authorizing an invasion of Iraq, consisted of United Nations Security Council resolutions that called for Iraq to eliminate its weapons of mass destruction. The final such resolution, 1441, passed the Council unanimously on November 8, 2002. In order to win passage of this crucial resolution, the U.S. was forced to acknowledge publicly that no war against Iraq would be acceptable to the U.N. unless authorized in a future U.N. resolution for that explicit purpose; in other words, no "automaticity" existed in 1441. Consequently, America's U.N. Ambassador, John Negroponte, said, on November 8th in the *Los Angeles Times*, "There's no 'automaticity' and this is a two-stage process, and in that regard we have met the principal concerns that have been expressed for the resolution."

America's U.N. Ambassador went on to make this commitment unambiguously clear in anyone's mind by saying: "Whatever violation [by Iraq] ... is [subsequently] judged to exist, will be dealt with in the [Security] Council, and the Council will have an opportunity to consider the matter before any other action is taken."

However, that commitment to the world was not kept by the U.S. The basis upon which 1441 was approved by the U.N. turned out to be this false American promise: it turned out to have been a lie.

Its having been a lie didn't negate the commitment on the basis of which 1441 was approved; the U.S. here was simply violating it. The United States (and its allies Britain and Australia) invaded Iraq without authorization from the U.N. to do so.

Since the increasingly rightist American public cares far less about international law than do the publics elsewhere, this illegality, per se, didn't much bother U.S. President G.W. Bush. It presented no real political problem for him; it didn't jeopardize his support among what all the polls indicated were a uniquely aggressive American people. (Similarly, the German people, during the 1930's, were standouts for their aggressiveness, and for similar reasons: they had been deceived.)

However, it did naturally greatly disturb British Prime Minister Blair, whose public was very concerned about international legality; he thus sought counsel about whether there would be any way to go to war legally without a further U.N. resolution concerning Iraq. The result of that inquiry was reported in the *Financial Times*, on October 6, 2002, which said that, "Tony Blair ... has been warned by his attorney-general that military action against Iraq to force a regime change would breach international law." The *FT* went on to note that the Prime Minister had been advised, "Were the government to breach international law, it could find itself before the International Court of Justice facing charges for breaching the UN charter." (The same man, who so advised the Prime Minister, nominally reversed himself on the very eve of war, March 17th, merely in order to minimize the Prime Minister's international legal vulnerability for a war to which the Prime Minister was already committed.) Scotland's *The Herald* further reported, on March 5th, an unfavorable opinion from the Prime Minister's wife, the lawyer Cherie Blair: "Blair's legal chambers ['Matrix Chambers'] dealt an embarrassing blow to the government yesterday after lawyers said military action with Iraq would be a clear violation of international law."

Although America's domestically popular President had already publicly expressed his contempt for the International Court of Justice, and had adamantly refused to have America join the International Criminal Court (sometimes also called the "World Court"), the British Prime Minister did not similarly have the political option to thumb his nose at international law and opinion. That's why Mr. Blair had assured his British public, only the prior month, that Britain "will always act in accordance with international law." When he subsequently joined Mr. Bush in invading Iraq, he likewise broke his promise to the British people.

U.N. Secretary-General Kofi Annan warned, on March 10th, "If the U.S. and others were to go outside the Council and take military action it would not be conformity with the Charter."

Here's why: The U.N. Charter states: "All members shall refrain ... from the threat or use of force against the territorial integrity or political independence of any state." It asserts that force may be used only in self-defense or if approved by the Security Council. Since force had not been approved by the Security Council, the only remaining legal basis for an invasion of Iraq would be self-defense. However, self-defense is a justification only "if an armed attack occurs." Therefore, so long as Saddam's regime continued to refrain from "an armed attack," no invasion of Iraq would be legal. This reality had, in fact, served as a great restraining-influence upon Saddam during recent years, especially given the precariousness of his regime after the early 1990's. But now, G.W. Bush was determined to do away with that restraining influence, and with Saddam.

During the run-up to the war, international-law experts in many countries issued public declarations that an invasion would be illegal. At www.the-rule-of-law.com, 317 American professors of law signed a joint declaration, dated October 22, 2002, and headlined "A US War Against Iraq Will Violate US and International Law." A body of 43 international-law specialists announced in Australia's *Sydney Morning Herald* on the following February 27th, "an invasion of Iraq could constitute a war crime." 16 top international-law experts in the U.K. signed a joint letter to the *Guardian* published March 7th, saying, "there is no justification under international law for the use of military force against Iraq." And Reuters also reported, at the war's start March 19th, that, "Justice Richard Goldstone of South Africa's Constitutional Court, who was the lead prosecutor in U.N. tribunals on the Rwanda genocide and killings in the former Yugoslavia, said the United States risked undermining international law."

This situation possessed profound historical irony. The U.S., in more liberal times, when it was led by Presidents from the Democratic Party, was the chief country that had instituted international law in Nuremberg Germany after World War II, and yet the U.S. was now acting to destroy international law, not just by expressing contempt for it and for the World Court itself, but by actively violating it through attacking Iraq.

Chapter 2
Bush's Lies

As was mentioned, the U.S. supposedly invaded Iraq in order to rid that country of "its weapons of mass destruction." In fact, the White House Press Secretary, Ari Fleischer, at a press briefing during the war, on April 10, 2003, said unequivocally, "That is what this war was about and it is about." At a subsequent briefing, May 14th, after a month's more of failure to find such weapons, Mr. Fleischer answered another reporter's question, "What are the chances that you were misled?" by saying, simply, "No," and, "We remain confident in all the statements we've made about it." The White House further argued that the Administration was carrying out the collective will of the American people in this matter. Thus, an unnamed "Senior Administration Official" was quoted by the White House press office a few months earlier, on January 22nd, as saying, "The fundamental issue is, does the country support the use of force to disarm Saddam Hussein," and he cited numerous polls showing that the American people were, indeed, favorable to invading in order to "disarm" Saddam. Those important comments appear in a "Background Briefing by a Senior Administration Official Aboard Air Force One En Route St. Louis, Missouri," published online by the U.S. Department of State, at http://usinfo.state.gov/regional/nea/iraq/text2003/0122maj.htm.

Astoundingly, as if the American people are ignoramuses, the President even went so far as to include in his speech to an audience at Northern Virginia Community College, after the war, on June 17, 2003, the following remarkable passage: "And we acted in Iraq, as well. We made it clear to the dictator of Iraq that he must disarm. We asked other nations to join us in seeing to it that he would disarm, and he chose not to do so, so we disarmed him." Was this "we disarmed him" supposed to be a comic punch line? No: to the contrary, the President went on to criticize "a lot of revisionist history now going on," presumably from the numerous commentators who were by then raising the question of where Saddam's weapons of mass destruction resided. That criticism, coming from this President, certainly ought to have made a good punch line, because if anything was actually "revisionist history," it was Mr. Bush's own claim that "we disarmed him" of weapons we had never even *found*. But instead of this "revisionist history" comment eliciting laughter from the audience, the transcript here, at www.whitehouse.gov/news/releases/2003/06/20030617-3.ht ml, mysteriously indicates "(applause)." Could the White House perhaps have brought in canned applause? Or else: Who, or even *what*, was actually sitting in those seats?

There were, of course, other reasons also cited for invading Iraq, even if not reasons under international law. One was to free the Iraqi people from Saddam's dictatorship. But the world is full of barbaric dictators, and George W. Bush had quite prominently and roundly condemned "nation building," such as freeing the Yugoslavian peoples from dictators and murderers like Slobodan Milosevich and Ratko Mladic. Mr. Bush had even belittled his immediate predecessor, President Bill Clinton, for doing that, and he criticized Presidential candidate Al Gore for having supported this Clinton policy. Nor was Mr. Bush now propagandizing to invade Zimbabwe and to remove its dictator, Robert Mugabe, whose thugs were robbing and murdering white farmers and thereby bringing ruin to the entire Zimbabwean economy. Nor was Mr. Bush propagandizing to invade Burma, so as to relieve its people of a brutal military dictatorship that was permitting its officers to rape women from minority ethnic groups and to perform sadistic acts upon these victims. A *New York Times* story, on May 12, 2003, was headlined "Burmese Women Are Reporting Systematic Rapes by Military," and indicated that a study had shown "that 25 percent of the rapes ended in death and that 83 percent were committed by officers." Yet Mr. Bush's propaganda machine avoided any suggestion that the United States must engage in "regime change" in *those* countries. And there were and are likewise many other tyrants whom President Bush remains satisfied *not* to remove.

---

from: http://bodyandsoul.blogspot.com/2003_06_01_bodyandsoul_archive.html

Saturday, June 28, 2003:

So the democracy in Iraq thing didn't work out too well, did it?

Something I heard Tom Friedman say before the war came to mind this morning. He said -- casually, the horrible thing about Friedman is the nonchalance he summons while saying things like this -- that we might discover after the war that Iraq could only be governed by a thug, and that we might have to be "the new Saddam Hussein."

From this morning's <u>Washington Post</u>:

"<u>U.S. military commanders have ordered a halt to local elections and self-rule in provincial cities and towns across Iraq, choosing instead to install their own handpicked mayors and administrators, many of whom are former Iraqi military leaders.</u>"

Now I really do understand the dilemma here. A popular election that brings a bunch of clerics with no respect for freedom or human rights to power is no accomplishment and not much (if any) of an improvement on the last thug's reign. I don't want to see a phony democracy rushed in. But, just out of curiosity, what exactly have we changed in Iraq?

"<u>Ten weeks into the occupation, the cities and towns outside of Baghdad are largely administered by former Iraqi military and police officers and people who had close ties to the Baath Party. Iraqi generals and police colonels, for example, are now mayors of a dozen cities, including Samarra, Najaf, Tikrit, Balad and Baqubah.</u>

"<u>The U.S. military contends that these people have been vetted and were not in leadership positions under the old government or associated with crimes it committed.</u>"

Sorry, but I find that last part pretty difficult to believe. We're purging Baath Party members from <u>universities</u> and the <u>oil industry</u> (*hmmmmmmm...*) -- two places where you'd expect to find plenty of people who just went along to keep their jobs -- but we continue to get along just fine with the Baathist police and military, and even install them in power.

Pardon my ignorance, but in a police state, aren't the police likely to be the people you most have to worry about? If a country is a military monster -- Iraq *was* a dangerous military monster, right? A threat to the entire world? -- are generals likely to be uncompromised?

Something stinks here.

by jeannedorleans@aol.com

But he convinced the American people to support invading Iraq to get rid of Saddam Hussein's WMD. How did the Bush Administration manage to convince Americans?

Here's how Gary Wills answered this question in *The New York Times Magazine*, during the war, on March 30th: "Bush has been very good at fooling the American people into thinking that Saddam Hussein was behind the attack on the World Trade Center in New York and the Pentagon in Washington and that he is an ally and supplier of

Al Qaeda, [and] that eliminating him is the best way to keep terrorism from our shores." Mr. Wills simply asserted this, without offering evidence to support it. However, the charge he made there is a very serious one, and it deserves to be documented, not just because it is serious, but because it is true.

Thus, here is the documentation proving Mr. Wills's severe charge that President Bush and his Administration lied to the American people in order to manipulate the nation into supporting and committing the war crime of invading Iraq. A major part of this documentation consists of proof that the Bush Administration lied to the public about possessing evidence proving that Iraq retained massive stockpiles of weapons of mass destruction.

The President's speech to the country on March 17th effectively declared war by giving Saddam 48 hours to rid his land of its (assumed) weapons of mass destruction. Mr. Bush argued that in the age of international terrorism, to wait until America's enemies "have struck first is not self-defense, it is suicide." The accusation that Mr. Wills made, that "Bush has been very good at fooling the American people into thinking that Saddam Hussein was behind" the 9/11 terrorist attacks, is here resoundingly confirmed by the President's unmistakable implication that Saddam posed the threat of a recurrence of the 9/11 terrorist attacks and *must therefore* be removed.

The President's speech was also in line with a similar characterization of his argument for war, which Linda Feldmann of the *Christian Science Monitor* had made earlier, on March 14th. She perceptively noted that, "In his prime-time press conference last week, which focused almost solely on Iraq, President Bush mentioned Sept. 11 eight times. He referred to Saddam Hussein many more times than that, often in the same breath with Sept. 11." She went on to observe that several polls were showing approximately half of the American public (44% in a Knight-Ridder poll, 51% in a CNN poll, 42% in a CBS/NYT poll, and 66% in a Pew poll) believed such things as that Mr. Hussein was personally involved in the Sept. 11 attacks and that most or some of the attackers were Iraqis, even though in the immediate aftermath of those attacks only three percent of Americans had believed that way (as was mentioned here at the outset). She further noted that none of the attackers actually had any connection at all with Iraq. She might also have pointed out that no evidence was ever provided by the Bush Administration (or anyone else) linking Al Qaeda to Saddam's regime, even though the Administration made numerous unsupported allegations of such a connection, the "evidence" for which was always subsequently proven bogus. (Remarkably, a *Newsweek* poll by Princeton Survey Research Associates, taken on July 24th and 25th, which was well after the invasion, reported 72% of Americans answering "Yes," and only 17% answering "No," when asked, "From what you've seen or heard in the news, do you believe that Saddam's regime in Iraq was harboring al Qaeda terrorists and helping them to develop chemical weapons?") She further cited a study (at http://people-press.org/rep orts/print.php3?ReportID=162) that had shown that "there is a strong correlation between those who see the Sept 11-Iraq connection and those who support going to war." This, too, supports Wills's charge, by demonstrating that the sneaky and factually false insinuations in the President's speeches were having their intended effect: they were deceiving the American public into supporting an invasion. Long after the invasion, obscure news stories appeared in Britain and elsewhere (most Americans never saw them) reporting that Anthony Cordesman, in notes from his interview with President Bush's chief WMD inspector in Iraq, David Kay, November 14, 2003 (which are available online at www.csis.org/features/031114current.pdf), recorded: "No evidence of any Iraqi effort to transfer weapons of mass destruction or [other] weapons to terrorists." Even the President's own WMD inspector, David Kay, *privately* acknowledged this.

However, such direct fear-mongering by the Administration to a gullible American public did not constitute the entirety of their sales-pitch for invading Iraq; this lie that American aggression would be good was supported also by the indirect "domino theory," which held that the fall of the dictatorship in Iraq will lead to the fall of dictatorships throughout the Arabic and Islamic worlds, and will thus, supposedly, yet again, help to bring about greater American safety against future terrorist attacks. Here, too, the Administration was keeping important truth secret from the American public. As Greg Miller revealed in the *Los Angeles Times* on March 14th, "A classified State Department report expresses doubt that installing a new regime in Iraq will foster the spread of democracy in the Middle East, a claim President Bush has made in trying to build support for a war." The classified report – which still remains "not publicly disclosed" but which was leaked by State Department officials who, presumably, didn't like the Administration's deception of the American public concerning this – called that domino theory simply "not credible."

Now, with this as background, we come to the key question of Iraq's supposed weapons of mass destruction (WMD). Why did the Bush Administration settle upon the WMD allegation as its justification for invading? There were actually two factors that virtually forced this pretext upon the Administration, like it or not, and regardless of what the actual main motivation for the invasion might have been: First, the entire international legal case justifying an invasion of Iraq consisted of this core issue of Iraqi WMD, since U.N. Resolutions 678, 687, and 1441, all dealt with that central matter. There was simply no other legal basis available to invade Iraq. That's critically important. And, second, the WMD problem was also basic to the alleged danger of Iraqi terrorism. The fear the American people felt, and which was shown in many polls, was that Al Qaeda terrorists could perpetrate something that would dwarf 9/11 if only Iraqi WMD were to become involved in the attack. If the American people did not believe that Iraq definitely possessed massive quantities of WMD, then they would almost certainly have opposed invading Iraq.

Consequently, Mr. Bush, being already determined for other reasons to invade Iraq, had to deceive the American – and especially the more legalistically interested British – people into sharing his (faked) certainty that Iraq possessed huge stocks of WMD. After all, the U.N. weapons inspectors were then working inside Iraq, and so, nothing less than *certainty* about this on Mr. Bush's part could conceivably have justified his kicking them out and invading. (For otherwise, the inspectors should simply have been left there, to do their job and disarm Saddam if he needed to be disarmed.)

Mr. Bush, needing Britain's participation, therefore had to argue that Iraq possessed banned weapons, even if it was not true. There was simply no other way for him to get the "coalition" partner he had to have in order to win the support of the American people to invade. (*All* polls showed that Americans were unwilling to invade *alone*.) The President did this not only by referring to Iraq's possession of large volumes of WMD as being a matter of certainty, but also by his offering "evidence" to "prove" it. As *The New York Times* editorially summed up the Bush charges on April 9th (relying primarily upon Mr. Bush's State of the Union Address on January 28th): "In making the case for the invasion, the administration suggested that Iraq's arsenal might be quite large: up to 500 tons of nerve and mustard agents, and 30,000 munitions capable of delivering them; materials to produce 25,000 liters of anthrax and 38,000 liters of botulinum toxin; and mobile or underground laboratories to make germ weapons." The *NYT* evidently (for reasons that will be made clear momentarily) didn't take the Administration's charges of the existence of an Iraqi nuclear program to have been sufficiently credible to mention. But all of the President's speeches had asserted, as a certainty, that the total volumes of Saddam's banned weapons stockpiles were huge, even if the exact quantities were still in doubt.

The denouement came just before the invasion. In two big blows, the Administration's credibility on WMD was crushed. One pillar upon which the Administration's case for war stood was that their allegations about Iraq's WMD were founded upon "vital intelligence" that had been obtained from Iraqi defectors: above all, from General Hussein Kamel, who had been the head of Iraq's WMD program, and who was a son-in-law of Saddam himself. However, late in February, Glen Rangwala of Cambridge University obtained, and made public in the *Washington Post* on March 1st (a tidbit of it appearing online February 24th) the notes of the actual classified briefing with the late General Kamel, dated August 22, 1995. Far from asserting that Saddam's regime was hiding WMD, Kamel actually said, "I ordered destruction of all chemical weapons; all weapons, biological, chemical, missile, nuclear, were destroyed." In direct contradiction of this, U.S. Vice President Dick Cheney, on August 26, 2002, had said of General Kamel's defection, that it exposed Saddam's *continuing* "secret weapons programs," and so "should serve as a reminder to all that we often learn more as the result of defections than we learned from the inspection regime itself." Mr. Cheney intentionally sowed seeds of doubt there, in the minds of the American people, about the effectiveness of the U.N.'s inspections-program. Thus, "Against that background," he continued, "a person would be right to question any suggestion that we should just get inspectors back into Iraq, and then our worries will be over." Cheney and Bush both emphasized this. However, Mr. Cheney's statements could only have been lies, because he had (and *acknowledged* that he had) seen what the defector actually said. Furthermore, the U.N. inspections regime itself is what had discovered the large volumes of WMD that remained in Iraq, and then destroyed them, in very large quantities. Although Mr. Cheney cited General Kamel's testimony as authority that Iraq still has WMD, the U.N. inspectors involved with the Kamel interrogation had concluded, "You have to take what he says with a grain of salt." Mr. Cheney was aware of *those* facts, too. Vice President Cheney's references to the Kamel testimony were thus all fraudulent. Should such a man be serving as the U.S. Vice President?

An even bigger blow to the Administration's case was revealed on March 7th, when the independent British press agency, Reuters, headlined, "'Proof' That Iraq Sought Uranium Is Fake," reporting that U.N. weapons inspectors had dismissed as forgeries intelligence documents that the U.S. and British governments were claiming to contain strong evidence that Iraq was importing uranium from Niger and was developing nuclear weapons. When asked about the matter two days later, Secretary of State Colin Powell casually dismissed it by saying simply, "if that information is inaccurate, fine." He offered no explanation, other than to assert that the U.S. Government had received the documents "in good faith, not participating ... in any way in any falsification activities." But the selective use of intelligence data to scare people into supporting an invasion is certainly a "falsification activity," and the use of forged documents while simultaneously ignoring contrary and much sounder evidence, is certainly selective use of intelligence data. Thus, "falsification activity" was undoubtedly present here.

This outrageous statement by Mr. Powell nonetheless went unquestioned by an American press that considers in bad taste the assumption that a high official of the U.S. Government is, or even might be,
lying. However, that's not in bad taste at all; it is instead the very
essence of professional journalism, even though it's almost absent
from the American major media. Executives in the American press fail
to consider journalistically unprofessional the mere *assumption* that
U.S. officials are truthful, even though that assumption is, indeed,
journalistically unprofessional. No *authentically* professional journalist *trusts* the word of *anyone*, least of all the word of a politician or any
other type of sales-person. The essence of journalistic professionalism
is: first, to distrust the statements from everyone (and especially from
sales-people, which all politicians, even the best of them, are); second,
to know how to test them; third, to perform the required tests; and,
fourth, to report only the confirmed facts. But, par for the course in the
United States, Mr. Powell's assertions were *not* tested by the requisite
follow-up questions, and so his lies were passed to the U.S. public as if
they were truths – as if the journalists' reports of Mr. Powell's statements constituted news not *only* about what he was saying, but also
about what was true. Mr. Powell was simply assumed *not* to be lying.
That's unprofessional journalism, but it's virtually universal in America's major media.*

---

*   One article provided unusually direct testimonial confirmation of this point. It
appeared in *New York* magazine on August 11th, and was titled and sub-headed, "The
Media at War: Did journalists working the Iraq beat botch the story of the year? At a
forum hosted by New York Magazine, The Guardian, and the New School, we turned
the microphone on the press." The first question discussed was, "Did the American
media sell out in covering this war?" Everyone except Michael Elliott of *Time* magazine
thought so. Next was, "Did the British press do better?" Everyone except Mr. Elliott
thought so. Then came, "The British vs. the American Press," in which the BBC's John
Kampfner crucially commented, "The impression I have from the U.S. media is that it
regards the people in authority, the people in government, as good men who need to be
proved otherwise. In Britain, we work from the assumption that they need to prove to
us that they're telling the truth." Mr. Elliott responded, "I would say that the attitude
that right now is very present in the British press – that a politician is a lying bastard
unless proven otherwise – has gotten to the stage where it is really, really dangerous.
Nobody elected us." Unfortunately, there was no follow-up to Mr. Elliott's actually *anti-
democratic* rejoinder. His basic, authoritarian, assumption was that the function of
journalists/reporters in a democracy should be limited by virtue of their lacking the
authority to challenge authority: only someone in authority has the right to question
what a person who possesses authority is saying. This falsehood is disastrous in a
democracy – especially when *journalists* accept it. A democracy cannot even exist
unless everyone has the right, and the authority, to question authority. To exercise this
right and authority is not a privilege at all in a democracy: not for the citizenry, and
certainly not for journalists. In fact, this is the most solemn professional *obligation* of
journalists in any democracy; and an aim of the following pages will be to demonstrate
that this was precisely the obligation that the American major media catastrophically
failed in regards to the Iraq war. I'll also explain *why* they failed it.

None of the journalists at that time covering Secretary Powell questioned him even about the directly contradictory earlier statement he had made in "Press Remarks with Foreign Minister of Egypt Amre Moussa," on February 24, 2001: "He [Saddam] has not developed any significant capability with respect to weapons of mass destruction. He is unable to project conventional power against his neighbors. So in effect, our policies have strengthened the security of the neighbors of Iraq, and these are policies that we are going to keep in place." To find this assertion by Powell, reporters need only to have looked on the State Department's own website: www.state.gov/secretary/rm/2001/ 933.htm.

What is even more incriminating is that President Bush's State of the Union Address on January 28th had highlighted these very same Niger forgeries as "proof" that Saddam Hussein's regime was still developing nuclear weapons. For six months, the Bush Administration was prominently citing this forged "evidence," without challenge by the U.S. press, as "proof" that Saddam still retained hidden banned weapons. Then finally, Seymour Hersh revealed to the public, in the *New Yorker* on March 27th, that U.S. CIA Director George Tenet, and Secretary of State Powell, in late September of 2002, had persuaded the Senate Foreign Relations Committee of Iraq's nuclear-weapons threat, citing this faked "evidence," and Mr. Hersh noted that, "The testimony from Tenet and Powell helped to mollify the Democrats, and two weeks later the resolution passed overwhelmingly, giving the President a congressional mandate for a military assault on Iraq." So, the President got his war okayed by the Congress on the basis, largely, of a forgery. Fuehrer Bush's re-dressed "Polish invaders" against Gleiwitz. And all other of his "evidence" similarly consisted of distortions and outright lies. Thus, when Mr. Powell said, "if that information is inaccurate, fine," he was casually dismissing not just *any* lie, but a crucial lie that had deceived Democrats – some of whom are Presidential candidates – into supporting, and essentially politically committing themselves to, this President's war policy. That helped to shape not only the immediate Senate vote approving the invasion, but the coming 2004 U.S. presidential race. Consequently, the *Independent* headlined about the Democratic Senator, and subsequently also U.S. Presidential candidate, John Kerry, on June 20, 2003, "Bush 'Misled Every One of Us', Says Rival for White House." Should a man like Mr. Powell, evidently with no conscience about truth, and obviously no practical respect for democracy and for democratic process, have been serving as the U.S. Secretary of State?

Numerous other "facts," asserted by the Bush Administration as "proving" Iraq's continuing WMD program, were also demonstrable lies, as documented at www.walden3.org, and elsewhere. For example,

Secretary Powell's U.N. speech mentioned a supposed Al Qaeda "poison factory" and training camp in northern Iraq, but actually this facility was in an area of the country no longer under the Hussein regime's control, and the Islamic fighters training there were not affiliated with Al Qaeda. Moreover, as the *Observer* reported about that camp on February 9th, under the banner, "Revealed: truth behind US 'poison factory' claim," nothing like a "poison factory" existed there; the charges were a tissue of distortions and outright fabrications.

Item after item of "evidence" that President Bush, Vice President Cheney, Secretary of State Powell, and others in the Bush Administration cited repeatedly as "proving" that Saddam Hussein's regime still possessed enormous quantities of WMD, were fraudulent. Not a single item of such "evidence" turned out to be authentic. Furthermore, Cambridge's Dr. Rangwala wrote an article in the *Independent* on June 1st, titled "The Lies that Led Us into War," which detailed repeated blatant misquotations that had been made of U.N. weapons inspectors' findings and reports. For example, U.N. inspectors estimated "that Iraq produced 1.5 tonnes of VX [nerve poison] before 1990," and that the toxin was of a kind "that lasted only six to eight weeks," but "US and British leaders repeatedly referred to" these 1.5 tons of VX as unaccounted for and a current and continuing Iraqi WMD threat. In fact, the White House had most prominently cited these 1.5 tons of VX on January 23, 2003, which was well over a decade after this poison would have expired. Obviously, the Bush Administration had read *both* of these facts; yet they chose to cite *only* the insignificant fragment that would deceive and frighten the public.

From such repeated lies, one might conclude that the U.N. weapons inspectors must have been furious at the American Administration when their inspection mission was aborted by President Bush; and they indeed were. CBS TV News correspondent Mark Philips reported on February 20th that, "The inspectors have become so frustrated trying to chase down unspecific or ambiguous U.S. leads that they've begun to express that anger privately in no uncertain terms. U.N. sources have told CBS News that American tips have led to one dead end after another. ... So frustrated have the inspectors become that one source has referred to the U.S. intelligence they've been getting as 'garbage after garbage after garbage.'" Similarly, newsman Dan Stuber was datelined March 18th in the (San Jose, California) *Mercury News*, under the head: "Nuclear inspectors reportedly angry: Checking false U.S. leads wasted time, source says."

These U.N. inspectors had worked very hard, and in retrospect, had actually been extremely effective at rooting out Iraq's WMD, while those weapons still, in fact, existed. Perhaps an isolated WMD cache remains yet to be discovered, perhaps not; but certainly, there doesn't exist in Iraq the vast WMD program that the Bush Administration was assuring everyone that they knew to a certainty to be there. Like the American public, the U.N. inspectors were deceived by the Bush Administration's repeated assurances of certainty that these vast WMD stockpiles still existed, and these inspectors therefore expected to find U.S.-supplied leads to be productive – but they weren't. None of them were. Mr. Stuber reported, "As United Nations nuclear inspectors flee Iraq, some of them are angry at the Bush Administration for cutting short their work, bad-mouthing their efforts and making false claims about evidence of weapons of mass destruction. ... None of the nuclear-related intelligence trumpeted by the administration has held up to scrutiny, inspectors say. From suspect aluminum tubes to aerial photographs to documents – revealed to be forgeries – that claim to link Iraq to uranium from Niger, inspectors say they chased U.S. leads that went nowhere."

And, of course, there were also the British frauds, such as were reported on February 5th via the BBC, "Leaked Report Rejects Iraqi Al-Qaeda Link: There are no current links between the Iraqi regime and the Al-Qaeda network, according to an official British intelligence report seen by BBC News." This information had been kept secret, and contradicted British Government pronouncements. The *Guardian*, two days later, bannered "UK War Dossier a Sham, Say Experts." This reported that, "Downing Street was last night plunged into acute international embarrassment after it emerged that large parts of the British government's latest dossier on Iraq – allegedly based on 'intelligence material' – were taken from published academic articles, some of them several years old" (and thus not *current* data on Iraqi WMD).

The U.N. weapons inspectors weren't playing games; they were not amateurs, either; they were, in fact, carefully selected and experienced professionals, who were trying their professional best to confirm the intelligence leads that they had received, from the United States, and from other sources. But none of those leads led to banned weapons. Didn't this say something, then, about the quality of the "information" that the U.S. Administration, and its British "poodle," actually possessed?

And yet the U.S. Administration kept on saying that it had absolute proof that great quantities of these weapons still existed in Iraq. How could President Bush claim to be certain that these huge stockpiles still existed, if all "evidence" he had about the matter was fraudulent? If Mr. Bush wasn't bald-facedly and intentionally lying about his being certain, then why did each and every one of his leads end up being simply bogus? How could he have even possibly been certain, as he claimed, of the validity of "evidence" that, time and again, ended up being proven not only false but fraudulently false? Was Mr. Bush actually that stupid? But if he was, then why didn't he just say, at some point, "I've been fooled by my people; time and again the evidence I've been acting on has turned out to be fraudulent, and I'm furious about it and am firing those people; I won't bring about massive death and destruction in Iraq on the basis of such mere lies," and thus free himself from guilt? He didn't fire these employees *even* after the fraud revelations were made public.

There is only one possible reason: it was President Bush himself who was lying; he knew that he was doing so, and his team were doing exactly what he had instructed them to do – lie to the public, cite mere allegations as if they were established facts, in order to fool the American and British publics into supporting an invasion. In fact, *New York Times* columnist Nicholas D. Kristof reported, on May 6th, that people who had actually been involved in the two most important falsehoods – concerning the alleged uranium from Niger, and the testimony from Hussein Kamel – told him that from the outset, the White House had been informed in no uncertain terms that these "facts" were bogus, and yet the Administration cited them, and continued to cite them, as conclusive "proof" regardless. Adding confirmation to this, Jonathan S. Landay, of Knight Ridder Newspapers, datelined from Washington on June 13th under the head, "White House Was Warned of Dubious Intelligence, Official Says," and reported, "A senior CIA official, who spoke on the condition of anonymity, said the intelligence agency informed the White House on March 9, 2002 – 10 months before Bush's nationally televised speech – that an agency source who had traveled to Niger couldn't confirm European intelligence reports that Iraq was attempting to buy uranium from the West African country. Despite the CIA's misgivings, Bush said in his State of the Union Address: 'The British government has learned that Saddam Hussein recently sought significant quantities of uranium in Africa.'"

Mr. Bush's falsehoods were clearly lies. Their intention was to mislead, not to inform. He had no interest in whether an allegation was true; he would report an allegation as a fact just so long as it suited his purpose, which was until its fraudulence became exposed to the public. That was Mr. Bush's consistent pattern, and it is the pattern of an inveterate liar. Nonetheless, Mr. Kristof presented himself as believing otherwise in his commentary on June 13th, which tried to shift the blame onto the President's underlings. It was titled, "White House in Denial," and it closed by asserting, incredibly: "I don't believe that the president deliberately lied to the public in an attempt to scare Americans into supporting his war. But it does look as if ideologues in the administration deceived themselves about Iraq's nuclear weapons – and then deceived the American public as well." In other words, Mr. Kristof was here saying that only the President's underlings were to blame, and that even they weren't "liars"; they were, somehow, merely "deceived." Perhaps Mr. Kristof was now attempting to mollify conservatives. But such "tact" is itself not professional journalism, but deceptive journalism, because it misplaces blame. And it's plain *false*.

After the war, the President and his tag-along Tony Blair naturally found themselves in a real bind about this. And what did they do then? Did they invite the U.N. weapons inspectors immediately back into Iraq, to continue the work that Mr. Bush's invasion had aborted? Did they have the U.N. resume its investigations immediately, before possible evidence-tampering by U.S. forces? No; in fact, they *prohibited* the U.N team from continuing inspections. Despite urgings from around the world, including from chief weapons inspector Hans Blix, and from chief nuclear inspector Mohammed ElBaredei, to let them back in immediately, for "credibility" on any WMD findings, the *Observer* headlined April 20th, "No Role for UN in Weapons Hunt," and reported, "The United Nations is to be cut out of any involvement in the hunt for weapons of mass destruction 'for the forseeable [sic] future', after Washington made it clear it sees no role for Hans Blix or the Unmovic inspections team." The same day a story in the *Independent* led off with, "Tony Blair has ruled out an inquiry into allegations that the public was misled about Saddam Hussein's alleged weapons of mass destruction, the main justification for the war."

Clearly, on both sides of the Atlantic, then, the wraps were being put onto the entire issue. As one expert was quoted in the *Observer*, "The credibility of the Bush administration and the intelligence community will be put at risk if weapons of mass destruction are not soon found in significant numbers." A former British Defence Minister said that if there was no discovery of WMD, the war would be deemed illegal. The report in the *Independent* quoted a Labour MP as asserting, "There is cynicism about the US, and a number of people have said this to me: they will find them [WMD] because they will take their own [WMD] in there with them." A Reuters story the same day quoted a junior defense minister for Mr. Blair as saying, "I have no doubt in my mind at all that Saddam possessed these weapons, that they've been well hidden, and with considerable effort, we'll turn them up." Mr. Bush was sending his own team of a thousand people in to search for the weapons that he had always said that he had irrefutable "evidence" still existed there. But, if all of that "evidence" consisted of fabrications in the past, as it assuredly did, then why should anyone think that this exclusion of the U.N. inspectors was anything else than a continuation of Mr. Bush's lies and fraud about the "evidence" he actually had?

A popular adage says, "Fool me once, shame on you; fool me twice, shame on me!" President Bush had already had his chances, again, and again, and again, and again. And, each and every time, he turned out to be a bare-faced liar. This is now certain, regardless of what specific things about Iraq's former WMD program might not be. What he was lying about was not the existence of Iraqi WMD, but his possession of proof that they existed. He actually possessed no such proof – only bogus "evidence." So, how many people are still stupid enough to believe any "evidence" a man like that turns up?

At the immediate end of the invasion, one Iraqi scientist after another came forth and said that Iraq had destroyed all of its WMD much earlier, and that nothing would be found. However, many interrogations took place in secret, unmonitored by anyone, much less by lawyers for the people who were being interrogated. Coerced or induced testimony is almost certain to be produced under such circumstances. Sure enough, then, on April 21st, came a front-page *New York Times* story from Judith Miller, that was datelined the day before, and that led with what ought to have been the non-reportable (because untrustworthy) "news" that, "A scientist who claims to have worked in Iraq's chemical weapons program for more than a decade has told an American military team that Iraq destroyed chemical weapons and biological warfare equipment only days before the war began, members of the team said." Here, it wasn't even the supposed "witness" who was testifying; it certainly wasn't a lawyer who was representing him. How many times have America's newspapers revealed that a confession was coerced or induced (such as plea-bargained) from a criminal defendant now recognized to have been innocent, and this *inside* the United States? It happens tragically often. Isn't it obvious, then, that the "defendants" in this particular case, inside a militarily defeated Iraq, subject to military rule by the conqueror, are even less protected than are those American citizen defendants inside America? Only a fool would take such a dubious second-hand or hearsay "news" story as "evidence" on anything, especially after the consistent string of lies and deceptions from Misters Bush and Blair that had been reported in the United States and Britain. Only international war crimes trials of Bush and Blair, which place them both onto the witness stand, might be able to validate such "evidence," assuming that the defendants (and American "weapons inspectors") wouldn't previously have tampered too much with any actual evidence before that can happen.

A May 7th story, titled "Pulitzer-Prize-Winning Reporter Crosses The New York Times' Line of 'Strict Neutrality'," by Daniel Forbes at GVNews.net/MediaChannel.org, revealed that Judith Miller is affiliated with the Middle East Forum, which is headed by the far-rightwing Daniel Pipes, and which has long promoted invading Iraq.

By May 10th, things were beginning to get desperate for President Bush; the international pressure on him wasn't disappearing in the wake of his "victory" as it seems he had expected. So the AP was

headlining, "U.S. Offers Rewards in Iraq Weapons Hunt: U.S. Author-
ities in Baghdad Use Radio Announcement to Offer Rewards for Help
in Banned Weapons Hunt." Odd, isn't it, that Mr. Bush was willing to
accept the "help" of everyone *except* the U.N. inspectors whom the
U.S. had kicked out of Iraq in order to start its bombing of that
country? Like clockwork, the *Observer* headlined the next day, "U.S.
Rivals Turn on Each Other as Weapons Search Draws a Blank." This
story was about "a struggle to avoid blame," and essentially concerned
the question: who in the Administration would take the fall for the U.S.
President? The Office of Special Plans at the Pentagon was where the
"cooking" of intelligence on Iraq had been coordinated, and so it
seemed to be a promising target to take the heat for the President
whom they were serving so effectively. However, CIA director George
Tenet was a Democrat and a holdover from the previous Clinton Administration, and so he, too, was vulnerable.

On the other hand, the unruly masses *outside* the U.S. were
setting their sights on targets far higher than such mere lackeys. Russia's Itar-Tass news agency the same day (May 11th) reported, "Thousands of people in Arab and other Islamic countries have signed a
petition demanding that U.S. President George W. Bush and British
Prime Minister Tony Blair be brought to trial for actions committed by
U.S. and British forces on Iraqi territory." This sort of thing caused the
drawbridges over the castle moats to be raised. Thus, the same day, the
Independent headlined, "US Blocks Return of UN Arms Inspectors,"
and led with, "The United States is continuing this weekend to block
the return of United Nations weapons inspectors in Iraq, even though
its own teams of experts have so far failed to find any definitive evidence of banned biological, chemical or nuclear materials in the country, let alone any actual armaments." Apparently, the only thing that
President Bush feared more than a possible inability – or, perhaps, unwillingness – of his own people to "find," plant or else contrive "evidence" of Iraqi WMD, was the potential conclusion by independent
experts that there simply *weren't* any WMD in Iraq.

Public recognition that the Bush Administration had lied was
nonetheless increasing gradually, until a climactic Reuters report from
Alan Elsner, on May 12th, quoting David Albright, the President of the
Institute for Science and International Security, and a former U.N.
weapons inspector in Iraq, as saying: "We can conclude that the large
number of deployed chemical weapons the administration said that
Iraq had are not there. We can also conclude that Iraq's nuclear
weapons program was not nearly as sophisticated as the administration claimed." Joseph Cirincione, of the Carnegie Endowment for International Peace, was likewise quoted in this article as asserting: "I
think it's safe to say the weapons do not exist in the quantities claimed

by the administration ... and there simply was not the imminent strategic threat that the President cited as his main cause for going to war." The invasion was now in the process of becoming retrospectively recognized officially as having been illegal.

At first, this created only minor political waves in the U.S. But on the opposite shore of the Atlantic, culturally less diseased with Christian theocratic imperial fantasies of "God's People" carrying out the "Law of God" instead of the United Nations and the laws of Man, and intent upon saving the souls of infidels for God instead of complying with U.N. edicts, this authoritative acknowledgment was found to be severely disturbing. The breaking of Man-made international laws is simply a bigger issue on the other side of the pond. Therefore, when British Foreign Secretary Jack Straw was reported on May 15th in the *Guardian* as reversing the previous line of the Blair Government, and as saying that finding Iraqi WMD was, after all, "not crucially important," one of Mr. Straw's fellow Labour Party Members of Parliament gagged and just blurted out, "The whole basis of the war is based on an untruth. ... This is making the war even more illegal." Bush and Blair were, indeed, war criminals, and their hopes that American weapons investigators would cap their lies by creating the "evidence" that would exonerate them of war crimes, had, it seems, finally collapsed. By May 21st, President Bush's harshest Senate critic on the war, Democrat Robert Byrd, asked, from the Senate floor, "Were our troops needlessly put at risk? Were countless Iraqi civilians killed and maimed when war was not really necessary? Was the American public deliberately misled? Was the world?" On May 29th, the *Washington Post* headlined, "U.S. Hedges on Finding Iraqi Weapons: Officials Cite the Possibility of Long or Fruitless Search for Banned Arms." However, most Americans cared little about international law: just as the President expected, his war still remained popular at home.

Then, everything seemed finally to spill out on May 30th, just as President Bush was leaving for a rare trip to Europe, hoping to drum up support for his international policies. But instead, statements from U.S. Defense Secretary Donald Rumsfeld, and from his Deputy Defense Secretary Paul Wolfowitz, downplaying the importance of the entire WMD issue, set off a firestorm among the assembling leaders of the Group of Eight industrialized countries, who were not so ready to dismiss the demands of international law as was the American Administration. London's *Daily Express* bannered that the Americans' prewar assertions about Iraqi WMD had been "Just Complete and Utter Lies." The *Frankfurter Algemeine Zeitung* asserted, "The charge of deception is inescapable." *Le Monde* said that the WMD deception was "the greatest lie told by statesmen in recent years." Approving references were being made to a statement from French President Jacques

Chirac, earlier the same week, in a May 26th interview in the *Financial Times:* "A war that lacks legitimacy does not acquire legitimacy just because it has been won." This view reflected European opinion, and it separated Europe from the United States of America by more than just the 3,000 miles of the Atlantic Ocean. However, stateside, the *New York Times's* Nicholas Kristof attracted more attention by the revelation that his earlier column on the WMD issue "drew a torrent of covert communications from indignant spooks who say that administration officials leaned on them to exaggerate the Iraqi threat and deceive the public. 'The American people were manipulated,' bluntly declares one person from the Defense Intelligence Agency who says he was privy to all the intelligence there on Iraq."

The next day, May 31st, the *Guardian* headlined, "Straw, Powell Had Serious Doubts Over Their Iraqi Weapons Claims," and reported on the "Waldorf transcripts" that "are being circulated in Nato diplomatic circles." The ten-page transcripts were reported to have recorded a dispute over intelligence data that had surfaced at a meeting between Foreign Secretary Straw and Secretary of State Powell, shortly before Mr. Powell's U.N. speech on February 5th. Mr. Powell purportedly then admitted that the speech might include falsehoods so gross as to "explode in their faces."

The real issue here is not, as some have maintained, whether there will ever be "a smoking gun" that "proves" that Saddam Hussein did *not* "have huge quantities of WMD" as of some specified date. Proving a negative is virtually impossible. Criminal convictions in court never require it. The real issue is, instead, whether President Bush was lying when he claimed, repeatedly, that he was in possession of evidence that proved, to a certainty, both that Saddam Hussein retained massive quantities of WMD, and that the inspections program by the U.N. was incompetent. Without a doubt, Mr. Bush and his entire Administration were lying repeatedly. That is what made their invasion of Iraq irretrievably criminal. They couldn't convince the world on the basis of the facts, and so they lied about what the facts were. They even selected the shoddiest allegations, which weren't acceptable to intelligence agencies as being "facts," and presented that trash to the world as facts. And the matter at issue here was not of only minor importance, either: to the exact contrary, it was a matter of life and death for many people, and could damage the future of entire nations. Misrepresentations of this nature are of vastly greater importance, both politically and morally, than any that Mr. Bush's predecessor, Bill Clinton, made regarding his sexual behavior, for which Republicans impeached him. But who is outraged at this? Ought not *all* Americans to be very concerned about this kind of deception?

from: http://bodyandsoul.blogspot.com/2003_07_01_bodyandsoul_archive.html

Sunday, July 20, 2003

Do you know how bad the intelligence about uranium from Niger was?

Via CalPundit, and the LA Times, I just learned that its source was an Italian journalist named Elisabetta Burba, who works for the weekly **Panorama**. But **Panorama** -- which, by the way, is owned by Silvio Berlusconi (yes, *that* Silvio Berlusconi), and which is not exactly a news source with high standards -- didn't print the story because it seemed fake. Nevertheless, after "discussions" at the magazine -- did I mention its owner was Silvio Berlusconi? -- Burba brought the Niger documents to the U.S. Embassy.

I'm not sure which is worse -- that our standards for intelligence are below those of *Sussuri e Gossip*, or that the information was passed on by someone working for the King of Denial.

Note to reporters: Berlusconi happens to be here, and there are some questions that need to be asked. These [asked by *Time* magazine] aren't the questions.

by jeannedorleans@aol.com

On June 9th (and featured on the web June 2nd), the normally conservative magazine, *U.S. News & World Report*, ran a blockbuster story, "Truth and Consequences," by Bruce Auster, Mark Mazzetti, and Edward T. Pound, which detailed the day-by-day debates within the White House that had produced Secretary of State Powell's speech of February 5th to the U.N. – America's global sales pitch to invade Iraq. This stunning account said, "The first draft of Powell's speech was written by Cheney's staff and the National Security Council," but mainly by the Vice President's Chief of Staff, Lewis "Scooter" Libby, who was known to have been promoting for several years the idea that the United States should invade Iraq. The magazine reported, "At one point during the rehearsal, Powell tossed several pages in the air. 'I'm not reading this,' he declared. 'This is bulls---.'" Nonetheless, on some contested issues, "The White House instructed Powell to include the charge in his presentation." There was, *U.S. News* said, a "fault line dividing the Bush administration. For months, the vice president's office and the Pentagon had been more aggressive than either State or the CIA when it came to making the case against Iraq." That was the Administration's purpose, stated right there, "making the case against Iraq," not adhering to the requirements of truth and of international law. The story continued: "Veteran intelligence officers were dismayed. 'The policy decisions weren't matching the reports we were reading every day,' says an intelligence official. In September 2002, U.S. News has learned, the Defense Intelligence Agency issued a classified assessment of Iraq's chemical weapons. It concluded: 'There is no reliable information on whether Iraq is producing and stockpiling chemical weapons.' At about the same time, Rumsfeld told Congress that Saddam's 'regime has amassed large, clandestine stockpiles of chemical weapons, including VX, sarin, cyclosarin and mustard gas.'" The article then quoted someone as saying, "'I don't think [administration officials] were lying; I just think they did a poor job.'" These commentators were so alienated from the truth that they couldn't even be truthful about lying. Those *were* lies – and a bold job of it, too.

On June 8th, Mr. Powell lied once more, telling Fox News Sunday that, "It wasn't the President's credibility and my credibility on the line [concerning Iraqi WMD]; it was the credibility of the United States of America." Only a week earlier, on May 31st, he was quoted in *The New York Times* as having admitted to reporters, aboard Air Force One, that he knew that what was "going to be on the line on the fifth of February" was "the credibility of the President of the United States, and my credibility." That's a direct self-contradiction.

How long can this continue to work: playing the American people for fools who can't even follow simple logic?

Diehard nationalist Americans may not be able to accept that their Fuehrer made fools of them. They refuse to let it into their consciousness. Far from being angry at Mr. Bush, they admire the man. Their lawn signs say, "SUPPORT OUR TROOPS," but, if only they knew how to do that, those same signs would have emblazoned instead, "NO WAR IN IRAQ," and then, "BRING OUR TROOPS HOME." America has a good role to play in the world, but conquest isn't it. The minds of millions of Americans were twisted into supporting aggressive nationalistic invasion, by this evil President who readily uses the word "evil" against rogues who happen not to be himself.

Meanwhile, at the opposite end of the conservative political spectrum, are tepid liberals who can't call a spade a spade, and who therefore blame lower-level fall guys for what are, in fact, the President's – and his aides' – lies. For example, on June 18th, the peripatetic Josh Marshall, of such liberal media as the *Washington Monthly*, the *American Prospect*, and his own talkingpointsmemo .com, headlined at www.thehill.com/marshall/061803.aspx, "Evidence Against Iraq Was Always Fanciful," asserting his lame view that, "It's not so much that the administration was lying – as in saying things it knew to be false – as it was happy to pass along or credit almost anything anybody said no matter how speculative the theory or how flimsy the evidence: uncorroborated tales from defectors, crackpot theories from think-tank denizens, worst-case-scenario speculations, anything." Two days later, the perhaps more comfortably conservative PBS TV commentator, and soon to be appointed *New York Times* columnist, David Brooks, similarly told the Lehrer NewsHour, "They said lots and lots of things which turned out to be 100% wrong. Now are they liars? No. They interpreted a fuzzy situation in different ways." To be generous to such commentators, their interpretations of what went on here were euphemistic. But their deceptions were mild compared to some others. Fox News Sunday interviewed the leading Republican and Democrat on the Senate Intelligence Committee, on June 22nd. Republican Senator Pat Roberts, when asked the least incriminating form of the pertinent question, "Did the president take speculative estimates and portray them to the American people as near certainties?" responded, "I have no evidence of that. I don't believe that is true." The interviewer, Tony Snow, then turned to Democratic Senator Jay Rockefeller, and similarly asked, "Do you know of any specific case in which, in your opinion, the White House or the president exaggerated intelligence?" This timorous Democrat responded, "I do not know of any." He wouldn't volunteer even a single instance of such "exaggeration."

But how much better documented could the case possibly be that Mr. Bush lied all the way to invading Iraq? Would the liar's admission, a confession from him, be able to add anything to the evidence? Not at all. Like the worst liars, Mr. Bush never admits what he isn't forced to admit. And what difference would it make, even if he did admit that he was lying? George W. Bush has proven by his record that his word isn't worth its air vibrations. Whatever he might admit to would have no credibility.

Further indicting the lack of credibility of the remarks by Senators Roberts and Rockefeller letting the President off the hook, was the revelation by the *Washington Post*, on June 25th, that, "A top State Department expert on chemical and biological weapons told Congressional committees in closed-door hearings last week that he had been pressed to tailor his analysis on Iraq and other matters to conform with the Bush administration's views." Under the headline, "Expert Said to Tell Legislators He Was Pressed to Distort Some Evidence," the reporters, James Risen and Douglas Jehl, noted that the official's "decision to speak out has caused a stir inside the House and Senate intelligence committees." And, of course, both Roberts and Rockefeller were on the Senate Intelligence Committee. However, whatever "stir" this whistleblower might have made there, failed to be reflected in either of the two Senators' public statements on Fox.

Clearly, the institutional forces were lined up against holding Mr. Bush accountable for deceiving the nation into an invasion. Furthermore, the Republican Congress has been, to put it mildly, reluctant to impeach the Republican leader. Impeachment proceedings against this President would therefore require proof beyond what any court would demand. Both houses of the Congress are controlled by the President's Party, and so Republicans would not convict him unless there were a "smoking gun" – something that courts can't require in order to convict anyone, but that is a practical necessity for this President's successful impeachment. Only a smoking gun would be so incontrovertible that if the Republicans in Congress were to stand against impeachment in the face of such decisive evidence, the Democrats in Congress would win politically, and would discredit the entire Republican Party. With smoking-gun evidence, virtually any Republican who stood against impeachment might be risking political suicide. Of course, if people were logical, then smoking-gun evidence would not be required – logical inference could be decisive – but people aren't so logical. For example, the mere observation should have sufficed, coming from the chief U.N. weapons inspector, Hans Blix, at the Council on Foreign Relations on June 23rd: "It is sort of fascinating that you can have 100 percent certainty about weapons of mass destruction and zero certainty about where they are." That observation would have simply closed the book on the matter, because it would have made clear, to anyone with an open mind, that President Bush's continuing "search" for Iraqi WMD itself constituted proof that the President's statements *prior* to the war had been lies. By contrast, a smoking gun doesn't require such astute reasoning abilities: it is a direct contradiction between what a person says he has done or seen, and what he has actually done or seen.

So, here's a "smoking gun," with the palm-prints, upon it, of both Bush and Blair:

In September of 2002, the issue was whether or not further International Atomic Energy Agency, and United Nations, sponsored inspections in Iraq were needed in order to be able to declare Iraq a WMD threat.

At www.whitehouse.gov/news/releases/2002/09/20020907-2.html on the web, is the transcript of "Remarks by the President and Prime Minister Tony Blair in Photo Opportunity Camp David, Maryland," from the Office of the Press Secretary, September 7, 2002. The critical question from the press was the first one: "Q: Mr. President, can you tell us what conclusive evidence of any nuclear – new evidence you have of nuclear weapons capabilities of Saddam Hussein?" His answer: "THE PRESIDENT: We just heard the Prime Minister talk about the new report. I would remind you that when the inspectors first went into Iraq and were denied – finally denied access, a report came out of the Atomic – the IAEA that they were six months away from developing a weapon. I don't know what more evidence we need." In other words, Mr. Bush said here that no further inspections were needed; that Iraq was definitely in violation, and was specifically a nuclear threat, based upon "the new report" from the IAEA; and that the IAEA was even reporting Saddam to be within six months from having the bomb. Blair concurred.

At www.iaea.org/worldatom/Press/P_release/2002/prn0211.s html is the then-latest press release from the IAEA, in Vienna, titled "Iraq and IAEA Inspections," dated just the prior day, September 6th. It said that, "the International Atomic Energy Agency would like to state that it has no new information on Iraq's nuclear programme since December 1998 when its inspectors left Iraq. Only through a re-sumption of inspections in accordance with Security Council Resolution 687 and other relevant resolutions can the Agency draw any conclusion with regard to Iraq's compliance." So, there was no such "new report," and the IAEA was emphatic that renewed inspections were essential. In order to reiterate this, their website posted also the statement from the IAEA Director General dated Monday, September 9th, saying, "Since December 1998 when our inspectors left Iraq, we have no additional information that can be directly linked without inspection to Iraq's nuclear activities. I should emphasize that it is only through resumption of inspections that the Agency can draw any conclusion or provide any assurance regarding Iraq's compliance." In other words, the IAEA officially contradicted Mr. Bush's Saturday, September 7th, statement, on Friday, September 6th, right before he said it; and, yet again, on Monday, September 9th, right after he said it. They clearly did everything they could to deny the Bush lie.

Furthermore, emphatically to the contrary of Mr. Bush's asser-tion that there had been a finding from "the IAEA that they were six months away from developing a weapon," the IAEA's last report after leaving Iraq (their 1999 report, which can be found at www.iaea.org/worldatom/Programmes/ActionTeam/reports/s_1999_127.pdf), con-cluded that Iraq retained no nuclear-weapons program at all. This final report was emphatic in line after line; for example, it said, "There are no indications that there remains in Iraq any physical capability for the production of amounts of weapons-usable nuclear material of any practical significance," and, "The entire inventory of research reactor fuel was verified and accounted for by the IAEA and maintained under IAEA custody until it was removed from Iraq." Thus, there existed no basis other than a bald-faced lie for President Bush's having said that a "new report" had been issued from "the IAEA that they [Iraq] were six months away from developing a weapon. I don't know what more evidence we need." I don't know what more evidence we need, to convict George W. Bush of high crimes.

Others have alleged that Bush "was dead wrong" here (Andrew Stephen in the *New Statesman*, on September 16, 2002), and that, "There is no such report, as far as I know" (David Albright on CBS 60 Minutes, December 8, 2002), but this *proves* it; and it proves also that both Bush and Blair concocted a fictitious IAEA report, and placed into that non-existent "new report" a grave allegation that the authentic IAEA documents of the time emphatically contradicted regarding Iraq. So, both Bush and Blair committed fraud here.

This is proven because when Bush and Blair referred to "the new report" from the IAEA, there were only three things that could have qualified to be referred to by that phrase: the press release of September 6, 2002; or that of September 9, 2002; or the final IAEA Iraq inspectors' report – the one dated 1999. *Each* of the three contradicted what Bush and Blair were saying about "the new report" from the IAEA. The question that, if asked of President Bush, will expose him as having committed the "high crime" of deceiving Congress and the public into authorizing this war, is: Show us 'the new report' from the IAEA that you referred to on September 7, 2002, which alleged that 'they [Iraqis] were six months away from developing a [nuclear] weapon.'"

A smoking gun doesn't consist of only an allegation. It consists of either a single piece of evidence, or else a very limited set of such items, that is suitable, in itself, for a conviction. In the present instance, the evidentiary set that convicts President Bush, and also Prime Minister Blair, is the transcript of their September 7, 2002, press conference, on the one hand, versus those specific three documents from the IAEA, on the other.*

---

* This has not been understood by the press. Indeed, many of the news stories about the September 7, 2002, joint announcement by President Bush and Prime Minister Blair, simply assumed that "the new report" from the IAEA was, somehow, intended to refer to the 1998 IAEA report, even though that report could not have been, by any reasonable construction, "the new report" from the IAEA, and even though that 1998 report (at www.iaea.org/worldatom/Programmes/ActionTeam/reports/s_1998_927.pdf) also contradicted Bush's allegation about "the new report," because it stated, "verification activities have revealed no indications that Iraq had achieved its programme objective of producing nuclear weapons or that Iraq had produced more than a few grams of weapons-usable nuclear material or had clandestinely acquired such material. Furthermore, there are no indications that there remains in Iraq any physical capability for the production of weapons-usable nuclear material of any practical significance." However, since that IAEA report was written before, not after, the IAEA's departure from Iraq, whatever it said wasn't even relevant to the question of what "the new report" from the IAEA said. The web additionally contains a September 7, 2002, story from NBC News, at http://truthout.com/docs_02/09.10B.msnbc.iraq.p.htm, headlined "White House: Bush Misstated Report on Iraq." It appears that the

President's press operation was at a loss to explain to journalists just what "the new report" from the IAEA actually was. Therefore, this NBC story said, "A senior White House official acknowledged Saturday night that the 1998 report did not say what Bush claimed. 'What happened was, we formed our own conclusions based on the report,' the official told NBC News' Norah O'Donnell." Mark Gwozdecky, an IAEA spokesman, was quoted in that story, furthermore, as denying that a certain three-months-old satellite photo of a former Iraqi nuclear facility, which had been referred to in a news story the day before in *The New York Times*, came from the IAEA. It was "simply a picture from a commercial satellite imaging company, Gwozdecky said." So, that old picture was likewise not "the new report" from the IAEA. Still, reporters remained confused, and failed to apply elementary logic to the testing or analysis of the President's veracity. Allegations were made by some reporters (as our text notes) that Bush erred, or falsified, but, amidst this pervasive confusion, few were willing to charge that he had outright "lied." On September 27th, a story by Joseph Curl in the *Washington Times*, "Iraq Report Cited by Bush Does Not Exist," contained yet another White House attempt to add to this confusion: "The White House says Mr. Bush was referring to an earlier IAEA report. 'He's referring to 1991 there,' said Deputy Press Secretary Scott McClellan. 'In '91, there was a report saying that after the war they found out they were about six months away.' Mr. Gwozdecky said no such report was ever issued by the IAEA in 1991 [which can be verified by examining the IAEA's 1991 documents, on its website, www.iaea.org/worldatom/Programmes/ActionTeam/index .html]." However, just a modicum of logic would have sufficed to alert a journalist to the fact that a 1991 report cannot possibly qualify as having been "the new report" in 2002, so that whatever that 1991 document actually said isn't even relevant to the question of whether Mr. Bush lied on September 7, 2002. Then, on October 24th, there appeared in the *Washington Post* a letter from White House Press Secretary Ari Fleischer, finally admitting, "True, the president stated that the International Atomic Energy Agency said Iraq could possess nuclear weapons in as few as six months. It was in fact the International Institute for Strategic Studies that issued the report. The source may be different, but the underlying fact remains the same." This desperate late diversionary lie was knocked down just four days later, also in the *Post*, via a letter from an astute reader, William Murphy, which said:

"I find it curious that the report the White House now claims the president's original statement was based on was released Sept. 9, two days after President Bush made his statement. Even more curious, just like the original source that has been disavowed, the new source that the White House cites as the basis for the president's statement does not say that Iraq was six months away from developing a nuclear weapon. According to the International Institute for Strategic Studies web site: 'Iraq does not possess facilities to produce fissile material in sufficient amounts for nuclear weapons. It would require several years and extensive foreign assistance to build such fissile material production facilities.'" Nowhere did the IISS report say that Iraq was "six months away" from a nuclear bomb.

Nonetheless, no matter how ironclad a smoking gun in a document-based case like this might happen to be, it probably won't be able to be recognized by people who have difficulty identifying what is logically relevant and what is not. If reporters fail at elementary logic, then their abilities to clarify *anything* for their audience or readership can be only minimal at best.

However, for anyone who recognizes that only those three documents could have qualified to have been referred to, on September 7th, as being then "the new report" from the IAEA, it doesn't require a high degree of intelligence to know that the President is trapped here. Unlike the situation with respect to Democratic Congressman Henry Waxman's efforts (posted at www.house.gov/reform/min/invest_ admin/admin_nuclear_evidence.htm) to nail the President with respect to the forged

To reiterate: there is plenty of evidence proving that President Bush deceived his country into invading Iraq, and such evidence has been amply presented earlier. But a smoking gun is different, and the evidence now being cited is precisely that.

Valuable historical context behind this smoking gun is provided by the testimony from Britain's former Secretary of International Development, Clare Short, on June 17, 2003, to the Foreign Affairs Select Committee of the House of Commons, and which was reported the next day in the *Guardian* under the heading, "Short: I Was Briefed on Blair's Secret War Pact." She informed Parliament that three aides to Mr. Blair had confided to her that the Prime Minister had secretly committed himself to President Bush by no later than September 9th of 2002, to the effect that "we will be with you" invading Iraq in February or March of 2003, regardless what the best intelligence might actually indicate regarding WMD. Ms. Short's explanation of

---

documents on Niger uranium shipments to Iraq, the IAEA matter provides the President no escape hatch, no opportunity to question whether the President knew about the given document, or whether he knew about the intelligence reports saying that the document was a forgery. Clearly, in an instance such as the forged Niger documents, the President can simply blame a bureaucratic breakdown, if things should ever happen to pass beyond mere stonewalling on his part. That's a "he said, she said" type of issue, which, at worst for the President, would require only the finding of a suitable fall guy, probably at CIA or DIA. By contrast, all that is involved here is to determine which of the only three possible IAEA documents was "the new report" that the President was claiming, on September 7, 2002, proved to a certainty that "they were six months away from developing a weapon."

The key difference between the two approaches will become clear if things should ever happen to get as far as an impeachment proceeding, in which the President would be required to offer testimony as to what "new report" he was speaking of, responsive to the question the reporter had asked him, "Mr. President, can you tell us what conclusive evidence of any nuclear — new evidence you have of nuclear weapons capabilities of Saddam Hussein?" and which the President then recklessly volunteered further to say proved "that they were six months away from developing a weapon." President Bush wouldn't be able to answer by merely blaming a fall guy. As the U.S. President, he possesses no authority over the IAEA; and it is he, himself, who referred to this "new report." He named his weapon; here, it's just being turned against himself. By contrast, if things should ever reach as far as an impeachment in which the Niger uranium documents are at issue, it would be extremely difficult, if even possible, to identify who knew what when and informed whom how and when. That would become just a prosecutor's nightmare.

This logical restrictedness is what's key to making a smoking gun in any type of white-collar-crime case that's based upon documentary evidence, such as here. The most common form of practical impunity for CEO's lies in precisely this: it's rare for a prosecutor to be able to narrow documents' semantic/referential wriggle-room so narrowly that even jurors of limited logical ability can recognize clearly a CEO's guilt of fraud. Mr. Bush is already well beyond the time when he could have contested the accuracy of that September 7, 2002, press conference transcript, which presented his quote; he's now stuck with having to defend his statement there as not being a lie. It's an impossible task. He'll be trapped, if only he'll be pursued.

why she inferred that "by September 9 they were both committed to
military action," can be found at the Parliament's webpage (locatable
by the search-string: "by September 9 they were both committed to
military action" short parliament). Her inference was virtually confirmed by the testimony Mr. Blair himself gave at the Hutton inquiry at
the Royal Courts of Justice on August 28th, where he said that in late
August 2002 he had a conversation with Mr. Bush by phone, "and we
decided: look, we really had to confront this issue, devise our strategy
and get on with it."

As for President Bush himself, his decision was actually
reached much earlier; the only problem for him was obtaining "the
evidence" to make the case to the American people. The now-retired
General (and subsequent U.S. Presidential candidate) Wesley Clark,
interviewed on NBC's "Meet the Press" June 15, 2003, testified, "There
was a concerted effort during the Fall of 2001, starting immediately
after 9/11, to pin 9/11 and the terrorism problem on Saddam Hussein."
The moderator, Tim Russert, then asked, "By who? Who did that?"
General Clark's stunning answer was, "Well, it came from the White
House; it came from the people around the White House. It came from
all over. I got a call on 9/11. I was on CNN, and I got a call at my home
saying, 'You've got to say this is connected. This is state-sponsored
terrorism. This has to be connected to Saddam Hussein.' I said, 'But –
I'm willing to say it, but what's your evidence?' And I never got any
evidence." His testimony corroborated earlier revelations through
other sources, such as a CBS News report on September 4, 2002,
"Plans for Iraq Attack Began On 9/11," and an interview with Deputy
Defense Secretary Paul Wolfowitz, at www.defenselink.mil/transcripts
/2003/tr20030509-depsecdef0223.html. The CBS News piece quoted
Defense Secretary Donald Rumsfeld, on the day of the 9/11 attacks, as
having said, "Go massive. Sweep it all up. Things related and not,"
referring there to removing both Osama bin Laden and Saddam
Hussein. Mr. Wolfowitz, in his interview, asserted that, in a policy
debate on September 13, 2001, "the President came down on the side
of the larger goal" of eliminating not just Osama, but Saddam.
Therefore, the joint statement from Bush and Blair at Camp David, on
September 7, 2002, was a major step along the road toward invading
Iraq, but this journey didn't begin there; for Bush, it was already under
way by 9/11, if not earlier – perhaps even when he entered office.

With that smoking gun, and all of his other lies, President Bush
convinced the U.S. Congress, so that, on October 16, 2002, he was able
to sign a joint Congressional resolution authorizing him to launch an
invasion of Iraq. In the signing ceremony at the White House, he
brazenly announced, "Either the Iraqi regime will give up its weapons
of mass destruction, or for the sake of peace, the United States will

lead a global coalition to disarm that regime." It was all based on lies about weapons of mass destruction.

On July 6, 2003, something that for a while seemed close to being yet a second smoking gun came to light: in a *New York Times* op-ed, a former U.S. Ambassador, Joseph C. Wilson IV, identified himself publicly for the first time by saying, "Those news stories about that unnamed former envoy who went to Niger? That's me." He was the person who had been anonymously referred to in the press as an ambassador who had been sent to Niger by Vice President Cheney in February 2002, to evaluate the authenticity of the documents which alleged to show that Iraq was trying to acquire uranium from Niger. He promptly reported back to the CIA, and to the Vice President, saying that the documents were bogus. Notwithstanding that repudiation, the Vice President and others in the Bush Administration continued to rely upon the documents' authenticity. These were the documents that the IAEA pronounced to the world, on March 7, 2003, to be forgeries.

Because Ambassador Wilson blew the whistle on Bush's Niger uranium lie, the White House retaliated by destroying the career of his wife, Valerie Plame, who was an undercover CIA officer in the *real* war against terrorism: it blew her secret cover and thereby also endangered her undercover agents. The Bush people leaked to their friend, conservative columnist Robert Novak, this anti-terrorism spook's undercover identity. As the former White House Counsel John Dean pointed out on August 15th at http://writ.findlaw.com/dean/20030815 .html, this was "a Worse-than-Nixonian Tactic," a "Deadly Serious Crime," and an impeachable offense.

In the days immediately following Ambassador Wilson's bombshell July 6th revelation, the White House press office admitted that the reference to the Niger uranium ought not to have been included in the President's State of the Union Speech on January 28th. Then, as this issue rose to dominate the daily news, CIA Director George Tenet announced on July 11th: "First, CIA approved the president's State of the Union address before it was delivered. Second, I am responsible for the approval process in my agency. And third, the president had every reason to believe that the text presented to him was sound." Tenet implicitly took the blame, and so took the fall, if only he would be pushed to resign. The President, naturally, chose to retain the keeper of the secrets, so as to retain also his keeper's loyalty.

However, by contrast, the September 7, 2002, statement by Mr. Bush leaves no such possible fall guy. It refers to a supposed "new report" from the IAEA, and *not* from the CIA that the President himself controlled. And the President claimed to know the contents of that "new report." So, without a doubt, he did not know the contents of this alleged "new report" as he implied he did, and it didn't say what he said it said, and it didn't even exist, and his statements to the contrary on each of these points were, clearly and demonstrably, lies.

Adding to the importance of this smoking gun, his State of the Union address on January 28th *also* referred to evidence from the IAEA. This brings the Niger uranium and the IAEA flaps together, and so reveals the totality of Mr. Bush's fabrication of the crucial charge that Saddam still had a nuclear weapons program. Here is *everything* Bush said on that key occasion about Iraq's alleged nuclear weapons:

"We're strongly supporting the International Atomic Energy Agency in its mission to track and control nuclear materials around the world. ... The International Atomic Energy Agency confirmed in the 1990s that Saddam Hussein had an advanced nuclear weapons development program, had a design for a nuclear weapon and was working on five different methods of enriching uranium for a bomb. The British government has learned that Saddam Hussein recently sought significant quantities of uranium from Africa. [Similarly, on September 26, 2002, Mr. Bush's "Global Message," which is posted at "The White House" website, had stated that, "*according to the British government* (italics added), the Iraqi regime could launch a biological or chemical attack in as little as 45 minutes after the order were given"; and this, too, was known *at the time* to be an unfounded charge against Iraq.] Our intelligence sources tell us that he has attempted to purchase high-strength aluminum tubes suitable for nuclear weapons production." That was the *entirety* of his speech's "evidence" against Saddam on the nuclear WMD issue. *Each* of these several charges is now publicly recognized to have been false.

What's especially significant here is that not only did the President rely upon the bogus Niger uranium documents, and upon a bogus inference about aluminum tubes in Iraq, but he also relied upon the outside agency, the IAEA. He even lied saying that he strongly supported the IAEA. Furthermore, this time, he was vague as regards which documents from the IAEA he was allegedly referring to.

The President should be *asked* which documents he was referring to. How old was that supposed IAEA information? Why was he basing his accusation, about supposedly current 2003 Iraqi weapons, on information that was so many years old it related to the situation in Iraq long before the IAEA found and destroyed Iraq's nuclear weapons program? Why did the President employ words that clearly implied the contrary? And why were all three of the President's assertions about Iraq's supposedly current nuclear program either false or intentionally misleading?

He was obviously lying. And this time, because of the IAEA reference there, he won't be able to be saved by George Tenet and the

President's other employees, because this (actually non-existent) "document" wasn't *from* the CIA or any other U.S. source.

It is clear, furthermore, that Mr. Bush was comfortably habituated as a liar, and that he was comfortably accustomed to getting away with it. So, on July 14th, he lied yet again. Closing a White House press conference with U.N. Secretary General Kofi Annan, Mr. Bush said: "The larger point is, and the fundamental question is, did Saddam Hussein have a weapons program? And the answer is, absolutely. And we gave him a chance to allow the inspectors in, and he wouldn't let them in. And, therefore, after a reasonable request, we decided to remove him from power." Of course, the reality, to the exact contrary, is that Saddam did let the inspectors in, and that President Bush ordered them out so that he could invade Iraq. And, of course, the question was never "did Saddam have a weapons program," but rather: Did Saddam *retain* his WMD?

Almost everybody who gets sent to the electric chair (including the numerous indigent people that Bush as the Governor of Texas signed death warrants for) is executed on the basis of far less solid evidence than is available against President Bush in the present case.

Mr. Bush had also managed to induce the Australian Prime Minister, John Howard, to send a token number of troops into this quagmire, and on August 22nd, Reuters headlined from Canberra, "Inquiry Told Australia Govt Lied About Iraq Threat." The reporter, Michelle Nichols, opened, "The Australian government lied about the threat of Iraq's weapons of mass destruction to justify its involvement in the U.S.-led war, an official inquiry on Iraq was told on Friday." On October 7th, the Australian Senate officially censured the Prime Minister for his having lied about the WMD matter in order to win approval to commit Australian troops to the U.S.-led invasion.

Similarly, London's Sunday *Times* on October 5th published excerpts from a new book by former British Foreign Secretary Robin Cook, saying that Prime Minister Blair confided before the war that he knew to be lies his allegations both that Saddam possessed quickly deployable WMD, and that Saddam was a "real and present danger." Prime Minister Blair confided at the time that *both* of his allegations were lies. Of course, if he knew this, then his master across the Atlantic must certainly have known it, *too* – and a great deal more besides.

Mr. Bush's record is conclusive, and it proves that Gary Wills was right when he said: "Bush has been very good at fooling the American people into thinking that Saddam Hussein was behind the attack on the World Trade Center in New York and the Pentagon in Washington and that he is an ally and supplier of Al Qaeda, [and] that eliminating him is the best way to keep terrorism from our shores."

Scientists Still Deny Iraqi Arms Programs

By Walter Pincus and Kevin Sullivan
Washington Post Staff Writers
Thursday, July 31, 2003; Page A01

... All of the [Iraqi] scientists interviewed have denied that Hussein had reconstituted his nuclear weapons program or developed and hidden chemical or biological weapons since United Nations inspectors left in 1998. ...

U.S. Suspects It Received False Iraq Arms Tips: Intelligence officials are reexamining data used in justifying the war. They say Hussein's regime may have sent bogus defectors.

By Bob Drogin,
Los Angeles *Times* Staff Writer
August 28, 2003

WASHINGTON — Frustrated at the failure to find Saddam Hussein's suspected stockpiles of chemical and biological weapons, U.S. and allied intelligence agencies have launched a major effort to determine if they were victims of bogus Iraqi defectors who planted disinformation to mislead the West before the war.

... According to a senior U.S. intelligence official, ... "We're reinterviewing all our sources of information on this." ...

Iraqi scientists say Saddam had no nuclear program after 1991

VIENNA (AFP), Tuesday, Sep 16, 2003

Iraqi scientists working under the new provisional government confirmed Tuesday United Nations claims made before the war that Iraq has not had any nuclear weapons program for over a decade.

"There was no way to revive those attempts. There was nothing left," Dr. Albas Balassem, of Iraq's new ministry of science and technology told reporters. ...

An IAEA official said ... "it's consistent with our findings" that Saddam had no nuclear program after the first Gulf War ended in 1991. ...

United States Department of Defense, News Transcript
www.dod.gov/transcripts/2003/tr20030916-secdef0682.html

Presenter: Secretary Donald H. Rumsfeld, September 16, 2003: ...

Q: "There have been a number of public opinion polls that show a fairly sizable percentage of the public believes that Saddam Hussein was involved in the September 11 attacks. Do you believe that?"

Rumsfeld: **"I've not seen any indication that would lead me to believe that I could say that."**

The White House, The Cabinet Room, News Transcript
www.whitehouse.gov/news/releases/2003/09/20030917-7.html
Remarks by the President, September 17, 2003: ...

Q: "Mr. President, Dr. Rice and Secretary Rumsfeld both said yesterday that they have seen no evidence that Iraq had anything to do with September 11th. Yet, on Meet the Press, Sunday, the Vice President said Iraq was a geographic base for the terrorists and he also said, I don't know, or we don't know, when asked if there was any involvement. Your critics say that this is some effort – deliberate effort to blur the line and confuse people. How would you answer that?"

THE PRESIDENT: **"We've had no evidence that Saddam Hussein was involved with the September 11th."**

Comment : **We are facing death in Iraq for no reason: A serving US soldier calls for the end of an occupation based on lies**

Tim Predmore [101st Airborne Division near Mosul]
The *Guardian*, September 19, 2003
Originally in the *Peoria* [Illinois] *Journal Star*, August 24, 2003

For the past six months, I have been participating in what I believe to be the great modern lie: Operation Iraqi Freedom. ...

From the moment the first shot was fired in this so-called war of liberation and freedom, hypocrisy reigned. ...

As soldiers serving in Iraq, we have been told that our purpose is to help the people of Iraq by providing them with the necessary assistance militarily, as well as in humanitarian efforts. Then tell me where the humanity is in the recent account in Stars and Stripes [the newspaper of the US military] of two young children brought to a US military camp by their mother in search of medical care [after they had toyed with an unexploded bomb] ... who were denied care. ...

So, what is our purpose here? Was this invasion because of weapons of mass destruction, as we have so often heard? If so, where are they? Did we invade to dispose of a leader and his regime because they were closely associated with Osama bin Laden? If so, where is the proof? ...

I once believed that I was serving for a cause – "to uphold and defend the constitution of the United States". Now I no longer believe that; I have lost my conviction, as well as my determination. I can no longer justify my service on the basis of what I believe to be half-truths and bold lies. ...

Joint Chiefs Chairman Worried by Morale Poll

WASHINGTON, Oct. 17, 2003 (Reuters) – Joint Chiefs of Staff Chairman Gen. Richard B. Myers expressed concern Thursday over a survey suggesting morale problems among U.S. troops in Iraq, saying he was worried that he and other top officers were sometimes allowed to talk only to "all the happy folks" when they visited service members.

"I want to see the folks that have complaints. And sometimes they won't let me near them," Myers said when asked about the Stars and Stripes newspaper survey in which half of 1,939 troops said morale in their units was low or very low and that they did not plan to reenlist. ... A third of the respondents complained that their mission lacked clear definition and that they would characterize the war in Iraq as having little or no value. ...

Saddam Seen to Have Backed Iraq Peace Envoys

By Joseph Logan, Fri. Nov 7, 2003

BEIRUT (Reuters) - Iraqi intelligence officials seeking a last-minute deal with Washington to avert war appeared to have [had] the backing of Saddam Hussein, a Lebanese businessman who relayed the offer to U.S. officials said on Friday. Imad Hage ... said the Iraqis were rattled by the threat of war and apparently chose him for his Pentagon contacts. ...

"The broad outline [of the deal] had to do with allowing as many as 2,000 U.S. agents, whether FBI or scientists, to visit Iraq and verify the absence of weapons of mass destruction," he said, adding it came to include turning over Abdul Rahman Yasin, wanted in connection with the 1993 World Trade Center bombing.

"This was to be in addition to concessions on oil deals for the United States, agreeing not to obstruct any U.S. peace deal in the Middle East and to having free elections within two years," he said. ... [He had told ABC News and *Newsweek* two days earlier that the Iraqi elections in this deal were to be supervised by the U.N.]

The White House said on Thursday it exhausted all peaceful opportunities before invading Iraq on March 20, without clarifying whether President Bush had been aware of the offer relayed by Hage. ... [Presidential press spokesman Scott McClellan simply declined comment when asked whether the President had been informed of Saddam's offer.] ...

'No President Has Lied So Baldly And So Often and So Demonstrably'

—

Case for War Confected, Say Top US Officials

By Andrew Gumbel, The Independent
09 November 2003

... "Watching what has happened with Iraq over the past several months has been like watching your daughter being raped," ... says Ray McGovern, who worked as a CIA analyst for 27 years, ... near the very top of his profession, ... preparing the President's daily security brief for Ronald Reagan. ...

"Now we know that no other President of the United States has ever lied so baldly and so often and so demonstrably" [he says]. ...

—

Says Mel Goodman, a veteran CIA analyst, ... "There was never a clear and present danger. There was never an imminent threat. Iraq – and we have very good intelligence on this – was never part of the picture of terrorism." ...

Saddam's Ouster Planned in '01?

from: cbsnews.com, January 10, 2004; 60 Minutes, January 11, 2004:

The Bush Administration began laying plans for an invasion of Iraq, including the use of American troops, within days of President Bush's inauguration in January of 2001 – not eight months later after the 9/11 attacks as has been previously reported.

That's what former Treasury Secretary Paul O'Neill says in his first interview about his time as a White House insider. ...

O'Neill ... is the main source for an upcoming book, "The Price of Loyalty," authored by Ron Suskind.

Suskind says O'Neill and other White House insiders he interviewed gave him documents that show that in the first three months of 2001, the administration was looking at military options for removing Saddam. ...

"There are memos," Suskind tells [correspondent Leslie] Stahl, "One of them marked 'secret' says 'Plan for Post-Saddam Iraq.'" ...

In the book, O'Neill is quoted as saying he was surprised that no one in a National Security Council meeting questioned why Iraq should be invaded. "It was all about finding a way to do it. That was the tone of it. The president saying 'Go find me a way to do this,'" says O'Neill in the book. ...

Chapter 3
The Duped Public

What, then, about the U.S. public itself? Why did the polls show such enormously high American support for invading Iraq, when there wasn't a single other nation in the entire world where polls didn't show the public strongly opposed to this invasion? (For example, The Pew Research Center for the People & the Press, at http://people-press.org/reports/print.php3?PageID=680, issued a report, on the very eve of the invasion, March 18th, "America's Image Further Erodes ... : a nine-country survey," showing that opposition to the invasion was 51% in Britain – and that only 39% of Britons supported it – and that opposition was overwhelming elsewhere: 81% in Spain, 81% in Italy, and 73% in Poland, just to mention some of the more prominent nations that President Bush said were "on our side" in this war.)

Of course, an important part of the reason has to be that no other nation in the entire world is ruled by George W. Bush. However, England's Tony Blair also participated in these lies, and in the invasion, and yet the British press and public were far less supportive of invasion than were the American.

The difference rests, to a major extent, on the relative meekness of America's press.

Although the facts that have been reported here are largely taken from the U.S. news media, those reports constituted perhaps only one to three percent of U.S. news on the Iraq issue, and were drowned out by American media serving essentially as public relations agents for the President's policies, transmitting his lies to the U.S. public, and serving as propaganda organs, instead of as investigative journalists. Most of the American people received their news about the war from television and radio, and these broadcast sources were even more biased in favor of war than were print sources.

Of course, after America's "victory" turned sour, and troops started coming home one-by-one in body bags, instead of all-at-once with peace being restored to Iraq, some in America's major media turned 180 degrees around, and became critical of the Administration and of its numerous lies. But by then it was already too late. The press had already failed. An American institutional catastrophe had already occurred.

There are two sides to this: first, we'll discuss representatives of the clearly partisan American right-wing media, which equated support of Mr. Bush with patriotism, and then we'll address the deeper and more insidious problem, which pervades the entire American major media.

Despite the overwhelming public support for this war by Americans, most who were joining the public demonstrations about it were marching against, and not for, this invasion. The relatively few Americans who recognized that their President was lying, tended to be sufficiently enraged to join these marches, but most of the war's supporters didn't feel quite so passionately about the war-issue. Nonetheless, some of the invasion's supporters *did* feel that passion, and *where* they did, this was often passion whipped up by the far-Right nationalist media, such as by Fox News Channel on television, and by Clear Channel Communications on radio.

Fox News Channel, run by former Republican President Ronald Reagan's propaganda chief Roger Ailes, is controlled by international newspaper-owner Rupert Murdoch, a dedicated far-Rightist, and the man who grubstaked the neo-conservative and longtime Iraq-war hawk, William Kristol, to become the publisher of Vice President Dick Cheney's favorite magazine, the *Weekly Standard*. This helped Mr. Kristol, in his "spare time," to organize the Project for a New American Century in 1998, which immediately, but unsuccessfully, lobbied the Democratic Bill Clinton Administration to invade Iraq. Now that their man and fellow Iraq hawk G.W. Bush was finally in the White House, Fox's "news" reporting about this war was naturally dominated by "patriotic" flag-waving propaganda for Our Great Leader.

Mr. Murdoch, as a global media baron, also did everything he could to encourage and to support British Prime Minister Tony Blair's crucial decision to *join* in the American invasion. After the invasion, on August 25th, Mr. Murdoch's potent bond with Mr. Blair's "New Labour" neo-conservative (or neo-liberal) corporate nationalism sparked the *Independent*'s Media and Culture Editor, Vincent Graff, to headline "BBC Launches Public Attack on Murdoch 'Imperialism.'" Mr. Graff reported: "The controller of BBC1 launched an unprecedented attack on Rupert Murdoch yesterday, calling the media billionaire a 'capital imperialist' who wants to destabilize the [BBC] corporation because he 'is against everything the BBC stands for'. Lorraine Heggessey said Mr Murdoch's continued attacks on the BBC stemmed from a dislike of the public sector. But he did not understand that the

British people 'have a National Health Service, a public education system' and trust organisations that are there for the benefit of society and not driven by profit. Her controversial comments, in an interview with *The Independent*, are believed to be the first time a senior BBC executive has publicly attacked the motives of the media tycoon. They follow an intensification of anti-BBC rhetoric from Mr Murdoch's side." Murdoch and the BBC were at war with each other.

Rupert Murdoch was, in fact, similar to the neo-fascist Italian media baron (and now Prime Minister), Silvio Berlusconi, in his using his press to promote the invasion of Iraq. However, whereas Mr. Berlusconi's media empire was only local (within Italy), Mr. Murdoch's was global. Furthermore, whereas Mr. Murdoch was no politician himself, Mr. Berlusconi had successfully used his control over Italy's three main commercial television channels, and of the newspapers, to win his own election as Italy's head of State. Thereby, Mr. Berlusconi now controlled even the three State-run TV channels, whereas Mr. Murdoch was waging war against the British public network, BBC. The BBC's worry was that Mr. Murdoch might obtain a similar grip upon the British media, not by his becoming Prime Minister, but by his currying favor with the existing neo-conservative/neo-liberal Prime Minister Blair, who exercises considerable influence over a British competitor, the State-run BBC. Mr. Blair was, moreover, at that time, himself in the midst of a huge battle against the BBC, on account of the BBC's having failed to support the invasion, despite the network's receiving State funds. The BBC didn't cave in to the Government on this invasion, even though the BBC was far more dependent upon the Government than were America's closest broadcast equivalents, PBS television and NPR radio. The British Government was, in effect, now threatening to pull the plug on the BBC for being more skeptical of Government lies than their American non-commercial counterparts. Mr. Murdoch naturally favored the Prime Minister's aim against the BBC, at least to bring them into line, if not indeed to eliminate the BBC from the British media competition altogether.[*]

---

[*] The *aim* of fascists is to reduce competition. Oligopolies and monopolies do that. As competition goes down, power proportionately increases, and fascists worship power. The actual aim of fascists is therefore to increase power, and they do this *by means of* reducing competition. Reducing or eliminating competition transforms what was formerly a competitor into a dependent, who might even (in the extreme example) be a slave. The increase in one's own power comes always at the expense of the freedom of others. Therefore, when a fascist says that he favors "freedom," the only individual's freedom he is actually promoting is his own, and he enhances it by weakening or eliminating competitors. This inevitably *reduces* the freedom of those others. Power is correctly called a "zero-sum game," with a "winner" and a "loser," because, as contrasted with positive-sum games like trade or exchange or any other form of purely economic competition, its benefits to one person come inevitably at the expense of the

Just the same way that media oligopolists such as Rupert Murdoch seek to eliminate competition within the media, the Bush Administration have been trying to eliminate competition in the international *political* arena. They oppose the idea that France's President Jacques Chirac was promoting, of a "multi-polar world," which entails competing nations. The Bush Administration favor instead a "unipolar world": everyone must submit to the lone super-power, the United States. Rather than competing powers, there should, they believe, be one almighty power – the United States – in the international arena, imposing its will upon the world. Ideologically, therefore, Mr. Bush and Mr. Murdoch are very close, and they have lots of company.

Clear Channel is the giant of American radio, owning over 1,200 radio stations, many of which carry nationalistic talk shows such as Rush Limbaugh. As the progressive columnist Paul Krugman noted in *The New York Times* on March 25th, Clear Channel organized most of the pro-war demonstrations around the country at the same time as it was lobbying the Bush Administration to permit the company to expand into television and other areas that could increase the firm's media control in many local U.S. markets and thereby enable it to reduce yet further the news function at the expense of propagandizing the public to support such conservative policies and politicians. (Another reason they would favor such conservative politicians is to strengthen their position against those of their employees and former employees who have charged Clear Channel with sexually harassing them, or else with firing them for whistle-blowing.) Mr. Bush's head of the Federal Communications Commission, Michael Powell, the son of the Secretary of State in this highly nepotistic Administration, was only too happy to oblige these media giants, and thus doggedly led this initiative on the part of those oligopolists. However, this medi-ocracy (or, to use the full phrase, media-aristocracy) position was too fascistic even for some conservatives. Even the conservative Nixonian political columnist William Safire, also in *The New York Times*, was headlining on July 24th

---

losses to other persons. Not everyone can benefit, but there must be individuals who are actually left worse off, with *less* freedom than they had before, because they've lost their freedom to this master, the winner in the power-game, *not* in any competition-game. Power is the two-person, zero-sum, game, that's the subject of political science. By contrast, competition is a four-person game, in economics, where both the buyers and the sellers have competition, and both the buyer and the seller in any given transaction benefit without hurting anyone. It is always (at least) a four-person game, in which always (at least) two players win, and always the others aren't (necessarily) affected by the exchange at all. When two people exchange goods, both do it in order to become better off, but bystanders are not necessarily hurt by the exchange. Even competitors are not hurt; they just are not helped. There are no winners or losers, but only two people freely choosing to exchange goods and/or services. Fascists lie and call the power-game the competition-game; it's not. Power *corrupts* the competition-game.

"Bush's Four Horsemen" (of the media Apocalypse), sub-heading a-
bout Bush, "He's embedded with media giants." Safire argued that the
four TV networks were bonded with this White House to their mutual
benefit, against the interests of an informed public in a democracy. But
actually, it wasn't *just* the four major networks. For example, Clear
Channel's top management had personally assisted Mr. Bush years
earlier in a business deal that made Mr. Bush, previously a failure in
business, very wealthy. Furthermore, Thomas B. Edsall and Sarah Co-
hen reported in the *Washington Post* on August 10th, under the banner, "Broadcasters Bank on a Combination of Interests: Parties Seeking FCC Approval of Hispanic Broadcasting Merger Are Big Donors to
Bush Campaign," describing the lobbying efforts of Clear Channel and
other big Bush contributors, who were aiming to win government approval to control access to 80% of the U.S. Hispanic television and radio audience. Mr. Bush's saying "yes" to his medi-ocracy friends provided a way to get his message out to Hispanic voters without spending
a cent. In fact, far from charging the President for such access, these
big media companies were helping finance his "re"-election. And then,
too, there was their friendly "news" reporting about this war. And
there was also their blocking popular and time-tested liberal local-ra-
dio talk shows from reaching any broader national network exposure
(such as is documented about the very popular talk show host Randi
Rhodes, at www.takebackthemedia.com/randi.html), by denying network syndication even to liberal program hosts who were drawing bigger local radio audiences than Rush Limbaugh and other conservatives. What the beer halls had been to Germany in the 1920's, talk radio had become to America in the 1990's, and Clear Channel Communications was an important part of that. Friends in high places don't say
or do things that would be unpleasant to friends in high places.

    Think of it as a club. Then think of that club hitting the Amer-
ican public very effectively between the ears. This is what has now
become American "democracy."*

---

*   Here's an interesting aspect of that "club": Freelance journalist Clementine
Wallace wrote in the July/August 2003 issue of *Extra!* magazine, headlining "Saying
Non to Rupert: More to Murdoch's France-bashing than just politics." She reported:
"In the U.S., NewsCorp recently acquired DirecTV, the country's biggest satellite
broadcaster, after the Bush Justice Department barred Murdoch's competitor Echostar
from bidding. This little favor, completed the same day the Saddam Hussein statue was
toppled in Baghdad, saved Murdoch about $15 billion." Consumers Union had testified
in Congress on May 6th against this merger, saying that it would "threaten to harm
meaningful competition between media companies." By contrast, on October 10th of
2002, the "Consumers Union Statement on FCC Rejection of Echostar - DirecTV
Merger" had protested against the FCC's action of barring *that* merger, saying that,
though "the merger of the two dominant providers of satellite TV naturally raised
concerns, ... this merger could have been structured in a way that actually helped
consumers by making satellite TV a legitimate competitor to cable TV."

Al Franken's 2003 *LIES and the Lying Liars Who Tell Them* does a very effective job of proving that America's overtly right-wing media (Fox, Ann Coulter, etc.) lie so consciously and so brazenly that to call them "news" media and commentators would have to be either ignorant or else a lie itself. The very fact that such premeditated fabricators are referred to in *other* U.S. media as commentators and purveyors of "news" is scandalous. This doesn't mean that every detail that these right-wing PR agencies report is false; only that the numerous falsehoods are there for purposes of political indoctrination, rather than being merely honest and incompetent blunders. Franken demonstrates these people's professionalism (as political propagandists) at the same time as he proves that they're not authentic journalists. In the United States, it took a *comedian* to do this!

A lesser known but crucial element of the media consists of media consultants, one of which, McVay Media, of Cleveland, Ohio, was urging radio stations around the nation, "Get the following production pieces in the studio NOW ... Patriotic music that makes you cry, salute, get cold chills! Go for the emotion!" McVay trumpeted surveys that supposedly showed the American people turning away from stations that report anything anti-war, such as protest marches, and tuning in to stations that are mindlessly nationalistic or "patriotic." Similarly, another broadcast consultant, Frank N. Magid Associates, of Cedar Rapids, Iowa, was advising television news executives that Americans change channels when they see scenes of war protesters. Perhaps it's true that the majority of Americans not only are fooled, but are bigoted against the minority among themselves who aren't. But even if this is so, the news business in a democracy cannot cater to such prejudices, or else the country won't continue to *be* a democracy. Perhaps corporate media sometimes gravitate toward fascism. If so, this was certainly such a time.

Therefore, Bush's FCC had, it seems, squelched a higher competing bid for DirecTV by Echostar, even though Murdoch's bid was worse for consumers, and though the FCC is supposed to protect consumers. At http://media.guardian.co.uk/rupertmurdoch/story/0,11136,879383,00.html appears "A History of Rivalry: News Corp, DirecTV and Echostar," which presents a time-line of the competing bids by Charlie Ergen of Echostar and by Rupert Murdoch of NewsCorp. Mr. Ergen's bid was far higher, and he seems to have been a pretty smart man, as a former professional poker player. However, he had not done the enormous favors for President Bush that Rupert Murdoch had done, and therefore, the Bush FCC prohibited the Ergen bid from going through, and the sellers of DirecTV were compelled to settle for the less lucrative offer from Mr. Murdoch. This is not capitalism; it's neo-feudalism, otherwise known as fascism. The same issue of *Extra!* provided also excellent and ample documentation of how Mr. Murdoch's media properties warped the news so as to propagandize Americans into supporting invading Iraq. All of this is the result of power corrupting the competition-game.

However, most of the American media tries to avoid such rank partisanship, and just to deliver the regime's propaganda straight, without "patriotic" icing on the cake. These are what used to be called "the mainstream media." The problem with them is that they still aren't reporting news. They're passing along government propaganda, some of which is news, and some of which is lies. (Probably an example of such transmission of lies was Judith Miller's report in the *NYT*, previously discussed, concerning an unnamed Iraqi scientist who was alleged to have said that Iraq had destroyed its WMD right before the American invasion.) Although a few of these mainstream news organizations (obviously *not* including the *NYT*) have made great efforts to sift out the falsehoods and to report only the actually confirmed facts, real journalism is investigative in nature, and investigative journalism is both expensive and a dying craft in America's increasingly oligopolistic media. Investigative journalism is also increasingly perceived by the American people to be offensive, or, in the case of a war, even unpatriotic. British news media consequently were far more aggressive in probing Prime Minister Blair's veracity on the war than U.S. news media were in probing President Bush's lies. The Bush Administration thus had highly effective means available to it for shaping "news" that might otherwise have come from any wayward reporter who took his journalistic assignment so seriously as to seek to report what the Administration preferred *not* to be reported.

For example, at www.gulufuture.com/news/kate_adie030310 .htm, is a pre-war report, March 10th, from veteran BBC war correspondent Kate Adie, saying that the Pentagon had outright threatened that they might shoot her, and could kill her, if she wouldn't embed herself with the invading troops. And during the fighting a month later, on April 8th, the *Guardian* bannered, "Military accused of targeting non-embedded journalists," reporting that, "The International Federation of Journalists has accused US military commanders of targeting non-embedded journalists." Several journalists were in fact killed, and not by anything like stray fire, but, as it turns out, by precisely targeted hits. The *Independent*'s Robert Fisk reported the next day, under the title, "Is there some element in the US military that wants to take out journalists?" The *Guardian* headlined, that day, "Iraq – the most dangerous war for journalists," and quoted a BBC correspondent as saying, "independent witnessing of war is becoming increasingly dangerous, and this may be the end of it." In another story that same day, the *Guardian* reported a BBC world affairs editor saying, "The independent journalists are upholding a great tradition, but my goodness they're taking a hammering." Bush's message seemed to be clear: report the war *our* way, or else don't report it at all.

The *Independent*'s Mr. Fisk became even angrier after ruminating for a few weeks and visiting in the hospital some of the journalists who had been struck by a shot from a U.S. Army M1A1 Abrams tank that had fired into the Reuters office high upon the 15th floor of the hotel where journalists were staying, the Palestine Hotel. Reuters had been reporting things that exposed some of the lies of the U.S. Administration. On April 26th, Mr. Fisk recounted of this fatal tank blast: "At the time, General Buford Blount of the 3rd Infantry Division, told a lie: he said that sniper fire had been directed at the tank. ... I was between the tank and the hotel when the shell was fired. There was no sniper fire – nor any rocket-propelled grenade fire, as the American officer claimed – at the time. French television footage of the tank, running for minutes before the attack, shows the same thing. The soundtrack – until the blinding, repulsive golden flash from the tank barrel – is silent." Mr. Fisk's account was seconded on May 27th by a study from the Committee to Protect Journalists. They interviewed "many" journalists who had witnessed the event. All agreed that the U.S. military's account of it was, as one of them put it, "impossible." Nonetheless, the military's account continued to be maintained by all spokesmen for the trusted but untrustworthy Bush Administration. Secretary of State Powell, for example, said, "the use of force was justified and the amount of force was proportionate to the threat against United States forces."

On the same day when the journalists' hotel was targeted, April 8th, the Baghdad office of the independent Arabic television operation, Al Jazeera, also took a precise hit from U.S. forces. Al Jazeera had broadcast many images of the war's victims. U.S. retribution thus hit these Arab newsmen, too, on that day when Mr. Bush was settling scores with unsubmissive journalists, and thereby warning those who survived. Mr. Fisk continued: "And on 8 April, less than three hours before the Reuters office was attacked, an American aircraft fired a single missile at the Al-Jazeera office." More innocent deaths. But hardly unexpected. Bush was here building upon his father's propaganda policy in the 1991 Gulf war; and so John MacArthur, the author of a book about that war, who was also a keen student of the younger Bush's 2001 invasion of Afghanistan, had accurately predicted, at the end of 2002, in a www.btlonline.org interview: "Whatever images we get of combat [in Iraq] will be from Al Jazeera or the BBC, I suppose. But probably from Al Jazeera, and that will be until the American Air Force bombs the Al Jazeera bureau in Baghdad, the way we bombed it in Kabul" (which had occurred on November 13, 2001). According to the Air Force's unclassified report "Operation Iraqi Freedom – By The Numbers," which was dated 30 April 2003, and prepared by USAF Lt. Gen T. Michael Moseley, the Air Force admits (p. 9), under the category "Information Warfare Physical Attack," that it hit 116 such targets, "which included 10 media facilities." The report didn't identify the 10 "media facilities" that were targeted. But Deputy Defense Secretary Paul Wolfowitz told Fox News, on July 27th, that Al Jazeera was "slanting news incredibly" about America's invasion/occupation of Iraq. He vaguely warned countries that permitted it to operate, "These governments should stop and realize that this is not a game." As he spoke, an Al Jazeera journalist who had filmed an attack on U.S. troops in the Iraqi city of Mosul went on a hunger strike to protest his imprisonment by U.S. forces; U.S. military officials refused either to confirm or deny that he was even in their custody.

After the war was supposedly over, the U.S. in August shot and killed another Reuters cameraman, and said that he had been fired upon because his camera looked like a gun. But on August 18th, CBS News headlined, "Reporters: U.S. Troops Negligent," and opened: "Fellow journalists accused U.S. troops of negligence in the shooting death of a Reuters cameraman, saying it was clear the victim was a newsman when soldiers on two tanks opened fire."

The way that these events happened can be likely inferred from what's behind the lines, or between the lines – or "implied" – by the postwar investigation that the Committee to Protect Journalists did concerning the Army's firing into the Palestine Hotel on April 8th. This report said that although commanders were aware that journalists were staying in the Palestine Hotel, troops on the ground weren't informed of that crucial fact. This would be the best possible environment to create the "accident": a field commander, under instructions from higher-ups to have the target fired upon, would simply ask an uninformed cannoneer a question such as, "did you see that guy up there with the gun pointing at us?" and when the frightened soldier says "Yes, Sir!" – if for no other reason than to avoid being seen as a slacker – the deed is as good as done. The cannoneer has no idea of what might possibly be up on the 15th floor of a tall building like any other; perhaps it's a perch for enemy troops. In this scenario, the man firing the shot would be entirely innocent, even while the chain of command above him is guilty of murdering journalists. Such a technique would provide superb "deniability" for commanders.

On August 26th, *Editor & Publisher* magazine headlined, "Press Groups Blast Pentagon Report" on these incidents, and noted, "International press-freedom groups say there have been other disturbing incidents by U.S. soldiers, who in recent weeks seized digital cameras from Turkish journalists and erased the images; beat and detained a cameraman for the Nippon Television Network in Japan; detained Al-Jazeera journalists, and ransacked the offices of a newspaper published by the Shiite Muslim party." This news story also mentioned that the Pentagon had changed its official line on how the April 8th incident at the Palestine Hotel had occurred: a Centcom (Central Command) statement was asserting that the crew that fired the cannon had "observed what they believed to be a [sic] enemy hunter/killer team on the balcony." No longer was the Pentagon claiming that hostile fire had been coming from this balcony.

On November 13th, *Editor & Publisher* headlined "30 Media Outlets Protest Treatment in Iraq: Claim: Reporters Harassed, Tapes Confiscated." AP, CNN, ABC, and many other media, signed a letter to the Pentagon, saying these incidents "appear intended to discourage journalists from covering the continued military action in Iraq."

Reporters Without Borders issued a report, January 15, 2004, titled "Two Murders and a Lie," charging the Bush Administration with "criminal negligence" in the April 8th Palestine Hotel tank blast, and with lying about how it occurred. The investigation confirmed, "the soldiers in the field were never told the hotel was full of journalists." It thus lent further confirmation to the guilt of higher-ups.

Under the Geneva Conventions, any military firing on media facilities, or upon journalists, is prohibited in all circumstances, even if hostile fire is perceived to be coming from a journalist's location. Mr. Bush simply ignored international law.

Nor were American reporters entirely safe even at home, in the U.S. itself. Well before the outright invasion of Iraq started, CBS News anchor Dan Rather told the BBC's Madeleine Holt, in a BBC NewsNight interview broadcast on June 6, 2002 (according to the transcript on the website), "It's an obscene comparison, but there was a time in South Africa when people would put flaming tyres around people's necks if they dissented. In some ways, the fear is that you will be neck-laced here, you will have a flaming tyre of lack of patriotism put around your neck. It's that fear that keeps journalists from asking the toughest of the tough questions." He further asserted that, "What is going on to a very large extent I'm sorry to say, is a belief that the public doesn't need to know, ... and I'm sorry to say that up to and including the moment of this interview, it has been accepted by the American people. And the current Administration revels in that, they relish that and take refuge in that." (Shades, again, of the American public's ignoring the adage, "Eternal vigilance is the price of liberty.")

Journalist Seymour Hersh, of Vietnam War My Lai Massacre and much other fame, presented the bottom line when he addressed The Harvard Crimson to accept their Goldsmith Award, right before the invasion, on March 11th. He started his speech by portraying the dangers that America's reporters face, especially in Washington: "I've never seen my peers as frightened as they are now." He continued, "There is no real standard of integrity because the White House does-

n't have any." Hersh was amazed by this Administration's aggressiveness, saying, "It's scary." On May 20th, the Rockford [Illinois] *Register
Star* reported that *New York Times* reporter Chris Hedges was booed
off the stage delivering a commencement speech at Rockford College,
for saying such things as, "War in the end is always about betrayal.
Betrayal of the young by the old, of soldiers by politicians, and idealists
by cynics." His microphone was unplugged after only three minutes,
amid catcalls, foghorns, and objects thrown onto the stage. After the
main war was over, on July 18th, Lloyd Grove reported in the *Washington Post*, under the headline, "Drudging Up Personal Details," that
an ABC TV journalist, who had aired a piece that the Administration
didn't like, had just been publicly "outed" by the White House press
office as an admitted homosexual and a foreigner. Was this White
House determined to confirm Mr. Hersh's charge that they had "no
real standard of integrity"?

Opposition to Big Brother's line took real courage. A June 30th
story in Australia's daily, *The Age*, was headlined "Freedom Fighters,"
and itemized a long list of America's free-speech casualties: "Actress
Susan Sarandon, a well-known political activist, was recently told she
would not be appearing as scheduled at a charity function because it
could divide the community. Dustin Hoffman, who has been out-
spoken about the Iraq war, was forced to cancel a pacifist speech he
was due to make in Los Angeles after receiving threatening emails and
phone calls. Sean Penn said his opposition to the war cost him a film
role." And it went on, and on, like that. Glasgow Scotland's *Sunday
Herald* headlined, on September 14th, "Even Cowgirls Get the Boos,"
describing the career problems of the Dixie Chicks country music
group. These singers were targeted by Clear Channel radio for career-
destruction, because these singing Texans publicly said, a week before
the invasion of Iraq, "we're ashamed the President of the United States
is from Texas." Many U.S. radio stations then banned their music.

American politicians who were in the Democratic opposition to
the war were likewise in a vulnerable position. On March 24th, *USA
Today* ran an article headlined, "Peace Movement Revives Old Party
Split for Democrats." It reported that Democratic office-holders were
reluctant to criticize the invasion, for fear of feeding stereotypes that
voters have of Democrats as being "weak on defense," even though
both World Wars were military victories for Democratic U.S. Presidents, *not* for Republicans. Republican politicians were eager to pan-
der to the American prejudice that falsely equates Republican military
aggressiveness with national strength: "Anti-war remarks by prominent Democrats ... 'reinforce the impression that Democrats are not
willing to do the hard things with the military to protect the country,'
says Whit Ayres, a Republican pollster. Some Democrats may be more

hawkish, he says, but 'the messages that penetrate most effectively are those that reinforce stereotypes' like the anti-war tag. Bill McInturff, another Republican pollster, says Democrats are 'digging the hole deeper and deeper. You've got issues that are critical to the next presidential election, and you're starting in a horrible hole on credibility.'" So, according to this American "news" report, the politicians who had a "credibility" problem were *not* the actually lying President and his lying Administration and lying Republican supporters in Congress, but were instead the few honest *Democrats* who were bold enough to *challenge* those lies and that lying war policy. The article even closed with a quotation from John Podesta, former Democratic President Bill Clinton's chief of staff, saying of anti-war Democrats, "'If you merely adopt their posture, last time I checked, you still can't get to be president with 15 electoral votes.' That's how many a candidate would get today by matching [anti-Vietnam-war Democratic Presidential candidate George] McGovern's 1972 performance." Thus, this American mainstream "news" story was spinning the line that even prominent Democrats *agreed* that Democrats, and *not* the President, had a problem of "credibility."

If those Democrats who might have felt this way were President Bush's opponents, then he actually had only friends. Among his friends were, certainly, NBC TV's influential Sunday news interview program, "Meet the Press," whose guest, on June 22nd, happened to be the anti-war Democratic Presidential candidate, Howard Dean. The interviewer, Tim Russert, challenged Dr. Dean's proposal to roll back the Bush tax cuts. As the *Washington Post*'s Mike Allen reported about that question the next day, the research behind the inquiry had been done actually not by NBC, but by the Bush Administration itself, and, "The research was prepared at the request of 'Meet the Press.'" Reporter Allen pointed out that there had been factual distortions in this "research" supplied by the Administration. However, the candidate, Dr. Dean, couldn't possibly have been aware of that at the time; he had to answer the question as if it were based on entirely truthful facts. Similarly, *Time* magazine's Martin Lewis had reported, on November 3, 2000, right before the U.S. Presidential election, that candidate Bush's opposition researchers, the people who were being paid to dig dirt on the Democratic candidate Al Gore, had been contacted by "Meet the Press" and by other "news" media, for questions and for allegations to throw against Mr. Gore. One such Republican National Committee researcher was even quoted by Mr. Lewis as observing, "It's an amazing thing when you have top-line producers and reporters calling you and saying 'We trust you. We need your stuff.'" And this "stuff" wasn't even checked for accuracy. That's the American mainstream major media, drawing their "facts" from the Republican Party's opposition research. This is the new American "democracy."

Agence France Press reported, on April 16th, under the heading "US Bans Media from Protests," that, "US forces yesterday tried to stop the media from covering a third day of anti-American protests by Iraqis outside a hotel housing a US operations base. ... 'They (the Iraqis) are only performing because the media are here,' said a marines colonel who would not give his first name or title. The crowd ... moved to a nearby square." Was this war a media event, controlled by the invader?

A report by Harry Bhaskara in the *Jakarta Post* on April 3rd, datelined from Berkeley, California, concerned the frustration that mere garden-variety anti-war Americans were experiencing when trying to have their voices heard. Mr. Bhaskara was, it appears, attempting to explain America's remarkably controlled press to Indonesians, who didn't understand such a thing happening in what they had *thought* was a democracy.

Is it? President Bush's National Security Advisor Condoleezza Rice opened an op-ed in the rabidly pro-invasion *Wall Street Journal* on March 26th, titled "Our Coalition," by claiming: "The coalition that is currently engaged in the hard, dangerous work to disarm Iraq is strong, broad and diverse. Nearly 50 nations are committed to ridding Saddam Hussein's regime of all its deadly, destructive and illegal weapons. To put this in perspective, the combined population of coalition countries is approximately 1.23 billion people." Her piece, like the pronouncements of Big Brother in George Orwell's novel *1984*, was filled with lies and distortions; it even repeated the fabrication about Iraq's WMD. She even said of this coalition, "each member shares a common goal. We seek nothing less than safety for our people. Many members have suffered from terror themselves; all understand the awful price of terrorism and the potentially catastrophic danger from weapons of mass destruction." But what was especially shocking here was the Bush Administration's assumption that countries like Spain, where 81% of the people were opposed to this invasion, and which contributed virtually nothing in troops and assets to it, were nonetheless being claimed by Mr. Bush as part of this "coalition," only because the given nation's leader had provided his lip-service to the invasion. (And – despite Mr. Bush's talk about his dedication to "democracy" – the Spanish leader was paying a heavy price for the *real thing*: Spain's premier newspaper, *El Pais*, bannered, "War Sinks Aznar's Popularity.") That lip service, from the country's leader, constituted his entire nation's membership in "the coalition that is currently engaged in the hard, dangerous work" of – of, really, *what*? Dangerous work of – lip service? But this wasn't even the *people's* lip service; it was *only* their very lonely *leader's*.

Such a "coalition" came also at a high price to the American taxpayer; and not merely because, unlike the first (1991) Gulf War, when an authentic coalition was freeing Kuwait from an Iraqi invasion, other nations weren't pitching in, this time, to help finance the war. This time, Americans had to pay not only for the war, but for the mere lip service to it by the leaders of other countries. On March 8th, even the pro-invasion *Times* of London (one of Rupert Murdoch's papers, no less) bannered, "'Bribes' Pushing UN Waverers into Support for War." Turkey, however, turned down America's thirty-billion-dollar offer. On March 2nd, the *Observer* headlined, "America the Arm-Twister: In the conflict over a second resolution that could trigger a war, the 'Middle Six' nations on the UN Security Council face a barrage of bribes, persuasion and blatant threats." On March 3rd, Mr. Bush himself told Copley News Service that if Mexico didn't support him in the U.N. vote, "I don't expect there to be significant retribution from the government," meaning that there would be a "retribution" from "the government," but not as bad as the "retribution" from masses of American bigots, against Mexicans living in America; and he explicitly warned that there would be some such "backlash" (which fortunately did *not* occur; the American people weren't as evil as their President was fantasizing them to be, and as he himself actually *was*). His outrageous comments were essentially ignored by the shameful American press, but the comments created a fury in Mexico. That demonstrates how Mr. Bush is no more interested in what the majority of Mexicans favor, or Spaniards favor, than he was interested in what the majority of Americans favored, when he himself "won" the U.S. Presidency by Supreme Court appointment, despite having lost to his opponent Al Gore by 543,000 votes, and despite post-election analyses that showed the majority of Floridians had preferred Al Gore, even if, according to some – but not all – of the vote-recounts, Bush edged out Gore in that state. Mr. Bush clearly is not a man who supports democracy. So, then, yet again: is the U.S. really one any longer?

The present discussion started out by exploring the question: Where are Saddam's WMD? But now, the questions are becoming far more serious (and less imaginary) than Iraq's surviving WMD. And the answers, for Americans, and for the entire world subject to American military power, are, frankly, grim.

What ought we to conclude from all this? The answer to that question is now becoming increasingly obvious: the United States is ruled by a tyrant and doesn't know it.

Chapter 4
America's Corrupt Media

Why don't the American people know that they live under a tyranny? The American press has failed to report it to the U.S. public. Or rather, the snippets of this reality that, at the time, did manage to become reported in the U.S. (and that have been presented here) were not placed by the American news media into a meaningful context. And these important snippets furthermore failed to ricochet throughout the American media even when they did appear. They didn't resonate within the American media, even though these facts made big splashes abroad. This is the reason why, as *Time* magazine reported on March 3rd, after polling Americans: "Again and again in interviews last week, Americans told Time that their faith in Bush is what ultimately overcomes their reservations about his policy in Iraq." One of these fooled Americans (whom the Administration might privately view with smug satisfaction as simply "fools," or else "suckers") expressed it this way: "He is keeping a lot from us to protect us." The press coverage of Mr. Bush was far bolder and more honest in every other nation, and so it's hardly surprising that polls around the world showed that only the American people supported this invasion. (Britons came to support it only after Britain's troops were already fighting in it. Then British sentiment swung quickly to favor pulling troops out.)

Why is this? One possible reason is that the U.S. press is more controlled than is that in the U.K. or most other democracies. (At least, America *used* to be a democracy.) As the *Christian Science Monitor* astutely observed on March 25th, under the headline, "World and America Watching Different Wars": "Some analysts note that European press ownership is less concentrated than its counterparts in the US." For a characteristic example of this: London has eight major daily newspapers; whereas New York City, though slightly larger, has only four. The big corporate members of the American media oligopoly receive policy favors from the Bush Administration, and repay this with favorable "news" coverage on matters of critical importance to the Administration; it's a trading of political and financial favors.

One example of this was already previously mentioned here; namely, that all of the U.S. major media had lobbied for a historic rule-change that President Bush's Federal Communications Commission, headed by Colin Powell's son Michael Powell, rammed through on June 2, 2003, in a straight party-line vote, and against huge public opposition. Here's how Catherine Yang described the immense stakes of this rule-change, in her critical commentary, "How Michael Powell Could Have the Last Laugh," in *Business Week* on September 22nd: "Opening the floodgates to allow local behemoths to combine newspapers, TV, and radio stations under one roof would change media ownership in towns and cities, concentrating it in the hands of a few. Even in midsize cities, such as San Antonio, for instance, one company might own the leading newspaper, two TV stations, eight radio stations, and several cable channels." That's a "democracy"? As reported by Charles Layton in the January 2004 *American Journalism Review*, there had even been a virtual major-media "News Blackout" leading up to the momentous June 2nd FCC vote.

One important result of big media's "cooperative" relationship with the President was the biased way this war was covered in the American "news" media. For example, while Americans during the early phase of the Iraq invasion were being inundated with patriotic propaganda passing as war "news," Britons and the rest of the world were receiving a heavy dose of the much harsher realities about the war.

To give here just a taste of the coverage outside the U.S., this is Robert Fisk, in the *Independent*, reporting about the early days of the U.S./U.K invasion of Iraq: on March 27th: "It was an outrage, an obscenity. The severed hand on the metal door, the swamp of blood and mud across the road, the human brains inside a garage, the incinerated, skeletal remains of an Iraqi mother and her three small children in their still-smouldering car. Two missiles from an American jet killed them all – by my estimate, more than 20 Iraqi civilians, torn to pieces before they could be 'liberated' by the nation that destroyed their lives." The next day, on March 28th: "Two British soldiers lie dead on a Basra roadway, a small Iraqi girl – victim of an Anglo American air strike – is brought to hospital with her intestines spilling out of her stomach, a terribly wounded woman screams in agony as doctors try to take off her black dress."

That was the war being reported from the standpoint of its victims. Americans, instead, received their "news" from "embedded journalists" who reported from the standpoint of the invaders. The U.S. press slathered over the victims' bloodshed with the "victory" reports from the Pentagon. As *Newsweek* observed (April 14th, p. 49), "the war Americans see on their television screens is wholly different from what's shown elsewhere. U.S. programming concentrates on victory. Arab and Muslim TV focuses on victims." However, even this statement from the U.S. press was distorting: it wasn't only "Arab and Muslim TV" that was reporting a different reality; it was only the American press – and virtually all of it – that was exceptional, in the sense of standing out as unusual, and also in the sense of its being exceptionally *bad*. America's press virtually lied to its public, with its one-sided and grossly oversized focus on "our heroic troops," reporting this invasion of an ancient Muslim nation by a young Christian one, as being, instead, simply a "liberation." Of course, after the invasion was over, Americans were shocked to see that Iraqis didn't perceive things in quite the same Pollyannaish way. And only *after* the war, not *during*, did the U.S. press start reporting the victims' perspective.

Americans had been shielded from the realities of what their own federal tax-dollars were purchasing in Iraq: the *confirmed* civilian Iraqi war dead reported in the world press, as of May 22nd, at www.iraqbodycount.net, were about 5,500, and this number didn't include the "merely injured," nor did it include the corpses that no journalist had managed to see. On May 18th, the *Los Angeles Times* provided some well-researched information on that; it headlined a story, "Baghdad's Death Toll Assessed: A Times survey of hospitals finds that at least 1,700 civilians were killed and more than 8,000 hurt in the battle for the Iraqi capital." The reporter, Laura King, assiduously checked the records of 27 Baghdad-area hospitals, serving the capital city that is home to about a fifth of Iraq's population. Her survey excluded any corpses or injuries that were not processed through the city's hospitals. However, many corpses were buried immediately, and some injuries also went untreated by hospitals. (As Paul Wiseman observed months later, reporting from Baghdad, on December 11th, in *USA Today*, "Iraqi hospital records are incomplete, and many Iraqi families buried their dead without reporting their deaths.") Projecting nationwide, then, the American/British invasion produced at least 5,500 civilians dead and 26,000 civilians injured (using the iraqbodycount.net base for corpses, and the Baghdad hospital survey for the injuries-multiplier); or, alternatively, perhaps at least 8,500 civilians killed and 40,000 injured (using the Baghdad hospital survey for the base, and a multiplier of five for the entire country). Late in October, a medact.org study at www.medact.org/tbx/pages/sub.cfm?id=775 estimated Iraqi deaths at 7,800-9,600 civilians, and 13,500-45,000 soldiers. In any case, the Pentagon invaders showed no interest to determine the *real* numbers, and this fact alone is going to be sending an ugly message to the Iraqi people, especially to the families of the victims.

Under the headline "Who's Counting the Dead in Iraq," Helen Thomas of Knight Ridder, on September 6th, reported that when she had asked the Pentagon "How many Iraqis have been killed in this war?" she was told, "We don't track them (Iraqi dead). ... They don't count. They are not important." Not only was that thinking cruel, but this invasion was *supposed* to be in the war against Islamic *terrorism;* and so, to believe that such callousness fueling Islamic rage, which creates needlessly many *new* terrorists, is "not important," is plain *stupid*. Naturally, then, some reports quoted Iraqi victim families as promising to wreak revenge ultimately upon Americans.

On December 10th, the AP headlined "Iraq to Stop Counting Civilian Dead," and opened, "Iraqi Health Ministry officials ordered a halt to a count of civilian casualties from the war and told workers not to release figures already compiled." Evidently, Bush didn't want the figures *ever* to become known.

Barbara Bush is the mother of the current U.S. President Bush, and the wife of his father, the ex-President Bush. She is a popular grandmotherly figure in America. Right before the invasion's start, Diane Sawyer, on ABC TV's Good Morning America, March 18th, asked her whether she was going to be watching the war action on television. She answered, "why should we hear about body bags, and deaths, and how many [get killed]? ... I mean, it's, it's not relevant. So, why should I waste my beautiful mind on something like that?" This Bush dynasty former queen and current king-mother acknowledged "my pettiness about that."* Evidently, the royal acorn hadn't fallen far from its tree. And the deceived American people were still loving it.

The body-count of dead U.S. soldiers, whom the President had sent on this miserable mission, was at least 136 as of President Bush's false declaration, on May 1st, aboard the USS Abraham Lincoln, that, "The Battle of Iraq is one victory in a war on terror that began on September the 11th, 2001." (See http://lunaville.org/warcasualties/ Summary.aspx for the latest revised figures.) More than thirty British

* ABC, perhaps being protective of the King's Mother in response to some websites buzzing at how barbarous Barbara had just then exhibited herself to be, simply removed this interview from their website. Therefore, here's the context of her comment:

The solicitous Ms. Sawyer, formerly an aide to President Nixon, was evidently aiming to raise the delicate subject of how much television Mrs. Bush was watching, given that a war was about to start. So, Ms. Sawyer sympathetically advised her friend, "You may be watching too much TV." The response to that comment was obtuse, and so Ms. Sawyer then *directly asked* the question: "You do watch?" This was the answer from the haughty self-styled "beautiful mind," who had raised the present King and other Bush brothers. Perhaps her hero is Marie Antoinette.

soldiers were also killed by that time. And of course the Iraq war goes on; those were the numbers only before "victory" was falsely announced. Mr. Bush was pretending that the Iraq war was over, and that just the war against Al Qaeda remained still to be won. However, 43 more American soldiers ended up being killed inside Iraq within little more than a month after that "victory," by just June 8th. The Pentagon initially refused to make public the number of Americans wounded in Iraq, but finally, on July 10th, it announced that the number injured till that time was 1,044. (As we'll soon see, this figure was a lie, a *gross* under-estimate.) And the Iraqi people were, to put it mildly, not at all happy that their country was under occupation by foreign, and culturally very alien, troops. Furthermore, even estimates of the number of dead Iraqi soldiers have also been kept secret, though many of these corpses had actually been civilians *forced* into this unnecessary battle, and they too leave bereft families. All estimates of dead Iraqi soldiers run in the low tens of thousands.

An obscure item from Germany's Deutsch Presse-Agentur was ignored by the American media except for www.dailyfreepress.com on April 18th. It said: "The U.S. Defense Department does not plan to financially compensate Iraqi civilians wounded during the U.S.-led invasion or the families of those killed," and, "The Pentagon also will not count how many Iraqi civilians were victims of what the military refers to as 'collateral damage,' despite a decision by Congress allowing compensation." The Pentagon's announcement that it would not announce such figures was an insult to the Iraqi victims and their families, and yet the American press evidently saw unfit to publicize *at home* this announcement of its non-announcement.

Bush actually cared only about winning American hearts and minds, for his own re-election, and though his cooperative U.S. media remained silent about this Iraqi compensation issue, the matter might be dealt with subsequently, in international war-crimes trials against American leaders. It would be relevant there.

The *Observer* headlined to its British readers, on September 14th, "America's Hidden Battlefield Toll: New figures reveal the true number of GIs wounded in Iraq." This blockbuster (though unfortunately ill-written) story opened: "The true scale of American casualties in Iraq is revealed today by new figures obtained by The Observer, which show that more than 6,000 American servicemen have been evacuated for medical reasons since the beginning of the war." The article explained that, though officially only "1,178 American soldiers have been wounded in combat operations since the war began," this is because, "It is [Bush's] ... policy to announce that a soldier has been wounded only if they [sic] were [sic] involved in an incident that involved a death." So, no matter how badly a soldier was wounded, it

didn't count as a "casualty" if no one was killed in the particular incident. Furthermore, these wounds were not merely minor battlefield
casualties. As the *Observer* went on to explain: "many of the American
casualties evacuated from Iraq are seriously injured. Modern body
armour, worn by almost all American troops, means wounds that
would normally kill a man are avoided. However, vulnerable arms and
legs are affected badly. This has boosted the proportion of maimed
among the injured." Consequently, military "hospitals are busy," and,
"Dealing with the aftermath of amputations and blast injuries is common." British readers, thanks to the U.K.'s prying press, were kept
informed of such facts about *America's* battlefield casualties.

Subsequently, it was left to Seth Porges of the press trade journal *Editor and Publisher*, to chastise America's newspaper owners and
editors for their failures to report the nation's war-wounded. Even so,
it happened only in the online edition of *E&P*. This stunning story,
dated October 23rd, was headlined "Press Underreports Wounded in
Iraq: Few Newspapers Tally Injuries, Accidents." It said: "*E&P* reported in July that while deaths in combat are often tallied by newspapers,
the many non-combat troop deaths in Iraq are virtually ignored. It
turns out that newspaper readers have also been shortchanged in
getting a sense of the number of troops injured, in and out of battle."

Within the United States, it was often left to local news reporters to obtain whatever hints they could of the disaster occurring in
Iraq. Consequently, on September 11th, San Francisco's KRON TV, and
kron4.com, interviewed local sources and headlined "Longer Iraq
Tours Cause Financial Strain." This story opened: "National Guard and
reserve units sent to Iraq will not be staying the promised six months
to one year. Instead, the Pentagon is ordering them to stay a year and a
half. The longer tours are putting Bay Area employers and families in
financial jeopardy." Two days later, the Milwaukee *Journal Sentinel*
similarly interviewed local people and bannered "Some Reservists
Ponder Quitting as Service Time Grows." The reporter found that there
were "concerns about retention and recruitment from commanders,"
because of "anxious moments for families" of reservists who were
serving extended tours in Iraq.

Finally, on October 21st, the *Washington Post* broke the prevailing press silence about another major cover-up by the Administration, and reported, under the headline "Curtains Ordered for Media
Coverage of Returning Coffins," that, "In March, on the eve of the Iraq
war, a directive arrived from the Pentagon at U.S. military bases.
'There will be no arrival ceremonies for, or media coverage of, de-
ceased military personnel" killed in Iraq. Unlike all previous wars, the
U.S. Government hid, rather than ceremonially honored, its fallen-in-
action. And the major U.S. media, which knew how unorthodox and

even unprecedented this control of the media for political PR purposes was, didn't protest. To the contrary, they played right along, and remained entirely quiet about the matter until October 21st, seven months later.

In fact, the first major wire service report on this important Administration propaganda/PR policy appeared from Alternet, at www.alternet.org/story.html?StoryID=17079, in a story by Christopher Scheer on October 30th, under the title "Bush Ignores Soldiers' Burials." It quoted as follows a veteran of the first (1991) Gulf War: "'I was really shocked that the president wouldn't attend a funeral for a soldier he sent to die,' said [Seth] Pollack, who is board president of Veterans for Common Sense. ... 'From the cuts in the VA budget, reductions in various pays for soldiers deployed, ... to the most recent things like those we've seen at Fort Stewart, where soldiers who are wounded are not being treated well, the Administration has shown a blatant disregard for the needs of the soldiers.' Pollack was referring to 600 wounded, ill and injured soldiers at a base in Georgia who were recently reported to be suffering from terrible living conditions, poor medical treatment and bureaucratic indifference. During a recent stop at Fort Stewart, President Bush visited returning soldiers but bypassed the wounded next door. 'Bush's inaction is a national disgrace,' said one Gulf War I vet, speaking off the record. 'I'm distressed at the lack of coverage – amounting to government censorship – of the funerals of returning U.S. service members.'" Right after Veterans Day, the *Washington Post* (Nov. 14) headlined "Pentagon Limits Funeral Coverage," and opened: "The Army tightened rules yesterday on press coverage of funerals at Arlington National Cemetery, directing that reporters be kept far enough away from the graveside that they would likely be unable to hear a chaplain's eulogy."

But, as king-mother Barbara Bush had said, "why should we hear about body bags, and deaths, and how many [get killed]? ... I mean, it's, it's not relevant." King G.W. Bush might as well have spat upon the graves of war-dead, for all he cared. On November 3rd, *Army Times* headlined "An Act of 'Betrayal': In the midst of war, key family benefits face cuts," and complained of "the latest in a string of actions by the Bush administration to cut or hold down growth in pay and benefits, including basic pay, combat pay, health-care benefits and the death gratuity paid to survivors of troops who die on active duty."

President Bush didn't attend the funeral of so much as a single American soldier. But the U.S. media ignored this historic fact, though he was the first American president to do that. Instead, on Veterans Day (Nov. 11), the AP headlined "Bush to Honor Veterans Today at Arlington." Even *that* story failed to note that this President had stayed away from every military funeral. However, the reporter did observe that nearly 400 U.S. soldiers had thus far been killed in Iraq.

The _Los Angeles Times,_ on November 9th, casually reported, under the innocuous banner "Hospital Front," that "More than 7,500 have come through since April," vaguely referring there to the number of U.S. soldiers who had returned injured from Iraq and "come through" military hospitals. The _LAT_ editors were much bolder two days later, on Veterans Day, running a commentary from Patt Morrison, "Consequences of War: What You Won't See on TV," quoting Democratic Senator Patrick Leahy saying, in the Senate, "The wounded are brought back after midnight, making sure the press does not see the planes coming in with the wounded."

Just three days later (Nov. 14), United Press International busted the prevailing press censorship with a story by Mark Benjamin, "U.S. Casualties from Iraq War Top 9,000." The director of the National Gulf War Research Center was quoted "We are shocked at the increase in casualties," but "The Army offered no immediate explanation for the increase."

The distorted perspective that the major U.S. media presented of this war was simply obscene. And at least a few Americans were greatly disturbed by it. According to "Americans turn to BBC for war news," by Jason Dean in the _Guardian_ on April 17th, "One viewer from New York wrote on the PBS website: 'The BBC seems to be the only decent source for news on this conflict. American networks are just appalling.' Another viewer from Norwalk, Connecticut, commented: 'I cannot trust any of the other stations to be truthful. They appear to omit what could be seen as critical of the US.'" Greg Dyke, director general of the BBC, was quoted in the _Independent_ on April 25th as saying, "Personally, I was shocked while in the United States by how unquestioning the [American] broadcast news media was during this war." He called it "gung-ho" coverage. That's not professional journalism; it's professional political PR. Another BBC executive who worked in the U.S. during the war, John Willis, wrote a commentary in the _Guardian_ on June 20th, "The War, Brought to You by the White House," concluding that, "For all the warts on British television, a year in America taught me just how lucky we are to have not just the BBC but also a range of diversely funded channels with different layers of public service ambitions and obligations. The lesson from America is that, if news and public affairs are left purely to the market, it will most likely give the government what it wants." He said that "media consolidation is a careless risk" like "playing with matches." On the same day in the _Washington Post,_ TV critic Tom Shales said that, "the Bush administration ... has had an ongoing love affair with the biggest of the media giants, for all the twaddle one hears about left-wing domination of the press." American media owners have long been heavily Republican, even if the newsroom reporters they've hired have (at least in *previous* decades) been heavily Democratic. But the free ride that the U.S. major media gave President Bush on the invasion of Iraq was a con from top to bottom.

By contrast, to cite just one example, the BBC on June 27th bannered "BBC Rebuts Downing Street Attack," saying BBC's news chief had written to the Prime Minister's press secretary, "I do not accept the validity of your attacks on our journalism." Does that sort of thing happen in the United States, or does the American President simply get a free pass to attack "revisionist historians" in the press, as Mr. Bush did on June 17th? If Tony Blair had likewise tried such a "revisionist historians" attack against the British press, he would – and rightly – have been criticized by virtually all of his nation's reporters. That kind of thing, which the U.S. President did, would have been pointed out right away as fraudulent.

Just the day before this BBC report, on June 26th, AFP (Agence France Presse) headlined, from London, "Navratilova Slams Censorship in U.S.," reporting that, "Nine-time Wimbledon singles champion Martina Navratilova has blasted what she sees as censorship in the United States," concerning the invasion of Iraq. The article said that, "Navratilova, born in the old communist Czechoslovakia but now a naturalized American, ... stressed freedom of speech was paramount in a democracy," and that America's right-wing-organized trashing of the works of anti-war protesters such as the Dixie Chicks "doesn't solve the problem. Then we go back to Nazi Germany."

Furthermore, there were some seedy aspects of the context of America's "victory" in this war that were simply scandalously under-reported in the "patriotic" U.S. "news" media. For example, how many American news reports on this conflict mentioned the crucial fact that America's annual military budget was more than 200 times as large as Iraq's? And how many American news reports mentioned the key fact that Iraq's entire Gross Domestic Product (GDP) had been estimated, in "The World in 1999" annual supplement to the *Economist*, at a paltry $5.7 billion, less than a tenth of pre-U.N.-sanctions Iraq's $59 billion, and less than half of 1999's Clinton Administration proposed $12 billion *increase* in *merely* the U.S. Pentagon's budget? Where was the news-objectivity? Where was the news-balance? Where was the news-context? Where was the real news *reporting*? Iraq's entire $5.7 billion GDP would have been able to purchase only four B-1 bombers, with nothing left over to feed and maintain the Iraqi people. America's propagandistic CIA, the number-crunchers for the White House, stuck to the old, circa 1990, $59 billion Iraq GDP estimate (in their misnamed "World Factbook 2002"), which was still about one 175th as large as America's $10 trillion GDP. The far more reliable and independent *Economist* estimate was almost 2,000 times smaller than America's GDP. America's "heroic liberation of Iraq" was, therefore, actually more like a giant's swatting a fly – hardly "heroic" at all, except in the images of this war that poured through the major American media.

And how many Americans were additionally informed that the much-publicized American victory tour of U.S. tanks into Baghdad at the end of the war, in early April, was a pre-arranged U.S. promotional stunt paid for by "Smart Bribes," or "The Pentagon's Secret Weapon," as Fred Kaplan called it, in retrospect, on May 20th at msnbc.com, and on May 21st at slate.com; and that, as Andrew Buncombe headlined in the *Independent* on May 24th, the "US Army Chief Says Iraqi Troops Took Bribes to Surrender"?

Putting these two facts together – a nearly 2,000-to-1 U.S. wealth advantage, and those bribes *applying* that monetary advantage – was this war really a serious *military* contest at all, or was it actually little else than a bloody staged political spectacular for the President? If it was the latter, then why was this political stunt, to bolster a President's chances for "re-"election, paid for by American taxpayers' money, and by primarily Iraqi but also American lives, rather than by the President's own "re-"election campaign, and by the U.S. Republican Party? Has there ever been a more "skillful" use of the "news media" in a "democracy" to promote the "re-"election of a "democratically elected President"? And all on somebody else's (i.e., on the U.S. taxpayers') tab. What a (corrupt) deal!

After the war, on May 5th in the *Toronto Star*, Mitch Potter's "The Real 'Saving Pte. Lynch'" revealed that the Administration's "heroic rescue," on April 2nd, of injured Private First Class Jessica Lynch from a Nasiriya hospital, had been no rescue at all; no Iraqi troops were there when the U.S. troops arrived, and she was receiving attentive treatment from the Iraqi doctors and nurses, who offered no resistance at all to her being removed by U.S. troops. Subsequently, Mr. Potter's account was reaffirmed and taken up by the BBC and others, even though Rupert Murdoch's Fox "News" network continued to suppress it and to promote instead the Bush Administration's fictitious story, and even CBS cravenly sought movie rights to it. Characteristically for America's unprofessional major "news" media, the nation's finest editorial commentary about this Bush Administration hoax appeared elsewhere, on June 2nd in the modest *News-Journal* of Daytona Beach, Florida, where editorial writer Pierre Tristam observed that the cinematic heroics near the end of the movie Rambo III had seemed "a terrifically funny bit of war fiction that looked impossible to top – until that front-page account in The

Washington Post of April 3rd about Pfc. Jessica Lynch: How she 'fought fiercely and shot several enemy soldiers' after Iraqis ambushed her company, 'firing her weapon until she ran out of ammunition,' how she 'continued firing at the Iraqis even after she sustained multiple gunshot wounds and watched several other soldiers in her unit die around her,' how she was 'fighting to the death,' how 'she did not want to be taken alive.' And all that just in the first three paragraphs of the story. The Post has been gloating over The New York Times' scandal of fabricated and ghost-reported stories. But it has yet to print a correction about the reporting on Lynch's capture and the subsequently invented stabbing she suffered, the bedside slap, a-la-Patton, by an Iraqi officer, and the allusions to torture ('Special Operations forces found what looked like a 'prototype' Iraqi torture chamber in the hospital's basement'). First the BBC, then the Chicago Tribune and the Associated Press, among others, have corrected the Pentagon's Rambo account of Lynch's capture and rescue. At this point it's doubtful whether the 19-year-old West Virginian fired a single shot, because her injuries were the result of a pretty bad vehicle accident. No gunshot wounds, no stab wounds, no torture. To the contrary: The Iraqi hospital staff where she was kept seems to have accounted for much bravery and compassion, treating her fractures, donating blood for her and protecting her from roving thugs. She 'sipped juice and ate biscuits,' reports the Tribune. But that version of the story didn't fit the narrative the Pentagon wanted. If the fabrication of the Jessica Lynch story is a harmless lie, it is nevertheless emblematic of the Bush administration's sordid deceptions that led to the very lethal, very costly Iraq war and its equally pointless aftermath. For the media, Vietnam had its Five O'Clock Follies. But Iraq was (and still is) an around-the-clock sham. At least in Vietnam the press learned to call trickery by name. Regarding Iraq, and admirable exceptions aside, much of the press remains a stooge." That's a commentary hardly likely to win a Pulitzer, even if it might be far superior to whatever does.

When Ms. Lynch recovered sufficiently to face cameras, an interview with her was telecast November 11th on ABC's Primetime. She condemned the overblown American media coverage of her, and denied being a hero, saying, "I'm not about to take credit for something I didn't do," and "I'm just a survivor." She asserted, "They [the U.S. media] used me as a way to symbolize all this stuff. ... It's wrong." Ms. Lynch specifically denied allegations that Iraqis had mistreated her, and asserted that instead, "From the time I woke up in that hospital, no one beat me, no one slapped me, no one, nothing. ... I'm so thankful for those people, because that's why I'm alive today." She could hardly say more: on November 7th, yet another soldier

Jessica – this one Sergeant Jessica Macek – was interviewed on her local AM radio station WNTA in Rockford, Illinois, and reported to her hometown listeners, "I believe it is in the forefront in the minds of many soldiers that we were lied to about the reasons for going to war. ... We have been there for six months now, and we have not found any weapons. ... If there were weapons it seems we should have found them by now." For those observations, this courageous young woman was threatened with court martial, the First Amendment notwithstanding. Such people are heroes not just of war, but of democracy.

On May 28th, CBS News revealed that the allegedly successful missile hit upon Saddam's bunker at the start of the invasion, much trumpeted by U.S. Defense Secretary Donald Rumsfeld and others, had also been fictitious: "U.S. intelligence was wrong," no bunker had been there, and no one was killed or injured by the bomb. The Bush Administration flew the Commander-in-Chief and "his" press corps to the wilderness of South Dakota, and staged there a photo-shot of the President's mug at the end of the string of great Presidents' heads that are so famously chiseled in stone at Mount Rushmore.

This war was called, by some, a Jerry Bruckheimer event. But the blood in this spectacular movie was all too real, as will be the hundreds of billions of dollars that U.S. taxpayers will be funding for years of occupation and reconstruction in Iraq. If this was a U.S. taxpayer-funded Presidential re-election spectacular, its bill will still be coming due to the American people in federal debt payments long after Mr. Bush leaves office. An obscure Reuters story on June 4th was headlined, "More Cash Headed Toward Iraq," and reported that $200 million had just been shipped "to war-torn Iraq as provisional authorities try to keep key civil service workers on the job, ... with another $358 million expected to be shipped soon." It referred to a planned "meeting of donor nations," but failed to mention that U.S. international appeals had produced few volunteers to become "donors" for this reconstruction, after an invasion widely viewed as illegal; the attitude of most governments was simply: You broke it; you fix it. The article mentioned that, "One problem is the external debt Iraq owes to other countries, which ... has been estimated at $60 billion to $130 billion." President Bush, on May 22nd, had already issued an Executive Order that unilaterally declared all such claims against Iraq and its oil revenues "a threat to the national security and foreign policy of the United States," and that simply nullified them by executive fiat; but still, the U.S. was now struggling to wrangle international agreements for Iraqi oil proceeds to pay these debts. However, this matter was a legal hornet's nest, and many Iraqis, for their part, were wary of America's stealing their oil to finance the restoration of their country after America had bombed it. Furthermore, the *Financial Times* reported

October 28th under the headline "Iraq Business Deals May be Invalid, Law Experts Warn," saying that the consensus of international legal experts was that the privatization of Iraqi State enterprises, and all other actions that the Coalition Provisional Authority was taking concerning Iraqi private and State property, were in violation of the Iraqi Constitution, the 1907 Hague Regulations, and the Fourth Geneva Convention, and would thus not be binding.

Also on June 4th, prominent Australian economist Jeff Schubert told a Sydney meeting of the Economic Society of Australia, that American taxpayers were going to be surprised by the cost of the occupation of Iraq. He noted that the U.S. Council on Foreign Relations had estimated that each American peacekeeper there would cost the U.S. treasury approximately $225,000 per year. Minimal estimates of the number that will be required in order to avoid Iraq's degenerating into rule by tribal warlords is 100,000 soldiers, with another 100,000 support personnel. That's $45 billion per year. (This estimate was in line with a Scripps Howard News Service story earlier in the year, on February 21st, which was headlined: "Economists Predict Occupation of Iraq Will Be Costly: 200,000 troops may be needed; bill could hit $48 billion a year.") And, just the day before, on June 3rd, *USA Today* ran a story, "Ex-Army Boss: Pentagon Won't Admit Reality in Iraq," asserting that, "The former civilian head of the Army said Monday it is time for the Pentagon to admit that the military is in for a long occupation of Iraq that will require a major commitment of American troops." A Reuters story datelined June 23rd was titled, "U.S. Senators Say Five Years in Iraq Likely," and opened, "Leading U.S. Senators from both parties said on Monday American troops could be in Iraq for at least five years but the White House cautioned it was too soon to set a time limit on U.S. involvement in Iraq."

So, that's a likely total of at least $240 billion, or over $2,000 per U.S. taxpayer. But even that figure is, in fact, unrealistically low. The July 21st edition of *Newsweek* headlined a major feature story: "$1 Billion a Week: And that's on the low side. So much for a 'self-sustaining' reconstruction. Parsing the real cost for U.S. taxpayers." The reporter, Christopher Dickey, noted that Defense Secretary Rumsfeld had finally admitted to Congress, that America's cash "burn rate" in Iraq was $3.9 billion a month (almost exactly the $45 billion annual figure that others had earlier estimated). The article then ominously noted: "But that billion a week is just the beginning. It doesn't include the cost of running Iraq's government and rebuilding it, which could be an additional billion a month, according to rough U.N. estimates made before the war."

So, we're now up to $57 billion annually. However, those U.N. reconstruction estimates didn't include the extra costs America has been stuck with to repair the constant vandalism by anti-American Iraqi guerillas. Certainly a modest estimate for the overall cost of the occupation would be $60 billion per year.

On July 31st, Paul Bremer, Iraq's U.S. Administrator, made a remarkable public admission. He told CNBC's "Capital Report" that, "It's probably well above $50 billion, $60 billion – maybe $100 billion. It's a lot of money." Even assuming the lower sum, just $60 billion per year, to fund a five-year stay, will be around $3,000 for each taxpaying U.S. household.

However, prior to the war, on December 3, 2002, the American Academy of Arts and Sciences had issued the most thorough analysis that has yet been published of how much this war will end up costing the United States. The American press essentially buried this crucially important and would-have-been eye-opening study. Most U.S. news media ignored the report entirely. It should have been front-page news at the time all over the country. It was a 37-page article, "The Economic Consequences of a War with Iraq," by Yale economist William Nordhaus, and it began by documenting that historically, wars invariably end up costing far more than had generally been anticipated. Dr. Nordhaus noted that the Bush Administration already possessed their own Iraq war cost-estimates (and this was in 2002!), which they refused to make available to the public, or even to Congress. "Nor are they likely to be released for a decade," he said. (This is a *democracy*?) Nordhaus's own detailed cost estimates covered a vast range of different possible war scenarios, and concluded that the most optimistic, for a short war and favorable and brief occupation, would be $99 billion. The most pessimistic, for a protracted war and long occupation, he described as follows:

"The high case is a collage of potential unfavorable outcomes rather than a single scenario. It shows the array of costs that might be incurred if the war drags on, occupation is lengthy, nation-building is costly, the war [such as an ongoing guerrilla war] destroys a large part of Iraq's oil infrastructure, there is lingering military and political resistance in the Islamic world to U.S. occupation, and there are major adverse psychological reactions to the conflict."

This seems to be pretty much what we've now got. Nordhaus continued about this worst-case scenario: "The outer limit of costs would be around $1.9 trillion, most of which fall outside of the direct military costs." Cutting that in half might be realistic if the United States gives up and leaves Iraq while the mess degenerates into quagmire. However, departing Iraq that way would subject the U.S. to not only massive global embarrassment, but a devastating legal liability. If *those* costs wouldn't amount to around $1 trillion, they'd still be a bargain.

On September 7, 2003, President Bush addressed the nation concerning Iraq. The U.S. taxpayer had already spent $73 billion in that country, according to the running tabulation at www.costofwar .com. But now, the President was requesting a quick additional $87 billion appropriation for his "war on terror." The vast majority of this sum, $71 billion, was for Iraq, a country whose entire annual Gross Domestic Product prior to our invading it had been only $5.7 billion. The question therefore naturally arises: What was going on here? Why have these expenses been so astronomical? An example will *demonstrate* why:

On September 3rd, Jon Carroll headlined in the *San Francisco Chronicle*, "Live from Iraq, It's the Real Story." The original account of this incident had appeared in more detail from an Iraqi blogger, "Riverbend," on August 28th at http://riverbendblog.blogspot.com/ 2003_08_01_riverbendblog_archive.html. The gist of the story is that the U.S. Coalition Provisional Authority in Iraq had contracted with an American firm to rebuild a bridge that we had destroyed. The U.S. firm's bid was $50 million. A highly experienced Iraqi firm, which had built many of Iraq's bridges, had bid $300,000, but they were passed over. Their bid was less than 1% of the American firm's price, and it included materials, engineering, everything. 65% of Iraqis were unemployed; they were desperate; they were eager to work for next to nothing. And Iraq has not merely millions of unemployed, but 130,000 trained engineers, many of whom are graduates of U.S. and British universities. Furthermore, Iraqis know Iraq; it's their country. Iraqis can rebuild Iraq *far* cheaper than Americans can.

So: Why should U.S. taxpayers have to spend almost $150 billion to occupy for one year a country whose annual GDP was only $5.7 billion? Part of the reason is to provide contracts for politically well-connected Republican U.S. corporations that gave Mr. Bush the biggest political campaign contributions in world history and so enabled him to become America's President. The Iraqi weblogger subsequently wrote, concerning this incident, an article that was submitted to many major U.S. magazines and newspapers, all of which turned it down. This article would have been the first publication, anywhere other than on her website, detailing the corruption that vastly inflates the costs U.S. taxpayers (in future generations) will be paying to rebuild Iraq. U.S. media expose such things only when they *have* to.

And still the story continued: on September 24th, this same Iraqi website posted another entry, "For Sale: Iraq." Here, "Riverbend" explained the skimming operation in further detail – again a worldwide first. It turns out that many Iraqi firms had been bidding on these contracts. But the jobs were being handed out instead to U.S. companies, especially to Vice President Cheney's Halliburton Corporation.

In turn, the selected U.S. firm would hire some politically well connected local Iraqi bidder to do the actual work. The U.S. firm was charging U.S. taxpayers at full U.S. wage (etc.) rates. The Iraqis who ended up doing the work, even at the managerial levels, were being paid only one or two percent of that. The roughly 98% difference – the skim – went to the U.S. Government-contracted firm, usually a major Republican Party contributor.

For example, www.capitaleye.org/iraqchart.3.12.03.asp discloses that, during the four years prior to America's invasion of Iraq, 1999-2002, Cheney's Halliburton had contributed 95% to Republicans, and only 5% to Democrats. This way, U.S. taxes being paid to this company on these military contracts were indirectly being skimmed to finance Republican political campaigns. Reconstructing Iraq is nice work – if you can get it. Pay (or else raise) at least $100,000 to (or for) the Republican Party, and you'll be in the *real* bidding for it. This neo-feudalism Republicans call "capitalism." To *them*, it's "freedom." It's serfdom to others, including to subcontractors.

But there was still more: the posting from "Riverbend" on September 27th discussed two "fixers," politically connected firms, influence peddlers, or whatever one might call them, who were promising, for a fee, to supply the grease on behalf of any serf or outside company that might want to bid on this Iraq reconstruction work. One of these "fixer" firms was headed by Joe Allbaugh, who had been the National Campaign Manager for the Bush-Cheney 2000 presidential campaign. The other was headed by Salem Chalabi, the nephew of Ahmed Chalabi, Richard Cheney's and Donald Rumsfeld's Iraqi friend the Administration wanted to become the head of Iraq's provisional government. Immediately after the capture of Saddam Hussein, Salem Chalabi was appointed to plan Saddam's trial. This guaranteed that the trial would *not* be a trial also of Saddam's former American benefactors, such as Donald Rumsfeld and George H.W. Bush. Mr. Allbaugh's colleagues included other former Bush family servants, plus one servant to the former Tory British Prime Ministers John Major and Margaret Thatcher. Of course, the Halliburton company didn't need to pay any of these fixers; Halliburton had already paid their political dues, in spades.

On September 25th, CNN headlined "Congressional Report Finds Vice President Still Has Financial Interest in His Old Company." Dick Cheney had blatantly lied about that eleven days earlier, telling NBC's "Meet the Press": "I have no financial interest in Halliburton of any kind, and haven't had, now, for over three years."

The *Washington Post,* on October 2nd, reported that a partner of Mr. Allbaugh was boasting, "One well-stocked 7-Eleven could knock out 30 Iraqi stores." A *friend* of Iraq? Or a *foe*? Iraqis knew which.

Mr. Bush, a proven serial liar, was telling the whole world that he was out to help the Iraqi people. But to the people of Iraq, Mr. Bush's friends and agents didn't seem much like friends at all.

The *Independent* headlined October 5th, "Democrats Warn of 'Profiteering' in Reconstruction Contracts," reporting revelations by the office of U.S. Senate Democratic leader Thomas Daschle, concerning the Bush Administration's corruption in this war. The article said: "The contracts uncovered by Senator Daschle's office include $3.6m for 400 handheld radios and 200 satellite phones – averaging $6,000 per item. The White House also wants to spend $10,000 a month per student on business school tuition in Iraq – double the fees for Harvard Business School. Congress has also been asked to approve spending $100m [per year] on protecting 100 Iraqi families, costing an average of $200,000 per family member whereas the US federal witness protection programme costs $10,000 per person per year. Another $400m is being sought to build and run two new prisons in Iraq to hold a total of 4,000 inmates. This will in effect cost $50,000 a prisoner, nearly twice the cost of each high-security prison place in the US." The Republican Congress nonetheless approved the $87b.

On October 15th, Democratic Congressman Henry Waxman sent a letter to President Bush's head of the Office of Management and Budget, asking him why he had failed to respond to a letter the Congressman had sent a month earlier seeking documentation for the White House's request for a Congressional appropriation of $900 million per year to pay Halliburton to import gasoline into Iraq. Mr. Waxman's letter cited experts who said that Halliburton's rates were "outrageously high," "a huge ripoff," and "highway robbery." The following day, the nonpartisan Congressional Research Service reported to Congress that Halliburton Corporation was, indeed, and provably, overcharging U.S. taxpayers at least $200 million per year for this fuel imported into Iraq. On October 21st, Congressman Waxman, having still not received a reply from the White House, wrote to the U.S. Army Corps of Engineers, supplying them with proof that Halliburton was charging U.S. taxpayers a base cost of $1.59 per gallon for gasoline coming into Iraq, while Iraq's State Oil Marketing Organization was paying less than a dollar per gallon of imported gasoline – similar gasoline, carried on similar trucks. Furthermore, Mr. Waxman said that Halliburton's excuse was that this inflated $1.59 base cost was what Halliburton was paying for the fuel (the Administration had, in fact, arranged it so), and that Halliburton thus enjoyed inflated "cost-plus" profits (in which raising costs raises profits) under the terms of their sweetheart no-bid contract. Nice work if you can get it.

On Friday, October 17th, Irwin Arieff of Reuters headlined "Bremer Fought to Weaken Iraqi Oil Watchdog," and opened: "During three months of tough negotiations, Iraq's U.S. administrator fought hard to trim the powers of an independent watchdog being set up to monitor how he spends Iraq's oil money, international agency officials said on Friday." The U.N. Ambassador from Russia – a country that thinks it understands corruption at least as well as the United States does – was quoted as being surprised that the monitoring board's "formation has clearly been delayed for too long, for reasons which we do not understand."

On Wednesday, October 29th, Reuters's Susan Cornwell bannered "Reps: U.S. Overpaying Halliburton for Gas," and revealed that a congressional inquiry had found that, "As of Oct. 19, Halliburton had imported 61.3 million gallons of gasoline from Kuwait into Iraq, and the company was paid $162.5 million for an average price of $2.65 a gallon. ... The U.S. government was then selling this gasoline inside Iraq for just four to 15 cents a gallon, subsidizing over 95 percent of the cost of gasoline consumed by Iraqis." So, this is how the Bush Administration was buying off Iraqi citizens at the same time as it was stuffing the pockets of its political contributors – all, of course, courtesy of U.S. taxpayers, or, more properly speaking, of *future generations* of U.S. taxpayers.

The same day, October 29th, France's AFP headlined "Halliburton Says KBR Unit Revenue Profit, Sales Soar," and reported that Halliburton's "profits rose fourfold and sales leapt 80 percent, boosted by work in Iraq."

---

from: www.christian-aid.org.uk/news/media/pressrel/031023p.htm

Iraq: the missing billions / 23.10.03

A staggering US$4 billion in oil revenues and other Iraqi funds earmarked for the reconstruction of the country has disappeared into opaque bank accounts administered by the Coalition Provisional Authority (CPA), the US-controlled body [headed by Paul Bremer] that rules Iraq. By the end of the year, if nothing changes in the way this cash is accounted for, that figure will double.

• Iraq: the missing billions - Transition and transparency in post-war Iraq

The financial black hole, uncovered by a Christian Aid investigation, is revealed as delegates gather for the donors' conference in Madrid. Before pledging money from their own countries' coffers to boost the reconstruction efforts, as requested by the US and UK governments, these delegates should first demand: "What has happened to the missing billions?" ...

In particular the British government, which has promised financial transparency in dealings with Iraqi oil funds, should use its influence to ensure that the missing money is accounted for. Christian Aid is calling on Prime Minister Tony Blair to deliver on his promises.

The fact that no independent body knows where this cash has gone is in direct violation of the UN resolution that released much of it for the rebuilding of Iraq's shattered infrastructure. The agency that is supposed to oversee these funds has not even been set up yet. ...

The entire matter finally climaxed late in the American media, on November 3rd, when the front cover of *Newsweek* bannered "Bush's $87 Billion Mess: Waste, Chaos, and Cronyism: The Real Cost of Rebuilding Iraq." Inside, an article titled "Waste, Fraud and Abuse" quoted one experienced observer as saying, "I've never seen corruption like this by expatriate businessmen. It's like a feeding frenzy." He told of a contractor who had demanded a $750,000 bribe from prospective subcontractors. Asked who that contractor was, all he would say is "No Iraqi would ask for a bribe that big." After all, Mr. Bush's friends are from Texas – and that's "Big Sky Country." But here they were robbing *America's taxpayers!*

Oliver Morgan of the *Independent* headlined on November 9th "US Bungling in Baghdad," concerning "the frustrations growing as Iraqis are locked out of their own reconstruction work." He reported that Mr. Bremer had set things up so that only Iraqis who were already cozy with the Bush Administration were being permitted to bid. This was creating among some Iraqis a seething hatred of America – fuel for future *real* terrorism against the American people.

On August 7th, an obscure local Connecticut AP story had been headlined, "President Appoints Greenwich Man to Iraq Position," and opened, "A Greenwich resident will serve as director of private sector development in Iraq, in an appointment by President Bush. Thomas Foley, 51, ... will report directly to the top U.S. administrator in Iraq, Paul Bremer. ... Foley ... was chairman of Bush's Connecticut campaign finance committee in 2000, after raising more than $100,000 for his college friend," the then-candidate Bush. Virtually *everything* was an inside job from the get-go, as Greg Palast further explained on August 31st, at www.baghdadbulletin.com.

Democrats inserted into the Senate's version of the $87 billion Iraq spending bill a provision to criminalize overcharging, fraud, and other "war profiteering" by government contractors in Iraq. Republicans in the House removed it: you don't bite the hand that feeds you. Another example of this – noted by Paul Krugman on September 30th in *The New York Times* – is that the contract to provide Iraq's cell phone service went to America's bankrupt and lately corrupt MCI Worldcom, which had contributed more than $1 million to U.S. politicians, two-thirds to Republicans. Both *existing* Iraqi cell phone companies were ordered shut down. This was Bush's way of serving Iraqis – serving them poverty and economic dependency.

On December 11th, Reuters headlined "Pentagon Audit Finds Halliburton Overcharged" for fuel it imported into Iraq, thus further confirming what Democrats in Congress were saying. But there was no danger of criminal penalties for the executives, because Republicans in Congress had blocked that provision from passing. During Bill Clinton's Presidency, when Dick Cheney headed Halliburton, the company was fined millions for overcharging the U.S Government. A firm like Halliburton's even *qualifying* for federal contracts is a scandal. But under Bush, Cheney's friends were simply handed huge *no-bid* contracts.

As if to insult the intelligence, and even the morality, of the American people, the Bush Administration did something stunning, just four days after that audit, and two days after the capture of Saddam Hussein. On December 15th, Reuters headlined "Halliburton Gets More Business in Iraq." This "new task order" of that date, for $222 million in "restoration of essential infrastructure," was likewise issued on a no-bid basis. The decision received little media play in the U.S. A December 30th Pentagon announcement got more publicity: the Halliburton contract to import gasoline into Iraq was cancelled. (This was soon *quietly* reversed.) The Administration perhaps hoped taxpayers would now pay less attention to Halliburton's excessive charges. On the same day, a more comprehensive Administration response to the emerging scandals was reported by Stephen J. Glain in the Boston *Globe,* under the headline "Pentagon Freezes Iraq Funds Amid Corruption Probes." The story led: "The Pentagon has frozen new funds approved for Iraqi reconstruction amid growing allegations of corruption and cronyism associated with the rebuilding process." On January 15, 2004, Pentagon auditors reported finding "suspected irregularities" in Halliburton's billing.

These turnabouts were not initiated by a good U.S. press that was doing its muckraking job. Instead, Democrats in Congress had exposed the corruption and pressed the issue. Overall, the U.S. major media minimized, when they didn't simply ignore, the corruption of the most corrupt President and war in American history. On November 6th, the *Washington Post* even published an article by Harvard professor Steven Kelman, headlined "No 'Cronyism' in Iraq," stating that any allegations of such corruption were "somewhere between highly improbable and utterly absurd," because "The premise of the accusations is completely contrary to the way government contracting works," and "campaign contributions have no effect on decisions about who gets a contract." Those blanket generalizations, applied to *this* President, must have given some members of the Bush Administration a chuckle. Other articles similarly reassured the public.

Repeated efforts by Iraqis to reach major American media on the corruption in U.S. Iraqi contracts failed. It was left to Malaysia's *The Star* on December 7th to headline "Firms 'Making Money' off Iraq," reporting that a U.S. contractor was receiving $180,000 for each school built, and paid the Iraqi subcontractor only $20,000 of that.

Perhaps there were other reasons than corruption behind Mr. Bush's invasion of Iraq; perhaps there was a higher strategic national goal that drove him, and those kickbacks were merely a *side*-benefit in his view. (Evidence will subsequently be provided here indicating that this was, in fact, the case.) But for many of the countries America bribed to join in this invasion, such as Poland and other nations in Donald Rumsfeld's "New Europe" (the formerly communist states) the corruption was sometimes *all there was*.

---

from: www.makethemaccountable.com/floyd/030711_BargePoles.htm
Moscow Times, Friday, July 11, 2003; *St. Petersburg Times*, Tuesday, July 15, 2003

Opinion: Chris Floyd's Global Eye

Barge Poles

In a political world blackened with the stinking pitch of lies, distortion and death-dealing hypocrisy, a shining knight of truth stepped boldly forth last week. With admirable – if ruthless – honesty, Polish Foreign Minister Wlodzimierz Cimoszewicz openly declared that his nation joined the Anglo-American crusade against Iraq for one purpose only: a share of the plunder from the conquered country's oil fields.

Here was no shifting, no spin, no crocodile tears about "democracy" and "liberation" such as are wont to dribble down the ever-flapping cheeks of Crusader George and his faithful page Tony. While each new day seems to bring another tortured "justification" for aggressive war from the Coalition's loquacious leaders, bold Cimoszewicz dispensed with pious cant and spoke plainly, the BBC reports.

"We have never hidden our desire for Polish oil companies to finally have access to sources of commodities," the minister told a group of Polish magnates gathered to sign an agreement allowing them to join the corporate hunting packs from the United States and Britain in tearing off chunks of the Iraqi carcass. Indeed, access to Iraq's oilfields "is our ultimate objective," Cimoszewicz told the press.

That's why Poland contributed a small combat force to the invasion: to seal its claims to loot in blood. It's the Bush Doctrine, you see: "If you wanna share the bread, you gotta pile up the dead." Now that the Poles have made their bones (figuratively and literally), the Busha Nostra will cut them in for a taste. ...

Under the headline "AP: Kennedy Says Iraq War Case a 'Fraud'," Steve LeBlanc of the Associated Press on September 18th reported that Senator Edward Kennedy was asserting not only that the case for going to war was a "fraud ... made up in Texas," but that 40%, or about $1.5 billion, of the approximately $4 billion monthly military expenditures in Iraq, were unaccounted for by the Bush Administration, and that, "My belief is this money is being shuffled all around to these political leaders in all parts of the world, bribing them to send in troops." If so, this was throwing good U.S. money after bad. But any country's bribe that entailed only a share of the spoils of this misbegotten war would be a loss for that deceived and bribed nation, not for U.S. taxpayers. This is why Mr. Bush was now working so hard to "internationalize" his disaster.

On September 23rd, Fox "News" headlined "Kennedy Faces Backlash From Colleagues Over Iraq Remarks." But it wasn't actually Senator Kennedy's Senate Democratic and Republican "colleagues," merely Republican politicians, who were being quoted against him: for example, "'These comments are obviously for political gain and are as disgusting as they are false,' [Republican] House Majority Leader Tom DeLay of Texas told reporters Tuesday. 'Unfortunately, Kennedy's brand of hate speech has become mainstream in the Democratic Party.'" That was Fox "News" reporting.

Yet, in confirmation of exactly the sort of thing that Senator Kennedy was saying, *Business Week* headlined on October 20th (p. 63) "Currency Quid Pro Quo," which provided an example precisely in line with the Senator's expectation that "money is being shuffled all around to these political leaders in all parts of the world, bribing them to send in troops." Here was the corrupt deal, which was rather complex: Japanese Prime Minister Junichiro Koizumi pledged 2,000 Japanese peacekeeping troops, and $5 billion for reconstructing Iraq, in return for which, American factory workers would suffer job losses that would go to Japan, because of Japan's being permitted artificially to prop up the value of the dollar and lower the value of the yen. As *Business Week*'s Brian Bremner said in his commentary about this agreement: "In the Bush Presidency, geopolitics trumps economic politics." So, pity America's unfortunate laid-off factory workers.

However, even *without* the Bush Administration's unprecedented U.S. corruption, the occupation of Iraq is bound to be extremely costly for the American people.

Conquest isn't cheap; this occupation is certainly going to cost U.S. taxpayers a mint, even under the best of circumstances. The economic impacts of the 9/11 attacks were puny by comparison. And President Bush brags that he's cutting taxes. But the only way he can continue doing that is to permit Iraq to degenerate into chaos, just as he is already permitting to happen in Afghanistan, which is a far less costly drain that, furthermore, is receiving additional financial help from some other countries. The U.S. will be bearing the Iraq burden almost alone. As a *Los Angeles Times* story on June 22nd headlined, "U.S. Enlists More Countries in Iraq, at Taxpayers' Expense: Bush administration has agreed to pay for several nations' participation in the peacekeeping effort." The American public was kept pretty much in the dark about this by the lying Bush Administration, which bragged about foreign troops joining Americans, and which carefully avoided mentioning that U.S. taxpayers were paying the entire tab.

The U.S. Administration continued holding out the tin cup: Reuters headlined, on June 21st, "U.S. Says Donors Must Come to the Aid of Iraq," and quoted a U.S. official as finally admitting, "There is not going to be enough (oil revenue) to do the reconstruction that is why this donor activity that is under way [which, of course, wasn't actually forthcoming] is so important." The rest of the world looked on with disgust at America's begging that followed an illegal invasion. Britain's daily *Telegraph* headlined, on June 17th, "America's Rebuilding of Iraq Is in Chaos," and quoted "a very senior British official in Baghdad" as saying that, "the American-led reconstruction effort in Iraq is 'in chaos' and suffering from 'a complete absence of strategic direction.'" The story further asserted that, "'This is the single most chaotic organization I have ever worked for,' the official said yesterday," and that, "Similar frustrations have been voiced privately in London, where British ministers are said to be fed up."

Did the American people know that they had made only a tiny down-payment on a huge disaster in Iraq? Hardly – the President's approval ratings on Iraq were continuing as they had been, at around 70%, throughout these revelations, until the President's request to Congress on September 7th for an additional $87 billion. In the American major media, bad news for conservatives travels *very* slowly.

But then, after the President's request for this additional $87 billion nearly became the straw that finally broke the camel's back of American public support for the invasion, and President Bush's poll numbers finally began to decline, the Administration abruptly changed course and decided to share with any cooperating foreign governments the spoils of this war. Steven R. Weisman on October 20th headlined in *The New York Times*, "U.S. Set to Cede Part of Control Over Aid to Iraq," and reported that the President's chief officer in Iraq, Paul Bremer, admitted, "I need the money so bad we have to move off our principled opposition to the international community being in charge." On December 9th, the Pentagon even posted on its website www .rebuilding-iraq.net an announcement that companies from the 63 countries that had not actively opposed the invasion of Iraq would be permitted to bid on the 26 remaining prime reconstruction contracts. This caused an increased rift with the *excluded* nations.

Going into an election year, the President's team were suddenly becoming desperate to stop robbing the American people for the benefit of the President's financial and political backers. Their "team" was breaking up: now it was becoming every man for himself – they just had to put a good face on it (not hard to do, given America's corrupt major media). A comprehensive review of the phenomenal stock-market gains that had already, even by this early time, been enjoyed by the Bush Administration's, and by the Republican Party's, financial backers, who had already received the major contracts for this war, is "A Band of Brothers: The Rebuilding of Iraq," at www.misleader.org/pdf/specialreport1_bandofbrothers.pdf, by Stephen Pizzo. Typical gains to these companies were 20-50% within six months of the war's start. In *USA Today*, on October 31st, Charles Lewis, chief of the Center for Public Integrity, condemned the "stench of political favoritism and cronyism" behind Mr. Bush's Iraq contracts. So, one hardly needs to feel sorry for this pack of Bushite wolves; it's the American people that they were eating, whom one should feel sorry for.

President Bush was even so callous that he had his Justice Department press a federal judge on July 29th to reverse the judge's earlier ruling that had granted almost $1 billion in compensation by the Government of Iraq to 17 American P.O.W.'s of the 1991 Iraq war, people who had been brutally tortured by their Iraqi captors. The Bush "Justice" Department argued that this money was needed instead for the reconstruction of Iraq – in other words, to pay to companies like Halliburton.

Other war-costs to the American people might be less direct, but not necessarily less important, than these war-fighting and reconstruction expenses. For example, the March 18th Pew Research Center poll in nine countries, previously mentioned, showed that "America's Image Further Erodes." After the war, on June 3rd, another poll by the same organization headlined in *The New York Times*, "World's View of U.S. Sours After Iraq War, Poll Finds." The Pew Research Center's Director, Andrew Kohut, summarized these findings by saying, "The war has widened the rift between Americans and Western Europeans, further inflamed the Muslim world, softened support for the war on terrorism, and significantly weakened global public support for the pillars of the post-World War II era – the U.N. and the North Atlantic alliance." The BBC did their own poll, and headlined it on their website on June 16th – and telecast the next day – "Poll Suggests World Hostile to US." This survey of 11,000 respondents in 11 countries confirmed that America's image was plunging.

As a natural consequence of this sinking U.S. image, international boycotts of American brands mushroomed. A Reuters story about one such boycott appeared, on March 25th, by Erik Kirschbaum datelined from Berlin, and it was published widely around the world, except – notably (of course) – in the U.S. It was headlined "Boycott of American Goods Over Iraq War Gains." The report opened, "No more Coca-Cola or Budweiser, no Marlboro, no American whiskey or even American Express cards – a growing number of restaurants in Germany are taking everything American off their menus." A typical weblog response to this news story was: "GREAT! I'm personally boycotting like hell. Some time ago me & my father cut our Esso credit cards in half. No more THAT goddamned petrol. No way I'm going to allow my hard-earned money to go to the USA to grant that nightmare administration some more cash for their disgusting war. I'm also a music fan, but the times of buying the albums of American bands are long gone." A few days later, on March 31st, there appeared an AP report by Melissa Eddy, datelined from Frankfurt, similarly saying that some "European restaurants are halting sales of Coca-Cola, Marlboro cigarettes and other U.S. brands in boycotts spurred by anti-war sentiment." This story received much more American coverage than the one from Reuters, but still it ran in only a half-dozen U.S. small-market areas. (No foreign media used the AP's story, and it didn't run in any major U.S. cities.) A Belgian-led "Boycott Bush" campaign was also spreading rapidly throughout the world, and it targeted numerous American brands and firms. This boycott, too, was ignored in the U.S. major media.

Then, something extraordinary happened: On April 4th, the nation's biggest newspaper, *USA Today*, broke this important story in a big way, headlining "Anti-War Protesters Take Aim at American Brands." Reporters Noelle Knox and Theresa Howard quoted Dr. Shih-Fen Chen, a marketing professor at Brandeis University, as saying, "if the war drags on for a long time, and there are a lot of civilian casualties and the rebuilding of the country falls below the expectations of people ... that could be a big problem for American brands." Their article unfortunately got buried under the surrounding torrent of contrary, more "upbeat," war stories, and it was foolishly even ignored by America's *anti*-war movement, which seems to have been biased against such mere "crass commercial concerns" as the threat to the nation's own brands. Furthermore, Knox and Howard shaped their story so as to make it comply with the Bush Administration's promotion of the invasion: the article insinuated that participants in anti-American boycotts are irrational because they "do not believe the real objective of the war is to liberate the Iraqi population." Such "liberation" had, of course, become by then the Administration's chief PR line on this invasion, due to their failure to find any Iraqi WMD. The article even contained what could reasonably be taken as a snidely intended description of a clearly anti-American foreign cartoon – but a cartoon that was no more anti-American than American cartoons at the time were anti-French: "An editorial on the front page of the French newspaper *Le Monde* last week showed a GI trudging through a sandstorm, walking over the bodies of dead Iraqi civilians, complaining, 'It's terrible, this sandstorm.'" No mention was made of the many similar American anti-French cartoons. The implicit *USA Today* message was: U.S. firms suffer because of unfair anti-American foreign bias and propaganda against our noble war. Nonetheless, readers who could see beyond that "patriotic" slant were being informed of an important and widely under-reported cost to American commerce, stemming from this invasion of Iraq.

An understanding in the U.S. that this invasion was bad for American business might have helped critics in the American public to recognize that this invasion wasn't really supporting American capitalism, as so many on the Left commonly charged; it was an invasion by, and in support of, American neo-feudalism. Beginning in 1980, a return of feudalism – rule by a power-elite of well connected insiders or "aristocrats" – has been on a tear within American culture, in the newer form of corporate feudalism, otherwise called "fascism." America's Founders had tried to defeat feudalism, but though that elitist political system lost the battle of the Revolution, it survived and is now surging again within the U.S. in its new 20th-Century corporate form, fascism. What used to be called the aristocracy consists now therefore of cartel/oligopoly corporate executives, and these people's political campaign contributions are purchasing the power of the State to crush their competitors and to advance their particular industries. This isn't anything like capitalism in the sense that America's Founders had promoted. In fact, it's more like the reverse: insiders self-righteously riding roughshod over outsiders, essentially like in older aristocratic times, but now using corporate forms of organization to do the job. They even have faith in a similar religiously founded belief attributing to themselves moral superiority as the explanation for their personal success, and moral inferiority as the explanation for the losers *being* "losers." Consequently, just as in olden times, the attitude of aristocrats toward the poor is condescending, to put the gentlest face upon it. These aristocrats feel that God, The Almighty, selects the "winners," and that the poor therefore likewise get only what they deserve. The arrogant attitude of aristocrats has remained unchanged, but the organizational forms have changed over time. The "little guy," the unconnected outsider, pays the brunt of the costs in an aristocratic system, now just as ever. However, some of these "little guys" are actually not so little. Not all of the "little guys" are poor. Most, in fact, are not. A few, in fact, are quite large.

The identification of some of these outsiders appeared in a story a few days later, on April 14th. Correspondent Margie Manning, in the obscure *St. Louis Business Journal,* headlined "War's Economic Fallout," and reported that numerous local Missouri manufacturers were experiencing plunging sales to Islamic countries. Then, about a week after that, a report from the U.S. National Council for U.S.-Arab Relations said that retailers selling American consumer products in Arabic nations had seen those sales plummet 40%. Of course, many small merchants were hit by this plunge. However, again, major brands – McDonalds, Burger King, Starbucks, and Kentucky Fried Chicken – were also hit hard. Another report from Reuters quoted Charley Kestenbaum, the commercial officer at the U.S. embassy in Saudi Arabia, as admitting, "The impact of the boycott is very significant. ... Yes, we are concerned."

The actual *insiders* in this war, today's political aristocrats, consisted of only a tiny group of companies, and of evangelical Christian organizations. Firms such as Vice President Dick Cheney's former employer Halliburton Corporation stood to gain, or thought they did; and so too did fundamentalist Christian organizations such as the Reverend Franklin Graham's Samaritan's Purse, the Reverend Pat Robertson's Christian Coalition, and others who were promoting this invasion to bring "Christian salvation" to the Moslems of Iraq. The Reverend Graham was the longtime Bush family friend who read the prayer at George W. Bush's inauguration. Pat Robertson's Christian Coalition provided the shock troops that won Mr. Bush the crucial South Carolina primary against Senator John McCain, and that then scooped up millions of dollars from fundamentalist Christians for Mr. Bush's culminating election battle against Democrat Al Gore.

However, with the exception of the one story in *USA Today,* Americans were essentially kept in the dark, by their major media, about the global boycotts against their nation's brands and goods. Subsequently, buried in the international trade figures from the U.S. Commerce Department, was this disturbing fact: during April-June 2003 (the second quarter) immediately after the invasion, U.S. exports fell 3.1%; U.S. imports rose 9.2%. America's trade-deficit was swelling.

All that most Americans ever heard about instead was the Bush Administration-backed campaign to boycott French products in retaliation for France having led what Donald Rumsfeld derogatorily called "the old Europe," in opposing the war. Columnist Thomas Friedman of *The New York Times* consequently headlined on September 18th "Our War With France," and opened, "It's time we Americans came to terms with something: France is not just our annoying ally. It is not just our jealous rival. France is becoming our enemy."

However, in fact, the U.S. was a relatively small market for French products. Meanwhile, outraged people in not just one country, but in all countries, were boycotting U.S. products.

During the lead-up to the war and the invasion, and the apparently "successful" immediate aftermath, the U.S. press was serving almost totally as an extension of the White House "press" office. For example, American media publicized widely the Administration's anti-French boycott. However, after the occupation of Iraq turned sour, major U.S. media had no choice but to begin significant reporting of the realities that they themselves had helped the Administration to cover up. Suddenly, the unaccustomed (since Vietnam War times) TV images appeared, of American troops fighting a bloody guerrilla war, and this ongoing bloodshed dragged in tow the economic news of the anti-U.S. boycott. *Newsweek*'s website (and, again notably, *not* the magazine) started the trend by headlining, on July 21st, "U.S. Brands on the Run: A new global poll offers the first strong evidence that consumers who have turned on America are now turning on American companies, too. Is it the end of an era?" On the opposite side of the Atlantic, a similar story made physical print in the *Independent*, on July 17th, under the heading: "Dire States: Americans are used to resentment of their global dominance. Since the war on Iraq, however, this hostility has begun to hit them where it hurts: in corporate balance sheets. David Usborne reports on the backlash being felt in the boardrooms everywhere from McDonald's and Nike to Microsoft and Coca-Cola." Reporter Usborne quoted, there, John Quelch, Dean of Harvard Business School, as saying: "Never before have global concerns about American foreign policy so threatened to change [international] consumer behavior. We are not speaking here of the frivolous grandstanding associated with temporary boycotts by a student minority. We are witnessing the emergence of a consumer lifestyle with broad international appeal that is grounded in a rejection of American capitalism, American foreign policy and Brand America." Usborne's article closed by trenchantly observing that, "The Bush administration considers itself to be business-friendly. Yet, it may have inadvertently soured the atmosphere around the globe for the very icons of American capitalism. These icons, from Coke to Nike to Levi's, may have only two choices. To underplay their American origins as far as possible. Or to wait for the President, or his policies, to change." Indeed, if Mr. Bush wins the election in 2004, these boycotts will likely soar.

Meanwhile, America's "newspaper of record," *The New York Times*, featured, instead, the petty story, "U.S. Chill Flattens Mood at

French Wine Fair." This extensive June 30, 2003, article (datelined from Bordeaux, June 26th, by reporter Craig S. Smith) focused upon a chart showing "French Wine in Decline" in President Bush's United States. These sales fell a substantial 20%. Buried in the report was: "The country's American-bound wine exports, which totaled nearly $1 billion in 2002, account for 16 percent of all the wine France ships abroad." So, that loss of 20% of that 16% would mean merely about a 3% decline in all exports of French wines. Hardly even deserving of notice. That's the difference between being the target of a boycott in only one nation (as is France), versus being the target of a boycott in just about every nation (as is the U.S.). President Bush – the "pro-business" President – and his American "news" media, had done this to the American people, *and* to American business.

Another way of looking at the matter is this: the August 4th issue of *Business Week* detailed "The 100 Top Brands." Of the world's 100 most valuable brands, 62 were U.S., with a total valuation of $707 billion; 7 were French, with a total valuation of $30 billion. So, America's global brand exposure was about 24 times as large as France's. In other words, if there were global boycotts against both countries' brands, the damage would be approximately 24 times greater in the U.S. But, of course, France, unlike the U.S., isn't subject to any such global boycotts. Therefore, the damage to America will actually be more on the order of 240 times as bad as the damage to France. And yet, with few exceptions, the American major media kept the American public in the dark about that damage to American brands, while promoting the damage that President Bush's boycott would cause to French commerce.

After the war, certain of the U.S. "news" media were admitting that some of the most egregious of their doctored stories during the war might possibly have been not quite right. But the damage had already been done. Thus, for example, a Knight Ridder story by Frank Davies, which was datelined well after the "official" war, on June 14th, opened: "A third of the American public believes U.S. forces found weapons of mass destruction in Iraq, according to a recent poll, and 22 percent said Iraq actually used chemical or biological weapons. But no such weapons have been found, nor is there evidence they were used recently in Iraq. Before the war, half of those polled in a survey said Iraqis were among the 19 hijackers on Sept 11, 2001. But most of [the hijackers] were from Saudi Arabia. None were Iraqis. How could so many people be so wrong about information that has dominated the news for nearly two years?" This befuddlement picked up on a similar confusion by the University of Maryland's pollster, at http://pipa.org/whatsnew/html/new_6_04_03.html, who had carried out these polls, and who resorted to such gibberish as "cognitive dissonance" to explain Americans' false beliefs. But why this befuddlement? Were that reporter, and that pollster, as ignorant of their own nation's "news" media, as the media-misinformed American public are ignorant about politics and public events? Shouldn't professionals in any field understand the business that they're in, in the country that they're in?

Not only are the U.S. major media meek; they are corrupt, which is *why* they are meek. How else can one explain the rampant American newsroom executive rot that's skillfully described by Katha Pollitt in her "White Lies," on June 16th at www.thenation.com/doc. mhtml?i=20030616&s=pollitt. And isn't corruption exactly what one would expect to find in the "news" media inside a country where the media are a propaganda organ instead of being truly independent? An even more damning indictment of the corruptness of the U.S. major media is to be found in "The Screwing of Cynthia McKinney," two days later, from BBC investigative journalist Greg Palast, at www.alternet .org/story.html?StoryID=16172. The American major media are so deeply deceptive that, even as early as December 16, 2002, the *Guardian's* Brian Whitaker was already headlining about "The Papers that Cried Wolf," exposing such leading U.S. newspapers as the *Washington Post* and *The New York Times* as mouthpieces for the White House. Even that early, this British media commentator was exposing falsehoods about Iraq's biological weapons program, known Bushite fabrications and distortions, which had been presented to the American people as if they were facts, misreported by "Judith Miller, the paper's 'bioterrorism expert.'" That's the contemptuous title Mr. Whitaker conferred upon this Pulitzer-Prize-winning *New York Times* reporter.

After the war, with the benefit of hindsight on July 25, 2003, Jack Shafer at http://slate.msn.com/id/2086110 headlined "The Times Scoops That Melted: Cataloging the wretched reporting of Judith Miller," and closed with, "Because the Times sets the news agenda for the press and the nation, Miller's reporting had a great impact on the national debate over the wisdom of the Iraq invasion. If she was reliably wrong about Iraq's WMD, she might have played a major role in encouraging the United States to attack a nation that posed it little threat. At the very least, Miller's editors should review her dodgy reporting from the last 18 months, explain her astonishing credulity and lack of accountability, and parse the false from the fact in her WMD reporting."

Just five days later, a study that the *Times* itself commissioned, to investigate some of its *other* false "news" stories, condemned the paper's authoritarian management, and reported that, although the newspaper's publisher "knew there were anxieties in the newsroom, ... the depth of the anger and frustration 'stunned' him." Either the man must have been more ignorant and stupid than is even believable, or else his previous concern about his employees was so hypocritical as to have been virtually non-existent. The commission urged that there should be "openness to dissent and appreciation of reasoned pushback from subordinates." Their report portrayed a corporate culture of arrogant power at the top, resentful fear down below, and purely one-way communication between the two levels. Lending confirmation to this, the October 2003 *Wired* magazine included a study that rated large corporations on the extent to which they either honored the privacy of, or else snooped upon, their workers. The New York Times Company ranked near the bottom: it was snoopy. One would *expect* this from such an authoritarian management.

The nation's second-most influential newspaper is the *Washington Post*. A superb "Post Watch" or "Washington Buzz" column in the September issue of *Washingtonian* magazine (www.washingtonian .com/inwashington/buzz/pincus.html) headlined "Why Doesn't the *Post* Love Walter Pincus?" Harry Jaffe there reported that prior to the war, Mr. Pincus, a star 70-year-old reporter at the *Washington Post,* was doggedly trying to get his stories published about the President's shaky evidence for invading Iraq. Jaffe said: "According to reporters, editors continually underplayed Pincus's scoops and discounted their stories that ran counter to Bush's call to arms. ... Pincus eventually prevailed within his own newspaper, but why did a veteran reporter have to bow and scrape to get his stories noticed and then printed?"

On September 14th, the ombudsman at the *Washington Post*, Michael Getler, headlined "Two Years and Two Cents," looking back on the *Post*'s coverage of the war against terror. He concluded: "my own sense is that the administration was more skillful in switching focus from Osama bin Laden to Saddam Hussein than the press was in detecting it early, and more skillful in linking Hussein to 9/11 in the public mind than the press was in challenging that, although it tried hard."

"Tried hard"? Did they try *at all*? Considering, as a point of comparison, the national press on the other side of the Atlantic, in Britain, one has to question the sincerity of Mr. Getler's statement that the U.S. media "tried hard" to detect the President's frauds. That statement is clearly a fraud itself, a lie from this supposed "ombudsman" at the #2 U.S. newspaper.

On the same day (the 14th), Peter Johnson, at www.usatoday .com/life/columnist/mediamix/2003-09-14-media-mix_x.htm, quoted CNN's leading war correspondent, Christiane Amanpour, as saying, "I think the press was muzzled, and I think the press self-muzzled. I'm sorry to say, but certainly television and, perhaps, to a certain extent, my station was intimidated by the administration and its foot soldiers at Fox News. And it did, in fact, put a climate of fear and self-censorship, in my view, in terms of the kind of broadcast work we did." Mr. Johnson then asked both Fox and CNN to comment. The Fox spokesperson said, "Given the choice, it's better to be ... a foot soldier for Bush than ... for al-Qaeda." (Where did "al-Qaeda" come into this? Amanpour was talking about the war in Iraq, *not* in Afghanistan. Al Qaeda didn't enter Iraq until *after* the invasion of Iraq.) But did the American public really expect *news* people to serve as a "foot soldier" for *either*? Why this "given the choice," anyway? Isn't there a *third* way – the way of *authentically* professional journalists, as opposed to such mere propagandists?

Propagandists have to choose which side to distort for, but do real *journalists* do that? CNN itself had "no comment." However, two days later, the website of the *New York Post* headlined "CNN Gives Christiane 'Private' Dress Down," and said, "CNN news chief Jim Walton had a 'private conversation' with reporter Christiane Amanpour after she accused her own network of being 'intimidated' in its coverage of the Iraqi war." Actually, though, that assertion by the *New York Post* was itself distorting: she had clearly accused the *entire* U.S. "the press" of that, and she *especially* accused Fox for its having provided much of the "intimidation" that she was condemning the most strongly of all. Furthermore, the report in the *New York Post* failed to note that this newspaper and Fox are virtually the same organization: they're both run by Rupert Murdoch. He was, in effect, using one of his newspapers to discredit his chief cable news competitor, CNN. And the wily Fox did no similar "dress down" of its own spokesperson, who publicly endorsed the network's being "a foot soldier for Bush."

Probably, along with the *New York Post*, Fox just secretly reveled in the entire situation, and enjoyed the same disdain, for its audience, that must have had Mr. Murdoch chuckling down his sleeve at the discomfort he was now causing for his *less*-indecent competitors such as CNN. Mr. Murdoch, after all, had become a billionaire in much the same way as had the U.S. tobacco companies (who have likewise been huge supporters of the U.S. Republican Party): namely, by despising his customers so much as to exploit their weaknesses – most especially, by exploiting their grossly misplaced *trust* in what he is selling/telling them. "A foot soldier for Bush": there is *finally* a statement from the Faux News Network that actually *fits* their trademarked "Fair and Balanced" and "We report. You decide." They reported it, and now we can all decide about it. And doesn't that look like a "Fair and Balanced" self-description coming from the *Faux* News Network? "A foot soldier for Bush" – this is the self-acknowledged *reality* behind their "fair and balanced" so-called "news" operation.

On October 31st, a veteran TV news producer, Charlie Reina, who had quit Fox News in disgust in April, posted a message about the network, on Jim Romanesko's Poynter Institute board, http://poynter.org/forum/?id=thememo. He said that, after having spent six years with Fox, and previously working more than twenty years at CBS, ABC, and AP, he decided that he could no longer tolerate the unparalleled management control of "news" that Fox imposed. "At Fox, if my boss wasn't warning me to 'be careful' how I handled the writing of a special about Ronald Reagan ('You know how Roger [Ailes] feels about him'), he was telling me how the environmental special I was to produce should lean ('You can give both sides, but make sure the pro-environmentalists don't get the last word')."

So, in a country like the United States, where there is rot at the top of the media, should real media-professionals be surprised to find that the public is suffering from delusions about public affairs? The University of Maryland researchers at pipa.org explored one of these delusions in particular, and found that it "is substantially greater among those who favored the war," which the vast majority of Americans did. Were those Americans following the "news" too little, or were too many of the "respectable" news sources, which they were following, actually trash? Maybe the more attention they paid to the "news," the less they knew and understood? Indeed, this seems actually to have been the case: the pipa.org press release also noted that, "Among Republicans who said they follow international affairs very closely ... an even larger percentage – 55% – said weapons [of mass destruction] have been found" inside Iraq. Therefore, the corruption of the U.S. press had the result that might reasonably have been expected: a deceived U.S. public. The more "news" these people were exposed to, the more *false* their beliefs about public events turned out to be. America's conservatives were receiving too much information – too much, because it was false information: *dis*information, *faux* "news." In fact, a subsequent pipa.org study found that viewers of Fox News had more misconceptions about the Iraq war than did the viewers *of any other network*.

Among these "news"-delusional American conservatives were, apparently, even top executives of major U.S. companies. For example, we've already documented the hit that America's brands were taking from this invasion. But Jeffrey E. Garten, Dean of the Yale School of Management, wrote in *Business Week* on November 10th, under the heading "Anger Abroad Is Bad for Business," that, "After the U.S. invasion of Iraq, I interviewed executives of U.S. companies in Germany, France, South Korea, and Mexico. All believed that American businesses would be unaffected by foreign opposition to the war." He went on to observe that, "Keith Reinhard, chairman of DBB Worldwide, a global advertising and marketing firm, says U.S. companies are already in trouble. Pointing to polls by RoperASW and surveys done by his own company in 17 countries, he told me that the value of American brands is being eroded by growing anti-Americanism." It seems that U.S. conservatives, people of faith, were ripe for feel-good "news." Mr. Garten closed by warning these American managers: "U.S. chief executives would be naïve to think their companies will remain unaffected. Wishful thinking isn't a policy."

On the other hand, there is also another reason, besides sheer political propagandizing, why America's press coverage of this war was less critical than the coverage in any other country: it was an American-initiated war. Even Britain's participation was generally considered to be in support of the Bush Administration's initiative, rather than on that of Mr. Blair. The United States might possess a more controlled press than other democracies (or "democracies"), but there is an unfortunate natural tendency in any nation for the press not to oppose a war that the nation itself has initiated. This is the warmongering danger that exists in a democracy, just as much as in any dictatorship. It's the reason why, as New York Long Island's *Newsday* bannered on April 16th, "Times Publisher Defends Paper's War Coverage" against ludicrous charges that the nation's most famous newspaper had an "anti-war bias."* The result is a press that's stiflingly "con-

---

* The overtly right-wing media have always charged that *The New York Times* and other major media in the United States have a "liberal bias." As is mentioned elsewhere herein, the *Times* does have a liberal slant in its editorials, but its news slant is conservative. This can be contrasted, for example, to the *Wall Street Journal,* which has extremely conservative editorials, but whose news reporting is un-slanted even when a story concerns political issues. The *Journal* is much higher quality overall than the *Times,* but, of course, is narrower in its scope. Many unknowledgeable people feel that the *Times* has a liberal slant to its news reporting because the paper's editorials have so clear a liberal slant. For example, the *Times* was editorially opposed to the impeachment of Bill Clinton, but its news reporting was slanted strongly in favor of his impeachment, even though many naïve readers were unaware of the fact. Gene Lyons, in the October 1994 *Harper's* was quite correct when he criticized the *Times* for having actually started the craze to impeach President Clinton. His article, "Fool for Scandal: How the 'Times' Got Whitewater Wrong," detailed that "it all began with the New York Times – specifically with a series of much-praised articles by investigative reporter Jeff Gerth: groundbreaking, exhaustively researched, but not particularly fair or balanced stories that combine a prosecutorial bias and the art of tactical omission to insinuate all manner of sin and skullduggery. ... [the] Whitewater investigation began in direct response. ... It is all the more disturbing, then, that most of the insinuations in Gerth's reporting are either highly implausible or demonstrably false." A 2003 book, by a naïve self-declared conservative, Bob Kohn, purported to see a liberal slant to the reporting in the *Times,* and was even titled on that basis *Journalistic Fraud: How The New York Times Distorts the News and Why It Can No Longer Be Trusted.* In order to understand and recognize propaganda and authentic slant, one has to know not only the subject that a given "news story" purports to discuss, but also what is being omitted from the account. Obviously, American news reporting on Iraq's alleged retention of its

trolled," even if only by its editors' pervasive fear of disturbing or even angering readers who have already become, supposedly, hopelessly duped. But duped by whom? By these media, of course. So, then, it's a vicious circle of duplicity and cowardice, feeding off each other. And this result is essentially the same as old Soviet *samizdat* censorship, even though the precise mechanism here is quite different. That helps to explain why America's war-criminal President Bush continued to be lionized in his own nation, even long after the supposed WMD pretext of his "glorious" invasion had drifted off into the imaginary ether.

Furthermore, some important aspects of the war's damage to Iraq were actually covered as well in the U.S. media as in the foreign press. Besides the massive human carnage from the invasion, perhaps one of the war's greatest harms to Iraq was its destruction of that ancient country's archaeological treasures, many of which were housed in the world's leading museum of ancient art and antiquities, the Iraqi National Museum, which was the world's premier repository of Mesopotamian art and antiquities, objects dating back to 3,500 B.C., documenting the ancient biblical cities of Ur, Nineveh, Babylon, etc. According to CNN on April 16th, this Museum had possessed "the most complete timeline of civilization that existed in any museum in the world." And the American major media matched their foreign counterparts in covering this museum's tragic sacking, which took place virtually under the noses of U.S. occupying troops.

WMD was the most strongly slanted in the entire world; no other nation's media even came close. Eric Alterman's 2003 *What Liberal Media?* is especially perceptive about slant, in that it makes the crucial distinction between the political orientation of a news medium's management, on the one hand, and of its reporters, on the other. The slant in news reporting comes almost invariably from management, only rarely from journalists themselves, whose careers are dependent upon their satisfying their managers. Of course, managers, in turn, are beholden to the controlling stockholders. Understanding news slant requires considerable sophistication, which unfortunately few people possess who write about the subject.

Someone who knows about slant first-hand, and yet who has been able to maintain complete freedom from the media-bosses, is Princeton University economics professor Paul Krugman, who, as a sideline, was invited by *The New York Times* to write a regular op-ed column. During an interview on September 11, 2003, at www.buzzflash.com/interviews/03/09/11_krugman.html, he explained, "I'm moonlighting. This is not my career. ... If I'm frozen out, if the *Times* finally decides I'm too hot to handle and fires me or whatever, that's no great loss. So I'm a lot more independent than your average journalist would be." He stated that "a good part of the media are essentially ... a propaganda machine." He tactfully avoided naming the *Times* in that category, but still admitted that "being critical at the level I've been critical – basically saying these [Bush] guys are lying, even if it's staring you in the face – is a very unpleasant experience. You get a lot of heat from people who should be on your side." A more vulnerable (from a career-standpoint) *NYT* journalist who had been forced out and who could never figure out what had hit him, was Sydney H. Schanberg, who wrote about the experience in the *Village Voice* on June 11-17, 2003: "Reviving the Good Gray Lady." Even after he left the *Times*, he remained fooled by its pretense.

Professor McGuire Gibson of the University of Chicago, interviewed on America's National Public Radio on April 13th, recounted that in January he had supplied to both the White House and the Defense Department a prioritized list of 115 archeological sites to be protected from bombing and also from looting in the event of a war, and that this Museum was number one on the list. He said that he had been promised that it would be secured and protected, but that it was not. Also on April 13th, *The New York Times* reported that one of the Museum's archeologists went up to an Abrams tank and urged American protection of the Museum against the looting that was occurring, and that the tank then proceeded to the Museum for 30 minutes and simply left. The tank evidently experienced no resistance. (Before pacification of the Museum's neighborhood prior to April 10th, some Iraqis had brought weapons into a wing of the Museum, and abandoned them there. The fighting was now over, and those arms were being looted along with the artworks.) The *Telegraph* reported, the same day, that virtually all of the Museum's treasures, "worth billions of dollars," were being carted off. Professor Gibson said that few of these items would reappear, because they "are in every ancient art book" and easily recognizable, and thus "too famous to show"; the gold items would simply be melted down. Also on the 13th, the *Washington Post* ran a story headlined, quoting an Iraqi, "'Our Heritage Is Finished.'" It noted that, "Some Iraqis ... question the allocation of U.S. forces around the capital," and that the Americans seem to have been obsessed "to guard the Oil Ministry" at the expense of everything else. "Why just the oil ministry?" asked an Iraqi. "Is it because they just want our oil?" Similarly, John Burns in *The New York Times*, the day before, quoted an Iraqi as saying, "'The cause is not Saddam, the cause is oil.'" Burns continued, "To press home his point, he contended that American troops who have taken control of much of the city have made no attempt to protect any government building from looters except the Ministry of Oil. 'They won't let the looters go anywhere near it.'"

One consequently understands Niko Price of the Associated Press, datelined on the 12th, headlining "Baghdad Seethes With Anger Toward U.S.," and quoting an Iraqi on the street as saying, "The coalition forces are responsible. Where is the law? This is the promise of the United States to Iraq?" Tragically, the looters just kept on coming, and the Museum's officials futilely kept on trying to save what was now left of their precious collection: stunningly, the *Guardian* was reporting even as late as April 14th, "US army commanders have rejected a new plea by desperate officials of the Iraq Museum to protect the country's archeological treasures from looters." That very same day, Joanne Mariner, a columnist at www.findlaw.com, wrote (ominously for the Bush Administration): "Under the laws of war, the

United States is obligated to ensure public order in territories that it occupies, and to prevent looting and other forms of lawlessness. More specifically, it is required to protect museums and other cultural property against damage. The primary international treaty on this point is the Convention for the Protection of Cultural Property in the Event of Armed Conflict, drafted in 1954." Nonetheless, the next day, CNN was reporting yet another futile "renewed appeal for U.S. troops to come and secure what is left of one of the most valuable collections in the world, ... and nobody has come, despite promises from U.S. officials, all the way up to the Secretary of State." The reporter, Jim Clancy, continued, "At the same time, Iraqis point to Iraq's oil ministry building, ... protected from day one, ... not a scratch on it. It was not looted. Many Iraqis ... [are] saying it shows where U.S. priorities are." And still a day later, on April 16th, Mr. Clancy was yet again speaking with the exasperated curator, who was saying, "Even in the news last night, we heard that [Secretary of State] Powell said that we will protect the Museum. And I was expecting this morning to come and see some of the armored cars here. But nobody is here." The next day, the 17th, Reuters reported that two cultural advisers to the Bush Administration resigned in protest. Said one, who had chaired for eight years the President's Advisory Committee on Cultural Property, "It didn't have to happen. In a pre-emptive war, that's the kind of thing you should have planned for." Said the other, "We certainly know the value of oil, but we certainly don't know the value of historical artifacts." Shortly afterward, yet a third cultural adviser to the President joined them in resigning. According to Frank Rich of *The New York Times* on April 27th, "It was on April 10, the same day the sacking of the National Museum in Baghdad began, that a subtitled George W. Bush went on TV to tell the Iraqi people that they are 'the heirs of a great civilization.'"

Perhaps the speechwriter forgot to explain to the American President what that passage meant. And Mr. Bush seems not subsequently to have learned its meaning. Even as late as May 23rd, the *NYT* was headlining, "Iraqi Looters Tearing Up Archaeological Sites." It reported: "President Bush's new civilian administrator for Iraq, L. Paul Bremer III, has moved aggressively to rein in looters in Baghdad, and the American armed forces have greatly expanded street patrols by military police. But with a few exceptions, the American forces have done little to protect Iraq's numerous archaeological sites, just as they stood by while Iraq's museums were looted in the days after the Hussein government fell." *Times* writer Edmund L. Andrews presented the details, datelined from Isan Bakhriat on the 22nd: "Mobs of treasure hunters are tearing into Iraqi archaeological sites, stealing urns, vases and cuneiform tablets that often date back 3,000 years and more to Babylon and Sumer, archaeologists say. Here at the site of what was once Isin, a city-state that first arose around 1,900 B.C., about 150 young men armed with shovels, knives and sometimes semiautomatic weapons have been digging from dawn to dusk and extracting ancient relics almost hourly. 'In two weeks, they have ruined all the work that was done over 15 years,' said Susanne Osthoff, an archaeologist ... with a German team."

But the looting just continued. AFP headlined, on June 11th, "Looting of Iraq's Archaeological Sites Continues," reporting that, "Looters continue to plunder Iraq's museums and archaeological treasures, many of them left unguarded since the end of the US-British-led invasion, the National Geographic Society said." Henry Wright, the curator of the University of Michigan's Museum of Anthropology, led the team of scholars, and said, "Irremediable damages are being inflicted, even as we speak." The next day, the *Washington Post* headlined, "Worst Looting May Be in Remote Parts of Iraq," and opened with, "While considerable attention has been focused on the looting and damage to antiquities in Baghdad, the scale of damage may be far greater in the rest of Iraq, home to some of the most ancient sites of human civilization, according to the most comprehensive survey to date." Thousands of years of human history were simply being carted off. Mr. Bush always had *other* priorities.

Fortunately, however, due to the foresight and planning of the Iraqi National Museum's curators and staff, Reuters was able to report, on June 7th, under the heading of "Missing Iraqi Antiquities Found in Secret Vault," that, "many of the items feared lost have been discovered. Some were taken home by staff for safekeeping, and others were found hidden elsewhere, including the large haul in a secret vault. Staff initially refused to reveal the location of the vault until U.S. troops had left Iraq, but later relented."

Now comes the most interesting part of this press story. The fact that the damage to the Museum turned out to be less severe than originally feared generated a vicious right-wing reaction against the journalists who had been reporting on the looting and on the scandalous absence of protection to the Museum and other cultural sites. For example, Andrew Sullivan, at Salon.com, on June 10th, headlined that these news reports and commentaries were the "Idiocy of the week," writing, "As to the critics – the Riches and Conasons who hyped reports they couldn't confirm in order to trash the administration? A correction would be nice, wouldn't it?" Mr. Sullivan identified not so much as a single factual falsehood in those news articles, yet he asserted that "a correction" of them should be published. The only thing that was even questionable in some of the news stories was the commonly cited estimate of how many objects had been in the

Museum's entire collection; but that figure, 170,000 objects, had still not been discredited. Furthermore, Sullivan's own outrageous commentary on the looting opened with a grossly false reference to "the alleged ransacking of the National Museum in Baghdad." The word "alleged" there was misleading, at the very least; it was no appropriate adjective for what indisputably went on. However, "gung-ho" is an appropriate adjective for such a so-called "journalist" as Mr. Sullivan, people who are in the business of duping the American public, not of informing them. Mr. Sullivan triumphantly asked: "Who was right – Rich and Conason or Rummy? Rummy, of course. He almost always is." (Sullivan was referring there, of course, to Donald Rumsfeld, the very same man who had outright lied about the evidence he had possessed concerning Iraq's chemical weapons.)

Similarly, on PBS television's Lehrer NewsHour, June 20th, David Brooks, from Bill Kristol's and Rupert Murdoch's *Weekly Standard* magazine, attacked the reporting "of the Iraqi Museum story where we had all these outrageous stories 170,000 artifacts are gone [that number, as was just mentioned, was actually reported to have been instead the alleged number of objects in the Museum's entire collection, not necessarily the number of objects that had been looted]. It turns out 30 or 40 artifacts are gone. [This statement, too, was false. The latest authoritative report was from Oxford's Eleanor Robson, writing in the *Guardian*, on June 18th, under the heading, 'Iraq's Museums: What Really Happened.' She indicated that, not "30 or 40," but 'between 6,000 and 10,000' of the Museum's artifacts were still missing, including 'some 30 major pieces.' Many other items had been broken or smashed by the looters – unsuccessfully looted.]"

These conservatives, such as Brooks (who has since become a columnist for *The New York Times*), had expressed no objections, and had even reported – as indicating established facts – the numerous unsubstantiated mere claims by this Administration asserting that Saddam Hussein was hiding huge stockpiles of WMD. However, when just so much as a single reported event, unfavorable to this Administration, later turned out fortuitously to have been somewhat less disastrous than had been accurately reported by journalists at the time, the honest reporters who were covering that event became, after the fact, demonized by conservatives in the press. Dan Rather might say "neck-laced." They were, in fact, being professionally lynched by the conservative "news" mob. Even if we ignore the archeological damage to the rest of Iraq, the reality is that what happened at the Iraqi National Museum was nothing less than an archeological catastrophe: According to Timothy Potts writing in the September 25th *New York Review of Books*, "As of July 11, a total of 13,515 objects had been confirmed as stolen, of which 10,580 were still missing, including all but a handful of the most important works." So much, then, for "the alleged ransacking of the National Museum in Baghdad," in which "It turns out 30 or 40 artifacts are gone." Did those conservatives ever correct their *lies*? No.

The noose should be turned. Such people as Mr. Sullivan and Mr. Brooks might satisfy the needs of a Joseph Goebbels, or of a PR firm, but not of professional journalism in a democracy. However, does this cravenness cause the careers of such conservative hacks to suffer? In the United States? To the exact contrary: in such a culture, this is the safest path to journalistic success, as was exemplified by Mr. Brooks's subsequent *promotion* to become a *NYT* columnist.

On September 9th, the online edition of *Editor & Publisher*, the trade magazine for U.S. newspaper publishers, essentially acknowledged that the American press had rolled over for the President in order to give him the war he had been seeking. In a "Shoptalk Column," the editor of *Editor & Publisher*, Greg Mitchell, headlined, "Will Press Roll Over Again on New WMD Report?" He described how the Bush Administration's chief Iraq WMD inspector, David Kay, was gearing up to "flood the zone" with "what may be largely assertion – not fact – as compelling proof. Would the media possibly fall for this? There are disturbing indications that they would." He cited especially a study that had been done for the AP by Charles J. Hanley. That investigation was summarized in the very same issue of *E&P* under the banner, "AP Staffer Fact-Checks Powell's UN Speech: Key Claims Didn't Hold Up." Mr. Hanley's full report had also been published on August 10th in the *Philadelphia Inquirer*, under the headline "Powell's Battle Cry Fails Test of Time." Mr. Hanley went through each of Secretary Powell's February 5th U.N. speech allegations, and concluded they were all bogus.

The trade journal for newspaper publishers was now informing its readers that they had been respectfully publishing White House propaganda all along under the guise of authentic journalism. The Editor, Mr. Mitchell, told America's newspaper publishers: "It's a depressing case study of journalistic shirking of responsibility. The press essentially acted like a jury that is ready, willing and (in this case) able to deliver a verdict – after the prosecution has spoken and before anyone else is heard or the evidence studied. A hanging jury, at that." Only the U.S. public is unaware that their "news" *was* mere propaganda. America's publishers (and broadcasters) don't want readers (and audiences) to know this embarrassing fact.

Of course, neither does the Government. So, on September 14th, the *Times* of London perfunctorily and briefly reported that "Britain and America have decided to delay indefinitely the publication of a full report on Iraq's weapons of mass destruction after inspectors found no evidence that any such weapons exist." The following day, considerably more details and background about this huge about-face appeared at http://fairuse.1accesshost.com/news1/monitor1.html. The public, especially in the United States, had simply lost interest in the subject, and the Bush Administration decided that it would be best not to re-ignite the matter. The London *Times* said that the findings of the by-then 1,400-person American weapons-inspection team would probably never be made public.

The crucial background for this Bush Administration decision to squelch its own WMD study was actually described the day before, by independent journalist Jason Leopold, at his website dissidentvoice .org, where he headlined "Dems Scrap Plans To Look Into Claims White House Manipulated Intel On Iraq." Leopold quoted a Democratic congressional aide as saying "We're past that." The Republican majority in Congress had successfully blocked the investigation. Politically, the issue seemed to be just dead.

Nonetheless, on September 24th, the BBC headlined "No WMD in Iraq, Source Claims," and reported that the weapons study would be issued some day, though it would show that Iraq retained no WMD, and no facilities for producing WMD. The report would instead accuse Iraq of having intended to produce WMD. Even if such allegation is true, so too do a number of other countries, and the success of the U.N. inspections program in Iraq at eliminating and monitoring Saddam's WMD remains impressive and indisputable. The United States didn't kick those U.N. inspectors out alleging mere hopes by Saddam; we kicked them out alleging existence in Iraq of huge stocks of WMD, and the failure of the U.N. inspections program there. Bush had lied.

Once the press has disastrously failed the public in a democracy, can they even *admit* this? If a "democracy" has degenerated into an elaborate sham, *who* will report it?

This is a far bigger scandal than any that the U.S. press has ever reported on.

The September 15th issue of *Newsweek* featured on its front cover this false headline: "Two years after 9/11, New Heroes, New Victims: 433 Americans Have Died in The War on Terror." Those 433 were *actually* almost exclusively casualties *in Iraq;* in other words, *Newsweek's* cover, even at this late a date, was falsely implying that the war in Iraq was a part in "The War on Terror," and was thus justifiable retaliation for the 9/11 attacks. Was *Newsweek* here practicing journalism, or simply raw propaganda? With subliminal support from the media such as this, President Bush was understandably applauded when he deceptively said in New Hampshire on October 9th, "The terrorists in Iraq believe their attacks on innocent people will weaken our resolve. ... They're mistaken. ... And beyond Iraq, the war on terror continues." What nation might he invade next? He had already transformed Iraq into a terrorist breeding-ground. Were more such breeding grounds to come?

Rubbing salt in the wound of the American people, but buried safely away from print as a "Newsweek Web Exclusive," Christopher Dickey on September 19th headlined "Pride and Prejudices: How Americans have fooled themselves about the war in Iraq," blaming *the American public:* "The problem is not really that the public was misinformed by the press before the war, or somehow denied the truth afterward. The problem is that Americans just can't believe their eyes."

This is rather like telling cigarette smokers: "Don't blame the people who advertise and manufacture cigarettes and who have profited from what harms you, and don't blame the politicians whom they finance. You're just a sucker!"

Expecting the major American media to report to the American people that the major American media have been political propagandists and corrupt deceivers is like expecting tobacco companies to say, "We're guilty, and we're sorry."

Are the American people simply trapped?*

---

* Further indications that the American people indeed *are* trapped, and that the country is a fascist dictatorship, are provided at www.projectcensored.org/publicat ions/2004/12.html, and at several other numbered pages at www.projectcensored.org /publications/2004/index.html. Although those academicians' generally Marxist viewpoints blind them to the role that religion plays in these and other egregious matters (the Marxist view being, of course, that religion is supposedly just an "opiate of the masses"), their selections are, nonetheless, far better picks for the year's outstanding journalism than, say, the Pulitzer's usually far inferior selections. Furthermore, the journalists who are honored at Project Censored are generally not only superior to, but unfortunately blacklisted at, America's mainstream "news" media. The Project Censored news stories demonstrate that the American press is, indeed, a right-wing mirror of what existed in the Soviet Union, and that press "diversity" in the U.S. is, itself, a lie.

This has been documented in a wide range of incidents, by a book that shows that America's best journalists have been forced out of the profession or else compelled to practice it in other countries not so rigidly controlled by fascist regimes: *Into the Buzzsaw: Leading Journalists Expose the Myth of a Free Press*, edited by Kristina Borjesson (2002). It's the best muckraking U.S. book in decades, and shows that there's no shortage of great American investigative journalists, but that no major media in the country will hire them. Still, the propaganda job that the U.S. major media did on the Iraq issue dwarfs any of the journalistic atrocities documented in that work. This is true despite one of those stories having been an even bigger scandal substantively, and actually involved in setting the stage for the invasion of Iraq: the theft by the Bush gang of the 2000 U.S. Presidential election. The invasion of Iraq couldn't have occurred if the U.S. press had done a professional job of reporting. But the theft of the White House by the Republican Party was only covered up (not also significantly *participated in*) by America's "news" media.

Here's what is perhaps the most depressing thing of all: www.pollingreport .com/media.htm shows that consistently during the reign of G.W. Bush, the American public overwhelmingly believes that the news media are "too liberal." This is truly Orwellian. Think about it: "1984" is today's U.S.A. It's right there – here and now.

On Wednesday, October 29th, Reuters headlined "U.S. Mulls Shifting Experts from Iraq Arms Hunt." This story opened: "The Pentagon is considering shifting intelligence personnel in Iraq from the so-far fruitless search for weapons of mass destruction to strengthen efforts to combat the intensifying resistance, officials said on Wednesday. ... 'There is a finite number of ... intelligence officers. And there are a lot of problems – dealing with the insurgency and other stuff. And so tough decisions have to be made,' a U.S. official said on condition of anonymity."

Then, on January 9, 2004, the front page of Dublin's *Irish Times* emblazoned "US Calls off Search for Weapons of Mass Destruction." This report opened, "The Bush administration has quietly withdrawn a 400-member military team it sent to Baghdad to scour Iraq for evidence of unconventional weapons. The move indicates that the US does not now expect to find illegal weapons, the main reason given by President Bush for the war last year that toppled Saddam Hussein."

Exactly a week later, Reuters bandered "U.S. Weapons Hunter Won't Return to Iraq," reporting that Bush's chief weapons inspector, David Kay, who had come to the U.S. supposedly to celebrate Christmas, had still not returned to his post in Iraq, and had no plans to. The January 2004 *Readers Digest* (p. 129) quoted Condoleezza Rice as saying, "The good thing is that, with weapons inspector David Kay, we will find the truth about what happened to his [Saddam's] weapons of mass destruction." Could she have been left out of the loop? Hardly.

On January 23, 2004, Reuters headlined "Ex-Arms Hunter Kay Says No WMD Stockpiles in Iraq." In a phone interview, Kay told Reuters "I don't think they existed."

The WMD charade was fading out, under the cover of media night in the United States. The *Atlantic Monthly*, which, even before the war, had turned down investigative articles that would have exposed the Bush frauds, featured in their January 2004 issue an article from longtime WMD propandist Kenneth Pollack arguing that President Bush didn't lie about Saddam's WMD. The American people had been had, and the U.S. media simply never reported the fact, because the U.S. media were themselves part of the President's scam that had deceived the U.S. public. (An interesting question, therefore, is going to be: What, if anything, will the U.S. media say about this book?)

Then, David Kay shocked the Bush Administration and testified to Congress. Democrats clamored for an independent investigation, which would report prior to election day. Republicans circled the wagons around the President. Finally, "truth," which had been controlled by the budding American dictator, was starting to be politicized.

Chapter 5
Bush's Motive for the Crime

"At the outset of the First World War, German Chancellor Theobald von Bethmann Hollweg handed the Allies the moral high ground and an unassailable propaganda advantage. At 3 P.M. on 3 August 1914, the day Germany declared war on France and two days after she declared war on Russia, he rose to address a packed and expectant Reichstag. He informed his fellow countrymen that German troops, advancing on France, had occupied Luxembourg and were 'already in Belgium.' Then, in a moment of candor he would almost immediately regret, he added, 'Our invasion of Belgium is contrary to international law but the wrong – I speak openly – that we are committing we will make good as soon as our military goal has been reached.'" **Diana Preston, *Lusitania*, 2002, the opening of the book.**

* * *

Above all, the great question is: why did such horrors even happen? Did they happen, as Gary Wills charged, because of the barbaric Bush lie that Saddam was behind 9/11? Did they happen because of the legally "obligatory" Bush lies that Mr. Bush possessed conclusive evidence that Saddam was hiding huge stocks of banned weapons? Why, then, those lies? And why the priorities that shaped this invasion, and which all of these lies served? The nefarious actual reason, behind Mr. Bush's lies and the entire war, was more complex, more ambitious, and more frightening, than simply oil, or even than simply the President's re-election, and it has been well reported in the European press; see, for example, the September 15, 2002, article in Scotland's *Sunday Herald* by Neil Mackay, "Bush Planned Iraq 'Regime Change' Before Becoming President," at www.sundayherald. com/print27735. Too bad that America's press hasn't reported it (with few exceptions, such as Jay Bookman in the *Atlanta Journal-Consti-tution*, fourteen days later). It should have been everywhere in the U.S. That was a huge failure of American journalism.* As Germany's *Spiegel*, on March 4, 2003, informed its millions of readers, in a long and fully documented background article about this illegal war-to-come, "It's not about [Saddam's] WMD, it's purely a war about world domination." Even before the U.S. invaded Iraq, Germans were thus being clearly informed that WMD were just a Bush ruse, and that conquest was the real goal driving this invasion. Germans recognized neo-fascism when they saw it. Americans were kept in the dark about it by a complicit national press. Even *after* the war, when the American television network ABC's John Cochran opened a report, on April 25th, by saying, "Officials inside government and advisers outside told ABC News the administration emphasized the danger of Saddam's weapons to gain the legal justification for war from the United Nations

---

*   The best summary history/bibliography of the presentation to the American public of this neo-imperial Bush scheme is to be found at www.jayware.com/us-plan. html. That web page mentions also a few early pieces on the subject that had appeared in the *New Yorker*. However, those articles, by Hendrick Hertzberg, Fareed Zakaria, and Nicholas LeMann were unfortunately written in the magazine's customary obtuse style, and so they all made very little impact. Because of the clearer writing style of the article in Scotland's *Sunday Herald,* that piece achieved far more web-mentions than any of the *New Yorker* articles. The first published mention of Bush's plan was actually the piece in the *New Yorker* on April 1, 2002, from Nicholas LeMann, titled "The Next World Order," which can be found in full on the web at www.newyorker.com/fact/ content/?020401fa_FACT1. Even though that was the first, it, too, was somewhat ignored on account of its obtuse style. (For example, it has only half as many web-mentions as does the Scottish newspaper article, even though appearing several months earlier in a supposedly far more influential publication.) But LeMann ought to be importantly credited with having been the first published journalist to notice this imperial thinking behind the Bush Administration. If his article hadn't been so pretentious, longwinded, and chatty, it might have had a salutary impact. (On the other hand, it would then have violated the style of the *New Yorker*, and so probably wouldn't have been published by that magazine; thus, it would probably have been impractical.) But the same can be said for the other early articles that the *New Yorker* ran on this crucial subject. That's why the scholars at Project Censored, when awarding the credits for news coverage of the most censored story of 2002-2003, "#1 The Neoconservative Plan for Global Dominance," at www.projectcensored.org/publicat ions/2004/1.html, they simply ignored all of the articles that the *New Yorker* had published on this subject. The reasons why Neil Mackay's and Jay Bookman's articles had bigger impacts, even though appearing in less prominent media, is that they were the first two articles that stated clearly and boldly what stood behind the Bush Administration's foreign policy – that it was a historic reach for hegemonic global military empire.
       None of these journalistic articles probed into the historical origins of this supposedly "neo" conservative thrust in foreign policy, and the purpose of the present chapter is to do that. While the neo-cons were the dermatological symptom, the source of this cultural disease went far deeper, more than a thousand years into history. In the closing chapter, a cure is proposed, based upon this diagnosis.

and to stress the danger at home to Americans," the falsehoods about the core context were left unchallenged: This invasion wasn't actually about "the danger at home to Americans" at all. That was just a subtle way of insinuating into this ABC "news" report the big Bush canard that the invasion of Iraq was a part in the 9/11 war against Al Qaeda terrorists. The propagandistic ABC "news" story continued, "'We were not lying,' said one official. 'But it was just a matter of emphasis.' ... Officials deny that Bush was captured by the aggressive views of neo-conservatives. But Bush did agree with some of their thinking."

That reference to Mr. Bush perhaps being "captured by" his subordinates was profoundly misleading, to say the very least. After all, the President, in fact, controlled these people; he selected his subordinates, and he gave them their instructions, which they dutifully executed. The insinuation here that George Bush was controlled or "captured" by some of his employees was a gross falsehood, whose only objective could have been to protect the President from blame for the disaster that was then just beginning to unfold. Such "news" reporting was pure deception, rank political PR.

The fact is that outside of a broader neo-Imperial context, specifically the restoration of the Holy Roman Empire with Washington as the new Rome, Mr. Bush's foreign policy, including his entire repudiation of international Law, makes no credible sense at all. Mr. Bush really does mean it when he calls the war against terrorism a new "Crusade." This *Amerika Über Alles* scares Europeans and just about everyone except Americans, who are kept ignorant of what their Government is doing and why. Americans are so ignorant about this, that even many skeptical Americans fail to probe beyond explanations that focus solely upon the greed of these conquerors (e.g., the Halliburton-Cheney links, etc.), and don't see the broader picture, in which empire is about far more than just money; it's about power and control. These imperialists, like Roman (and other) conquerors during the Holy Roman Empire, really do believe that they are the Chosen Ones of God; they feel that they deserve conquest, that it's their *right*. They believe that they're the good guys, and that their opponents are evil.

The deeply religious Hitler believed it, too. He even had his troops carry "GOTT MIT UNS" – God is with us – stamped onto their belt buckle (in a design along with only the eagle and swastika), because Nazis, too, were convinced that they were approved by "The Almighty." This was part of Hitler's "might makes right" ethic: powerfulness *proves* goodness. The more powerful one is, the closer one is to The Almighty. Hitler was therefore proud to lead a powerful nation, and he was determined that Germany must become the *most* powerful in the entire world. Naturally, other countries perceived such an attitude as being arrogant and frightening; and it was, in fact, both.

But Germans couldn't understand that then, and Americans can't understand it today.

An essentially similar arrogant attitude permeated the likewise devoutly Christian President Bush's "National Security Strategy of the United States" (NSSUS), which he presented to Congress in September 2002. This crucial document assumed that weaker nations necessarily occupy a lower moral plane than the world's lone superpower. It asserted that therefore the superpower, the United States, should stand above international Law; the superpower should dictate, not follow, the Law, because of its (actually only self-assumed) superiority; the entire world will benefit from America's (self-righteously believed "benign") rule. In Part IX, this strategy document stated: "We will take the actions necessary to ensure that our efforts to meet our global security commitments and protect Americans are not impaired by the potential for investigations, inquiry, or prosecution by the International Criminal Court (ICC), whose jurisdiction does not extend to Americans and which we do not accept." That is the *core* of the NSSUS, and of the entire Bush approach to international relations: God's America stands *above* merely Man-made international Law. This viewpoint is also widely shared among President Bush's political base, which includes Fox "News," a major cheerleader for the invasion.

Here is how Brit Hume, the Managing Editor of Rupert Murdoch's Fox News Network, expressed this self-righteous view, employing the standard public nonsectarian style of language, in the June 2003 *Imprimis*, a newsletter that serves as a speech digest from the far-right-wing Hillsdale college. This is from a speech he gave there on the subject of "The American Media in Wartime":

"Look at the assumption behind most of the reporting on the debate over the United Nations and the legitimacy of American unilateralism, which immediately preceded the war. The assumption was that the United States, with its marvelous record of beneficial military action around the world over the past century, needed to go before a tribunal at the United Nations – where the Human Rights Commission is presided over these days by Libya, and which has a long list of failures before it, e.g., Rwanda and Kosovo – before taking action against Saddam Hussein. This idea – the idea that we have to go pleading before such a body and receive its stamp of approval in order for our conduct to be legitimate – strikes me as more than a little nutty.

"There is a reasonable argument that says that international support of our foreign policy is desirable because we don't want to have to bear the whole burden of it ourselves. Certainly we should always welcome every bit of support we can get. For one thing, this argument has nothing to do with legitimacy. For another, at the end of the day, it is the U.S. military that's going to get the job done. Our country has made the necessary investments in its military, although many argue that we need to invest more."

Like the Emperor in the White House, Mr. Hume thought that the only problem with the American military is that perhaps "we need to invest more": perhaps it's not enough that America already spends *half* of the world's entire military budget; we're the *good* guys, so shouldn't we outspend all of the possible *bad* guys put together? And why should we submit to international Law? As opposed to, say, countries like Belgium, Germany, Finland, etc., *we* ought to be exempt. International Law is only for *bad* people – such as the Libyans. It should be used only against them, not against us *good* guys.

On November 4th, *New York Times* columnist David Brooks headlined about the war, "A Burden Too Heavy to Put Down," and subheaded "Defeating the scum of the earth." Urging rejection of any change in course, he said, "The President will have to remind us that we live in a fallen world." The same moral sentiment pervaded the Bush White House. In the famous CBS "60 Minutes" interview with President Bush's former Treasury Secretary Paul O'Neill, on January 11, 2004, Mr. O'Neill said that the Administration's first three National Security Council meetings were obsessed with getting rid of Saddam Hussein, because, "From the very beginning, there was a conviction that Saddam Hussein was a bad person and that he needed to go." This was a religious Crusade for Mr. Bush, well *prior* to 9/11.

Some commentators have said that this war was about oil, and they're right, as far as it goes, because oil nowadays fuels empire. But America didn't need to conquer Iraq in order to have access to its oil; this was about empire – power, pure and simple. This is not to deny that members of the Bush Administration, such as Vice President Cheney, or perhaps even President Bush himself, might profit from invading Iraq. They see that as fine: after all, "the good guys" would be profiting from it. They "deserve" this. God's with them. They really *believe* it. However, an aspiring Emperor wants far more than wealth; he craves power. To view the "National Security Strategy of the United States" as nothing more than a corrupt business plan, is to fail to see the big picture. Anyone who, like Adolf Hitler or George W. Bush, seriously aspires to establish a global political empire, views money as just another tool to attain and wield power. That's the basic distinction between people such as Bill Gates or Warren Buffet, on the one hand, and individuals such as Hitler and Bush, on the other.[*]

---

[*]   Sometimes, statements taken out of context are cited to the contrary, and create unfortunate misunderstanding. An example is an assertion by Paul Wolfowitz, during the Q&A after his keynote speech to an Asian security conference in Singapore on May 31, 2003, sponsored by the International Institute of Strategic Studies in London. Asked why Iraq was invaded whereas North Korea was not, Mr. Wolfowitz

said, "Look, the primary difference – to put it a little too simply – between North Korea and Iraq is that we had virtually no economic options with Iraq because the country floats on a sea of oil." This assertion reflects a longstanding imperialistic view, that maintenance of empire depends upon the security of the natural-resource base. On these grounds, for example, the copper mines in Chile were central to the CIA's sponsoring the coup against the democratically elected President of that country, Salvadore Allende, in 1973, and America's installation there of the fascist Augusto Pinochet. Similarly, Rome and every other imperial power sought control of what its rulers viewed to be vital resources. They felt it was their right. This doesn't mean that Rome's emperors were necessarily motivated like acquisitive modern business people, regardless of whether that motivation be called greed, need for achievement, or whatever. Wolfowitz has made clear, during more than a decade, that his commitment isn't to individual personal wealth, but rather to the American elite's global imperial control. The key documents on this come up in two web-searches: one containing the two terms (without quotation-marks): Wolfowitz 1992; and the other containing the three terms: PNAC Wolfowitz 1998. The first concerns Wofowitz's 1992 draft Defense Planning Guidance, which called for unilateral control of the entire planet by the United States — in effect, a modern American version of the Holy Roman Empire, with Wolfowitz using the phrase "democratic 'zone of peace,'" instead of "Pax Romana." The second concerns two letters: one dated January 26, 1998, to President Bill Clinton, and signed by Paul Wolfowitz, Donald Rumsfeld, Richard Armitage, R. James Woolsey, Richard Perle, and several other subsequent Bush II proponents of "regime change" in Iraq; and the other, less than a month later, an "Open Letter to the President," dated February 19, and signed by virtually the entire right wing U.S. foreign policy elite. The February 19 letter was the more extensive; it called specifically for establishing a "government of Iraq based on the principles of the Iraqi National Congress," the group headed by Ahmed Chalabi, subsequent chief source for fabricated and doctored intelligence documents used by the Bush and Blair governments to "prove" the presence of WMD in Iraq. These three documents, and especially the one from 1992, provide the background from which the PNAC's September 2000 "Rebuilding America's Defenses" and the White House's September 2002 "National Security Strategy of the United States" ultimately drew.

Another example to make the distinction between imperialism and capitalism is that the Soviet Union was imperialist, even though it was not capitalist. Yet another is that Rome itself was not capitalist; in fact, throughout the period of the Holy Roman Empire, up to even modern times, it was feudal. Imperialists are addicted to power; capitalists desire, and can be addicted to, wealth. Imperialists favor monopoly and oligopoly; non-imperial capitalists favor competitive markets, a free economy. Imperialists and capitalists aren't identical. Capitalists want to compete, whereas feudalists/imperialists want to control. The capitalist seeks to please his customers, but the imperialist dreams of dominating or else destroying his enemies, including not only his competitors but even his customers, dictating to them all, leaving no choice but submission. The power motive and the economic motive aren't identical, but some people combine or confuse them.

Furthermore, Wolfowitz's May 31st comment continued: "In the case of North Korea, the country is teetering on the edge of economic collapse and that I believe is a major point of leverage whereas the military picture with North Korea is very different from that with Iraq." Although this former academic's syntax here makes even George Bush appear coherent by comparison, what he seems to have meant is that Iraq's oil made that country relatively freer to do what it likes than was the case with North Korea. It is hard to imagine that Dr. Wolfowitz could actually have been stupid enough to believe that North Korea's poverty caused that nation's acknowledged nuclear weapons to be *less* of a strategic threat than whatever Iraq might have had and posed.

Both Hitler and Bush believed that they were empowered, ultimately, not by what they felt to be the contemptible masses below them, but by The Almighty Himself above them, as His Chosen One. They felt that they were answerable *only* to The Almighty.

This American thrust for world empire is the object of loathing in other countries; it isolates the United States. The playwright Harold Pinter might have sounded crazy to some Americans, but he was merely expressing with shocking articulateness views that are widely held about the current American government, when he was quoted on June 11, 2003, in the *Guardian*, under the headline, "Pinter Blasts 'Nazi America' and 'Deluded Idiot' Blair," as having said: "The US is really beyond reason now. It is beyond our imagining to know what they are going to do next and what they are prepared to do. There is only one comparison: Nazi Germany. Nazi Germany wanted total domination of Europe and they nearly did it. The US wants total domination of the world and is about to consolidate that. In a policy document, the US has used the term 'full-spectrum domination', that means control of land, sea, air and space, and that is exactly what's intended and what the US wants to fulfil. They are quite blatant about it." The article went on: "Pinter blamed 'millions of totally deluded American people' for not staging a mass revolt. He said that because of propaganda and control of the media, millions of Americans believed [that] every word Mr Bush said was 'accurate and moral'."

Such views, concerning the United States, have become almost commonplace everywhere except inside the U.S. For example, the Pew Study of World Attitudes, previously referred to, which was released on March 18, 2003 – just when the invasion of Iraq was starting – showed "U.S. Image Plummets," sinking in Britain from 83% favorable

---

But even if Mr. Wolfowitz's real sentiment here was that Iraq's oil was strategically important to the U.S., this still would not mean that the invasion of Iraq was motivated by financial greed. Such an interpretation would not fit the long previous record of his strategic policy writings.

A more interesting variant of the theory that "this war was about oil" is the following: OPEC denominates barrels of oil in U.S. dollars, making the dollar the world's reserve currency. If OPEC re-denominates either to euros or else to a "market basket" of currencies, then the U.S. economy will suffer a historic blow. Of course, the gargantuan fiscal deficits due to George W. Bush make this outcome virtually inevitable; knowledgeable people recognize this. However, some commentators, especially in the international petroleum community, have theorized that Bush attacked Iraq (and also that the CIA tried to overthrow Venezuela's Hugo Chavez) in order to have friendly voices within OPEC to retain the dollar. That theory flies in the face of the way Bush, and even neo-cons such as Wolfowitz, actually think. There is no indication whatsoever that Iraq was invaded on the basis of such thinking. Furthermore, the invasion of Iraq is turning out to *expedite* the end of the dollar as the world's reserve currency. Not only is this war going to make U.S. deficits soar even faster, but it's hurting the value of American brands and otherwise more directly *boosting* the incentives to *replace* the American currency as the world's standard.

in 1999-2000, down to 48% favorable in 2003; in France, from 62% to 31%; in Germany, from 78% to 25%; in Italy, from 75% to 34%; in Spain, from 50% to 14%; in Poland, from 86% to 50%; in Russia, from 37% to 28%; and in Turkey, from 52% to 12%. As was previously mentioned, polls, worldwide, further showed overwhelming opposition to the invasion of Iraq, and also indicated that George W. Bush was overwhelmingly viewed to be the most dangerous leader in the world.

There is, consequently, a tragic disconnect between the way that the vast majority of Americans see their country, and the way that it is viewed by everyone else. Until recent times, the American people would simply not have tolerated a President who had grand designs to turn their country into the world's policeman over a global Empire. However, during the past few decades, there has been a huge surge in America's religiosity, and the Christian fundamentalists and aristocrats who placed this President into office see no problem with that goal. Indeed, it's part of their longstanding Crusade for Christian world control. It's *central* to evangelical Christianity, *and* to American nationalism.

To the extent that America's liberals recognize that a problem exists, they tend to misunderstand its source, because they share the conservatives' assumption, that their enemy – whoever that is – is evil on account of greed pure-and-simple, and so he lacks a value-system that's just as religious, just as patriotic, and just as sincere, as their own. However, these conservatives tend to be very religious indeed. Liberals basically misinterpret conservatives.

For example, the liberal columnist at the Boston *Globe*, Derrick Z. Jackson, wrote a number of commentaries in June 2003, asserting that what motivates George W. Bush is pure greed. One (June 18th, "What Are Americans Dying For Now?") opened, "Oil is to die for," and concluded that, since "No weapons of mass destruction have been found": "Without the weapons of mass destruction, it has to be for the oil" that this war was fought. In other words: it was for greed, as if that were the *only* alternative. Two days later ("Bush Fries Climate Change"), Mr. Jackson similarly explained the President's approach to the problem of global warming, by saying, "Bush is in the control of oil interests." He ignored the fact that Mr. Bush feels deeply that these "oil interests," like himself, are among God's elite. And equally important is that this President rejects science, on global warming, and on a lot of other things, because he has *faith* that God will protect and provide for His People, *including* that oil-elite. Earlier in the month (June 4th, "A Tax Cut for the Selfish"), Mr. Jackson likewise attributed the President's tax policy to greed, pure and simple. No mention was made that this President apparently believes that rich people are *closer to God*.

Mr. Bush put this matter succinctly in a July 9, 2002 speech he gave on Wall Street: "There is no wealth without character." He seems to have meant this to apply not just in the U.S., but in *any* land where Adam Smith's supposed "invisible hand" of God controls things. As Bush went on to explain, "There can be no capitalism without conscience." But this President actually hasn't the foggiest understanding of capitalism, and he failed miserably at it whenever he tried it. He's been a winner, however, whenever he has relied instead upon feudalism, including his own aristocratic genealogy, contacts, and all the rest – the things that (unlike capitalism) made him become appointed as President. Now, serving in that capacity, his catastrophic misunderstandings of capitalism are wrecking the capitalist economy for future generations of Americans, because his economic policies are so bad that he has difficulty even finding respected economists willing to serve on his Council of Economic Advisers. This man is actually no capitalist at all. Yet in the view of religious liberals, it's politically irrelevant that he *is* a passionately committed fundamentalist Christian; these liberals even suspect that his religiosity is just another part of his act, merely another lie.

They're dead wrong. There is every indication that belief in The Almighty as the source and ultimate judge of right and wrong is the authentic foundation of this President's values, just as it is the source of conservative values, and as it was the source of virtually everyone's values during feudal times, which were the "good old days" for all the good old boys. Furthermore, Mr. Bush's fellow fundamentalist Christians, through the John Birch Society, the Council on National Policy or CNP, the Christian Coalition, and other such organizations, have lobbied extensively for many years for all of these policies – and for virtually the entire George W. Bush agenda, which is neo-feudal. Empire is just a part of that religious agenda.

When the President used the word "Crusade" to describe his goal after 9/11, he knew what that meant, and it meant Empire, in the sense of a forceful international imposition of "God's Law," and *not* of laws from the U.N., nor of *any* Law that's made by mere men.

Stephen Mansfield's 2003 *The Faith of George W. Bush* quotes Mr. Bush as having said before he won the Presidency in 2000, "I feel like God wants me to run for president. I can't explain it, but I sense my country is going to need me. ... I know it won't be easy on me or my family, but God wants me to do it." Mr. Mansfield also claims that after Governor Bush won his prize, "Aides found him face down on the floor in prayer in the Oval Office. ... And he framed America's challenges in nearly biblical language. Saddam Hussein is an evildoer. He has to go." Mr. Bush's employees (Colin Powell, Paul Wolfowitz, etc.) don't necessarily retain from childhood this same credence they too were raised with, but religious-based values are deeper than mere *conscious* belief, and often remain even if a believer subsequently comes to reject religion intellectually. Often *still*: might makes right. One doesn't have to be (consciously) religious in order (still) to feel so.

Osama bin Laden has an Islamic Imperial agenda; George W. Bush has a Christian Imperial agenda. Both men are Imperial, and both are fundamentalists. And both are feudal in their outlook. They lie about lots of things, but that's not a religious violation, and all evidence suggests their religious commitments are authentic, despite their lies. Even Saint Paul rhetorically raised the question, in *Romans* 3:7, "If my untruth serves God's glory, should I be declared a sinner?" And this founder of Christianity effectively answered his own question in *1 Corinthians* 9:22: "I become all things to all men, so as to bring men to salvation by any means possible." A True Believer can lie for his God. It doesn't mean he's no True Believer. It can even be an expression of the person's deep faith. George W. Bush lied concerning what he knew about Saddam's WMD, but he did it out of motivation that's entirely consistent with his religious values. He's enough of a politician not to say honestly what his motivation is. ("Empire" is no longer considered politically correct, and so he calls it by such terms as "unilateral" and "pre-emptive war.") But this fellow gives every indication that he hates Man-made international Law, and really believes he's serving God through his campaign to destroy and replace it by his standing *above* it.*

---

*   When conservatives such as Bush are in power, many liberals sprout conspiracy theories against them and say that the President is doing what he is doing *because* he is simply greedy. When liberals such as Bill Clinton are in power, many conservatives sprout conspiracy theories against them and say that the President is doing what he is doing *because* he simply craves power. Neither side can understand the motives of the other, and this is the reason why conspiracy theories are always popular, and why they tend to come most from those who are out of power, and to be directed most against those who are in power. However, political conspiracy theories are based upon mere caricatures of the motivations of the other side, and are therefore always false. They are essentially the views of the members of one culture, looking upon the supposedly "conspiratorial" members of a different culture, which they don't actually understand. This does not mean that conspiracies don't exist. In fact, "conspiracies" necessarily play an important role in political campaigns, because every political campaign has to keep some aspects of its strategy secret from outsiders. However, conspiracy theories that are grander than that become more false the grander they reach, because understanding culture and society – and politics on that basis – from the standpoint of conspiracies is to *mis*understand culture and society (and therefore politics). While individual events (even important events) can be conspiratorial, the deeper underlying realities are always cultural, and that's what conspiracy theorists don't comprehend. They don't understand how a culture works. That's why they are intellectual slaves to their own culture. This prohibits them from understanding their culture. In order to understand oneself, one has to understand one's own culture. It's easier just to believe in conspiracies.

Each time the press blames "the neo-conservatives" for this invasion, they're pandering, not reporting. They blame just the employees, while absolving the employer who hires them.

One astute person who doesn't do that is Mark Crispin Miller, author of the 2001 *The Bush Dyslexicon,* and the most careful analyst of George W. Bush's character. He was interviewed by Murray Whyte in the November 28, 2002 *Toronto Star,* under the headline "Bush Anything But Moronic, According to Author." Miller put it clearly there: "Bush is not an imbecile. ... This is a guy who is absolutely proud of his own inflexibility and rectitude." So, too, was Adolf Hitler, and on sincere religious grounds in both cases.

The headline on the cover of the November 17, 2003, *Newsweek* was thus an implicit buck-passing-downward lie: "How Dick Cheney Sold The War – The Inside Story: Why He Fell for Bad Intelligence—And Pitched It to The President." The *owner* of this invasion was G.W. Bush, *not* his mere hires.

Another major failure of journalists has been to take seriously the supposed benignity of U.S. foreign policy, and to all but ignore the real background of America's sanctimonious "liberation" of the used-and-abused Iraqi people, such as the American CIA's having installed the Baath Party into power in 1963, and assisted Saddam's seizure of the Baath leadership in yet another coup in 1968. Both events were recounted by Roger Morris, in a rare (op-ed) article about these events, in *The New York Times* on March 14, 2003, titled, "A Tyrant 40 Years in the Making." Mr. Morris noted there that, in 1968, "Serving on the staff of the National Security Council, ... I often heard C.I.A. officers ... speak openly about their close relations with the Iraqi Baathists." Those people had placed Saddam into power. Now the United States was "liberating" Iraq by conquest and removing Saddam. Mr. Morris's article spurred a follow-up report from UPI's Richard Sale on April 10th, "Saddam Key in Early CIA Plot," which detailed Saddam's employment by the CIA even earlier, in 1959, as an assassin, a CIA "hitman." Saddam was America's man, even during the worst of his atrocities. In 1986, the U.S. blocked Security Council resolutions condemning Saddam's use of chemical weapons, and the U.S. Department of Commerce licensed exports of anthrax to Iraq. A web search for the phrase "We came to power on a CIA train" will bring up much of this history. Now Saddam's sponsors demonize him.

The Iraqi people had been sacrificed upon the altar of America's cold war against the Soviet Union, and then of our hot war against Iran. Later, the U.S. sponsored the Islamic fundamentalist Taliban in Afghanistan, and did the same thing to a nation on the U.S.S.R.'s very border, likewise with disastrous consequences for the local population – and ultimately, for Americans, too.

Mr. Bush's war against Iraq, however, is quite different from such old ones during the Cold War, which were authentic U.S. reactions against authentic strategic threats to America. The enemy this time is not international communism. Nor is it really fundamentalist Islam, either, which is the force that drives the international terrorism that exploded with such horror on 9/11. Just as Hitler's fake-anticommunist Nazis would have existed even if communism never had, President Bush's variant of fascism is likewise no authentic reaction against any opposed form of extremism – in this case, against fundamentalist Islam, instead of against communism. After all, Saddam Hussein's Iraq was itself dogmatically secular, adamantly opposed to fundamentalist Islam. Saddam was, ironically, more like the neoconservatives who work for Bush: he saw himself much as a "philosopher king," a wise man whose deep insight surpassed anything the "inferior masses" could understand. Perhaps he worshiped Allah, but certainly he worshiped himself. His submission – his "Islam" – could never be complete. This doesn't mean that he was less tyrannical than an Osama bin Laden, but only that the two did not agree. Therefore it was always ludicrous for Mr. Bush to charge that the Baathist leader was a supporter of fundamentalist Islamists who, in fact, despised Baathism, and who, in turn, were despised by the Baathists.

Part of George W. Bush's reason for going to war against Saddam Hussein might well have been Mr. Bush's frankly expressed personal hatred resulting from Saddam's having tried to assassinate his father, the Senior President Bush, following the first Gulf War. G.W. Bush was not shy about expressing his desire for personal revenge against the former Iraqi leader. There was certainly the element of a personal grudge match between two dynastic families here, the Bushes versus the Husseins, much like the legendary Hatfields versus the McCoys. Unfortunately, on both sides, lots of "inferior" (because less powerful) people became crushed along the way. After all, this was "Global Politics" – *big* stuff. So, such leaders didn't mind that. However, until 9/11, there was no pretext available for actually executing revenge. 9/11 opened the way to settle the grudge. But even before 9/11, the people Mr. Bush had appointed to run American diplomatic and military policy – Donald Rumsfeld, Paul Wolfowitz, Richard Perle, Richard Cheney, Richard Armitage, and others – had long been on record as favoring a much *bigger* objective: America's becoming, in essence, the New Rome: the world's sole military superpower, and the sole authority and source for international Law, in effect replacing the United Nations and all of post-WWII international Law.

In fact, President Bush's very *first* initiatives upon coming into office were against the International Criminal Court, the Kyoto Protocol, the Anti-Ballistic Missile Treaty, and many other elements of "merely" Man-made international Law. The new President made clear right at the start that the United States had to be accepted by other nations as being not merely the first among equals, but a rule apart, which simply mustn't be judged like other countries. All he needed was a major opportunity to *make* the point – something positive, not just more of saying no to the merely Man-made international Law he was religiously so deeply set against.

9/11 provided this opportunity. But attacking Afghanistan couldn't be sufficient for so grand a purpose; the world would never think that such an attack violated international Law, the United Nations, and the rest of the post-WWII international legal order. The invasion of Afghanistan was, to the contrary, widely viewed as justified retaliation for the 9/11 attacks; the world accepted it on this basis. Not so the invasion of Iraq. Invading that country would be sufficiently illegal to establish the necessary precedent that the United States stands *above* (merely Man-made) international Law, and yet it was still sufficiently arguable within the prevailing WMD context so that it might be able to pass the legal "smell test" of the international community. It was therefore uniquely qualified to serve this bigger *strategic* purpose of establishing a *precedent* that would destroy Man-made international Law and establish the global reign of "God's Law."

The invasion of Iraq, consequently, offered the perfect opportunity that had been sought by politicized fundamentalist Christians for, actually, decades. The origins of their quest to break the back of Man-made international Law started at least as long ago as the formation in 1958 of the John Birch Society, the fundamentalist Christian political organization that demonized the United Nations. But only after fundamentalists took over the Republican Party, and Ronald Reagan thereby became the U.S. President in 1980, did the movement become really serious.

The grand international design behind this war was first rigorously formulated by Mr. Wolfowitz at the Senior President Bush's Pentagon in 1992. Because it was still so controversial at that time (except in a few places like the Birch Society, which since its founding had lived and breathed such thinking), it wasn't adopted then.

The basic outlook this "neo-conservative" view propounded, that America stood *above* (Man-made) international Law, was an extension of a long ideological tradition on America's far Right, which can actually be traced all the way back to Republican international isolationism during the years between the two World Wars.* American

---

*   It mustn't be forgotten that isolationism was part of, and grew out of, the American imperialist movement. For example, the Republican Henry Cabot Lodge, who led the Senate's defeat of the League of Nations after WWI, was a passionate imperialist. One of his most famous speeches was titled "For Intervention in Cuba" in

exceptionalism in that period was reflected by the belief that this country would become the Saint Augustinian City on the Hill, the model for all nations to emulate. This isolationism resisted America's becoming opposed to the fascist Hitler. It was a right-wing "peace" (with Hitler) movement. After World War II, and the subsequent anti-Communist crusades on the far Right, the United Nations emerged as the dreaded international equalizer, which seemed to them suspiciously like "Godless communism" itself. These American exceptionalists never could accept the idea that the United States had any equals, and *especially* not equals such as the *atheistic* U.S.S.R.

As was mentioned, this emerging new right-wing worldview gelled most famously in the John Birch Society. The group took their name in honor of the Reverend John Morrison Birch, a fundamentalist Southern Baptist minister from rural Georgia who preached the Gospel in China and ended up being killed there by communists in 1945. The Birch Society openly announced their hatred of the U.N., and even tried to portray it as a threat to American democracy (which they actually despise because the U.N. is based upon Man's Law, rather than the "Law of God"). The Birchites' fury against the Council on Foreign Relations (CFR) and the rest of the old Rockefeller-Morgan establishment was not against their imperialism, but against their secularism. The Rockefeller-Morgan group endorsed multilateralism and condemned unilateralism; they formed the Trilateral Commission in 1973 to forge a common global international economic policy, which included the U.S., Europe, and Japan, cooperating to lead the world. There was nothing religious about this vision. Neither Christianity nor any other religion was to control the world. Law, to these multilateralists, was strictly a human matter; not divine. The Birchites, as fundamentalist Christians, had contempt for that view. To them, it was "communist," because it stood opposed to Man's submission to "God's Law," and because it endorsed Man-made international Law; it was secular, and thus Satanic.

After the leaders of the Birch Society, in the late 1970's, recognized that they couldn't succeed unless and until they supplanted the "Godless" Rockefeller-Morgan-dominated Council on Foreign Relations, which had been the catalyst behind the very creation of the Trilateral Commission that the Birchites railed against, the Birchites established their own mirror-organization to the CFR in 1981, the sectarian (Christian, of course) Council for National Policy (CNP).

All three of the CNP's co-founders were leaders of the John Birch Society: the two fundamentalist Christian oil heirs T. Cullen

1896 (www.mtholyoke.edu/acad/intrel/lodge1.htm). Also see Daniel B. Schirmer's 1972 *Republic or Empire*, Ch. 4 (www.boondocksnet.com/ai/dbs/re04.html).

Davis and Nelson Bunker Hunt, and the fundamentalist preacher Tim LaHaye. The latter was also the co-founder, with the fundamentalist Jerry Falwell, of the Moral Majority that largely made Ronald Reagan President. More recently, the Reverend LaHaye has been the co-author of the best-selling "Left Behind" series of Apocalyptic novels. Mr. Hunt (according to Perry Deane Young's 1982 *God's Bullies*, p. 79) contributed $1,000,000 in 1981 to the Reverends LaHaye and Falwell, to help them establish the Moral Majority as the public organization promoting the political agenda that was being pushed behind the scenes by their elite secretive CNP.

This Birch/CNP agenda aimed ultimately to restore the Holy Roman Empire, with Washington as the new Rome.

Another prominent member of the CNP was the Reverend Pat Robertson, who introduced the phrase "compassionate conservatism" into American politics during his unsuccessful 1988 U.S. Presidential campaign, and who thereafter used his Christian Coalition to become Republican kingmaker and the political godfather of George W. Bush.

At www.pubtheo.com/page.asp?PID=1191 appears a 2003 "Christian Coalition Petition" for invading Iraq, dated March 17th, saying, "The news media proudly plays up the marches and screams of the anti-war crowd. Roberta Combs, president of the Christian Coalition of America believes that it is time to let their faith-filled President know that he has the solid support of Grassroots America." A Christian Coalition poll a few months earlier, on January 17th, had reported that 90% of members believed "Islam is not a religion of peace," and that, even this early, 75% of these Christians answered yes to "I support a war with Iraq." Likewise, Gallup reported, on February 27th, that "those who identify with the religious right [are the] most likely to favor military action" to invade Iraq. Later in the year, on November 5th, the Pew Research Center reported that White Evangelical Protestants were America's only religious group that were almost 2-to-1 Republican.

Unfortunately, the CC survey didn't include another question: Would these Christians who want to invade Iraq agree also with the statement that "Christianity is not a religion of peace"? Perhaps they're so self-righteous they would somehow find a way to answer no to that. Every religion claims to be a "religion of peace." It's only their believers who kill each other in religious wars, inflamed by religious passions.

The higher a person was in the leadership of the Christian Right, the more passionate he tended to be for invading Iraq. A *particular* focus of the Religious Right's contempt became the U.S. State Department, which they felt wasn't sufficiently aggressive against Islamic, and especially Arabic, countries. Thus, on October 9th, France's AFP headlined "US State Department Protests Televangelist's Nuclear

Threat," and opened by saying, "The US State Department has lodged a vehement complaint with prominent conservative televangelist Pat Robertson for comments suggesting that its Foggy Bottom headquarters should be destroyed with nuclear weapons." Rev. Robertson, hosting his TV show, had endorsed a guest's statement in which he said, "If I could just get a nuclear device inside Foggy Bottom, I think that's the answer." The program transcript at www.cbn.com/CBNNews/News/031007d.asp indicates that the guest also said there explicitly "We've got to blow that thing up." It further shows that Mr. Robertson agreed and even volunteered to condemn the State Department *specifically* on the issue of the Iraq war, saying that "They have supported the enemies of George Bush in the war on Iraq." The State Department's spokesman, Richard Boucher, naturally expressed "disdain" for the "despicable" idea of nuking Foggy Bottom, which, of course, would have meant his own murder.

The hard-line religious purists in Christianity, Judaism, Islam, Hinduism, etc., are all essentially equal, even though they would all deny this. Not every extremist is an Islamist, such as Osama bin Laden. Most in Israel are Jews. In India, most extremists are Hindus. Most American extremists are extreme Christians, and George W. Bush happens to be one.

The religions may differ, but the extremism is the same. And all the blood they spill is red.

At www.commondreams.org/headlines02/1010-02.htm can be found an article reporting another poll that showed, as the story is headlined, "Conservative Christians Biggest Backers of Iraq War." By Jim Lobe of Inter Press Service, it was published a year earlier, on October 10, 2002. Fundamentalists were *consistently* in the vanguard of the invasion of Iraq.

Subsequently, during the very height of the invasion of Iraq, on April 4th, an article by Bill Berkowitz at www.workingforchange.com/article.cfm?ItemID=14780 indicated what the main hoped-for Christian fundamentalist payoff was to be from this invasion. The article was headlined "The New Christian Crusades," and reported: "When the war against Iraq is over and occupation begins, the Bush Administration plans to establish an American-led government. ... Closely behind ... will follow a host of fundamentalist Christian leaders, plowing the sand for new recruits. Over the past ten days, several fundamentalist Christian organizations announced plans to prop further open the window of opportunity in the rebuilding of Iraq. ... The Rev. Franklin Graham recently said that his organization, Samaritan's Purse, will lead the way. ... Along with several other U.S. and Canadian-based fundamentalist Christian groups, he is organizing Christian welcome wagons stuffed with Bibles and band-aids." These people, like the President whom they had voted for, believe in a higher Law, the Law of The Almighty, the Law of the Bible. It's their Crusade. Such hopes were delayed by the chaos of post-invasion Iraq. But on December 27th, the *Telegraph* headlined "Bible Belt Missionaries Set Out on a 'War for Souls' in Iraq," quoting about this "war" a high Southern Baptist official. He promoted the urgency of beating "pseudo-Christian" groups to Iraq.

There's nothing specifically Roman Catholic about this evangelical vision, just as there was nothing specifically Roman Catholic about the Holy Roman Empire. Indeed, today's Pope had nothing to do with the attack against Iraq; he even opposed it, as did many religious leaders. The kind of religiosity that's reflected in this invasion goes historically much farther back, and it was the norm well *prior* to modern times:

When the Holy Roman Empire was first established, after the Caesars or Emperors became Christians themselves, the religion (Christianity) considered itself to be universal (that is, "Catholic"). Protestantism didn't even yet exist. The idea of the Holy Roman Empire, in that era, was simply a kind of fusion of Church and State, or a theocracy, whereby the source of the Law was not the people who were being ruled by it, but rather The Almighty, who ruled over everyone. This was a top-down political ideal, which was opposed to everything that's bottom-up. In other words, an *imposed* Law was considered to be not only acceptable, but the only truly *moral* legal order. (After all, Man was *naturally* sinful.) However, in order for it to *be* moral, the Law had to derive from the laws of the Bible, the laws of God. The Law, in other words, had to be imposed by none other than The Almighty God Himself. The Emperor therefore received his legitimacy from the Christian clergy, originally from the Pope in Rome. (*Ergo*, the phrase, "Holy Roman Empire.")

After the Church split, local kings or potentates sought to be *legitimized* by local clergymen. In return, those local clergymen won the favor of being proclaimed by that potentate as the established Church in the given area. This is how Protestantism grew. The Holy Roman Empire after the schisms was no longer specifically Roman, but rather Christian in the more inclusive sense, still deriving the constitution or basic Law from Roman Catholicism's Bible, which had now become simply Christianity's Bible.

The dream of the Holy Roman Empire was always that instead of there being stand-alone local kings, there should be a single mighty Christian Emperor over them all, representing the one, universal, Almighty "God's Law." This was especially the ideal represented by the Holy Roman Empire prior to the Reformation schisms, but it became less and less viable to the extent that the dream of one universal (Catholic) Christian Church broke up into more and more pieces.

A close analogy in the Moslem world was the Caliphate, the Muslim emperorship, which Osama bin Laden has likewise set as *his* primary goal to restore.

In order to achieve such a unified Christian force in the modern age, there must be a single *political* superpower, which would have to be not just theocratic but Christian, truly a *new* Rome: a Rome for modern times.

President G.W. Bush was now trying to carry out the plan, and to become this new Christian Emperor of the world. The theocratic "Law of God" is to replace the Man-made, democratic, international Law of the United Nations and other such dreaded "multilateral" bodies. The evangelicals who were organizing to follow after God's Army and to invade Iraq on their "holy mission," were much like the clergy during the original Crusades. The Christian Emperor was supposed to be preparing the way for them to convert those new souls to Christ. This, in turn, would prepare the newly converted people to accept the Law of the Christian Bible, thus spreading the Gospel. These evangelicals would save souls, even if by force.

In fact, the critical moment for Mr. Bush's Presidential election campaign came on October 9, 1999, when the candidate presented a secret speech that galvanized the CNP's support. One can infer what he promised the group. The Rev. LaHaye's 2000 book, *Mind Siege*, reprints, in its "Appendix A," the "questions for candidates" to answer, in order to receive his group's support. Naturally, but in the most tactful way, the first of the 18 questions asks whether the candidate favors replacing democratic Law (which in the domestic American case is actually the U.S. Constitution itself) with "God's Law": "Do you agree that this country was founded on a belief in God and the moral principles of the Bible? Do you concur that it has been departing from those principles and needs to return to them?" According to their view, in other words, the Bible is the *ultimate* constitution, the only *true* basis for *all* laws.

This is actually a common belief among American conservatives. For example, Alabama Supreme Court Chief Justice Roy Moore was passionately supported by conservative Alabamians when he placed a stone monument with the Ten Commandments at his courthouse; and on August 28, 2003, CNN reported that "The new CNN-USA Today poll found 77 percent of the 1,009 Americans interviewed earlier this week disapproved of U.S. District Judge Myron Thompson's order to remove the monument." Just as Sharia Law from the Quran is supported by conservative Moslems in many countries, Biblical Law is supported by conservative Christians in the United States.

Fundamentalist Christians voted overwhelmingly for G.W. Bush in 2000, and he is carrying out their program now as the President. In fact, the October 6, 2003, *Newsweek* reported, concerning "pro-life" Defense Secretary Rumsfeld, that "the vetting process" for Iraq "got so bad that even doctors sent to restore medical services had to be anti-abortion."

There's no mystery about where the support for these political policies comes from. When Nicholas LeMann in the *New Yorker* on May 12, 2003 "asked [President Bush's political strategist Karl] Rove to lay out the basic American political correlation of forces – who's a Republican and who's a Democrat – he started with Republicans. 'First of all, there is a huge gap among people of faith,' he said. 'You saw it in the 2000 exit polling, where people who went to church on a frequent and regular basis voted overwhelmingly for Bush.'" Rove next listed two categories of the population as Bush-supporters, who tend also to be strongly religious: small-businesspeople, and "married with kids." Of course, he didn't at all mention aristocrats, including oligopolistic *big*-businesspeople, because they're too few in numbers to constitute a substantial *voting*-constituency; they're the *money*-constituency; they merely *buy* elections via financing their favored Republican candidates. However, other statements from Rove (such as the rationale he has given for the Republican Party's "tort reform" campaign) have indicated that he's fully aware that this tiny group, the financial beneficiaries of conservatism, are the concentrated source for the Republicans' political funding, the money-fountain to propagandize the religious masses (and especially the eager evangelicals) to vote for conservatives. Rove spoke only about the people who provide the votes for conservatism, not about the people who provide the big financial inputs and so receive virtually all of the financial benefits from conservatism.

In another public forum, *Newsweek* (p. 31) on October 6, 2003, appeared the following additional confirmation of the central role that fundamentalist Christians play in the U.S. Republican Party: "The primary demographic objective of BC04 [the Bush-Cheney 2004 campaign] is more obvious: to increase turnout among families that consider themselves evangelical Christians. The GOP defines them as voters who say they are 'born again' and who attend church regularly, at least four times a week. Rove and his team – led by campaign manager Ken Mehlman and regional director Ralph Reed – have carefully scrutinized exit-polling data in recent elections, and the Bushies frankly admire the success labor unions have had in recent years in turning out not only their members, but their members' extended families. One reason the GOP did well in last year's midterm elections, strategists say, is that it was able to best the labor unions at their own turnout game. In 2002, evangelicals composed 21 percent of the electorate, according to the polls. The Bush-Cheney aim this time is 24 percent."

Some of these evangelicals are furthermore top soldiers in this President's war against Islam. On October 16th, the *Los Angeles Times* published two stories about Lt. Gen. Wm. G. "Jerry" Boykin, who had just recently been appointed Undersecretary of Defense for Intelligence, and placed in charge of tracking down both Osama bin Laden and Saddam Hussein. Richard F. Cooper headlined "General Casts War in Religious Terms," and William M. Arkin bannered "The Pentagon Unleashes a Holy Warrior." General Boykin was reported to have said that the United States was being attacked "because we're a Christian nation ... and the enemy is a guy named Satan," and because "We're the army of God." General Boykin asserted that, in conflict, he knew he'd overcome a Muslim opponent, because "I knew my God was bigger than his. I knew that my God was a real God and his was an idol." The same day as this story appeared in the *LAT,* the Pentagon was asked to reply, and the AP headlined "Pentagon Defends Gen. Who Chided Muslims." They reported that Defense Secretary Rumsfeld praised the General saying that "He is an officer that has an outstanding record," and that "We're a free people" and so General Boykin has a right to express his views. End of story: the Bush Administration doesn't object to one of its generals, in its war against Islamic terrorism, boasting that Christianity is superior to Islam, and insulting Islam as idol worship: it's freedom of speech, not incitement of opponents.

A good introduction to the theocratic movement that Mr. Bush represents is www.4religious-right.info/index.htm, "The Rise of the Religious Right in the Republican Party." Among the topics of special interest there is "Judiciary," which discusses Presbyterian minister Rousas J. Rushdoony. He arose in 1973 as the movement's intellectual leader, because of a tome that he wrote on what the Bible says the laws should be in a Christian nation. Citing chapter and verse of the Bible, this massive 1973 work, *The Institutes of Biblical Law* argued, for example, against the American Declaration of Independence: "All men are NOT created equal before God; the facts of heaven and hell, election and reprobation make clear that they are not equal. Moreover, an employer has a property right to prefer whom he will in terms of 'color' creed, race or national origin." The late Rev. Rushdoony became a leading member of LaHaye's CNP, and his work was generously financed by fellow-CNP member Howard F. Ahmanson, the heir to a savings-and-loan fortune, as well as by Richard Mellon Scaife, Joseph Coors and other conservative aristocratic fortunes, almost all of which are likewise represented in the CNP. Indeed, the CNP, even though it is a relatively young organization, is one of the premier organizations of the American aristocracy – if not the most powerful one of them all.

---

from: www.4religious-right.info/religious_right_new_leader_bush2.html

Religion in the White House

As Falwell withdrew from politics and Robertson arose to take his place, so Robertson is now fading from political prominence, the Christian Coalition is not as strong as it once was, and a new leader has arisen. "I think Robertson stepped down because the position has already been filled," said Gary Bauer, former President of the Family Research Council who challenged Bush in the Republican primary. "Bush is that leader right now."

Ralph Reed notes that the religious conservative movement "no longer plays the institutional role it once did," in part because it succeeded in electing Bush and other friendly leaders. "You're no longer throwing rocks at the building; you're in the building." To read the *Washington Post* article, 12/24/01, "Religious Right Finds Its Center in the Oval" Click Here.

This article from *The American Prospect* titled "W's Christian Nation", June, 2003, documents the ways Bush, through his actions and appointments, is turning this country into a Christian Nation. Click Here.

Rev. LaHay's book, *Mind Siege*, didn't cover merely homosexuality and other such "domestic" concerns, but it focused extensively upon international Law. Here, too, its views were far right-wing. And here, too, LaHaye's viewpoint reflected that of Mr. Bush, but expressed in the direct words of a preacher, rather than in the more tactfully hedged words of a politician who must make an appeal broader than sectarian. The book's central Chapter 6, "The Humanist Bible," condemns the United Nations as genocidal, and makes clear that the commitment to "God's Law" as opposed to Man's Law must apply not just nationally, but also globally. In this chapter (p. 129), he explicitly opposes the view (which he complains is pushed by the U.N.) that, "The principle of moral equality must be furthered through elimination of all discrimination based upon race, religion, sex, age, or national origin." In fact, the book's very first chapter, "It Could Happen," ominously describes the direction Rev. LaHaye believes the modern world is headed: toward a nightmare global dictatorship, by the United Nations, which imposes upon everyone the laws of "the Humanist Bible." Those laws, he says, demand worldwide mass murder, suicide, sex education, acceptance of homosexuality, etc. The third chapter,

"The Wisdom of Man," even claims that the source of this "Humanist Bible" is Satan, who, as the snake in *Genesis* 3, offered Eve the apple of prohibited knowledge, the source of Original Sin. Rev. LaHaye claims it's all an evil war against God, and urges Christians to rise up politically against this "Mind Siege." As President, Mr. Bush has been doing so, but with "compassionate conservatism" and other such verbiage to mollify the naïve.

At www.livingston.net/wilkyjr/link20.htm can be found a good introduction specifically to "The Religious Right and the John Birch Society." The sources referred to there are sound. Most of these sources come from non-mainstream American publishers, and they raise this political boulder and expose in detail the theocratic underside of American politics, which is censored out of the U.S. mainstream media. This side of politics now occupies the White House. Therefore, to censor it out of mainstream media – to think that because it's "wacky" we should just pretend that what is now controlling U.S. politics doesn't even exist – is to leave the American people in the dark about the biggest real threat that the nation faces: a large and extremely well financed domestic subversive organization, which is already well on its way toward achieving many of its objectives. As the Rev. Rushdoony's son-in-law, fellow CNP'er Gary North, slipped up and wrote down in Spring 1982, in *Christianity and Civilization, #1* (p. 25), "We must use the doctrine of religious liberty to gain independence for Christian schools until we train up a generation of people who know that there is no religious neutrality, no neutral law, no neutral education, and no neutral civil government. Then they will get busy in constructing a Bible-based social, political and religious order which finally denies the religious liberty of the enemies of God." Just as the Saudi princes finance their Islamic fundamentalist madrasas to "train up a generation of people" to impose Quranic Sharia Law, American princes are doing the same in the U.S., only Biblical Christian. It's the same thing; the only difference is that it's in a different culture: these are *America's* fundamentalists.

At http://garciapublicaffairs.com/council_for_national_policy .htm, is described the CNP, the actual coordinating council for today's Republican Party. Other "research" pages on that website provide a comprehensive overview of the aristocratic money that has financed into power this political agenda. Further information (not all of which, however, is reliable) about this underside of American politics can be obtained in a web-search for: lahaye "john birch society".

An excellent and intellectually far higher-level summary statement of the view of the Law that LaHaye expresses (and a statement of it with no explicit and hostile mentions of the U.N.) can be found in an unexpected source, which occupies the top rung of the U.S. legal system. This is a speech by a U.S. Supreme Court Justice who, prior to his appointment to the high Court by President Reagan, was one of the three co-founders of the Federalist Society, the elite organization of lawyers who have dominated both the Reagan and the G.W. Bush Justice Departments and White Houses, and which crosses over heavily with the CNP. Antonin Scalia is, in fact, President G.W. Bush's favorite Supreme Court Justice, and on January 25, 2002, at the University of Chicago, he delivered this speech. His bond to this President is further suggested by the fact that only little more than a year earlier, on December 9, 2000, Scalia himself chose Mr. Bush to become President, thereby effectively settling the contested 2000 U.S. election in his friend's favor. This speech powerfully endorsed that theocratic vision, though without much reference to its history.

Addressing this friendly crowd, on the conservative campus where he had formerly taught, Scalia condemned "democracy" because it "tends to obscure the divine authority behind government," and he said that, "government, however you want to limit that concept, derives its moral authority from God," instead of "from the consent of the governed" as Thomas Jefferson had said in the Declaration of Independence. Scalia likewise was there repudiating the U.S. Con-stitution, where it stated, "We the people of the United States ... do ordain and establish this Constitution for the United States of America." To Supreme Court Justice Scalia, *only* God possesses such authority: the actual moral authority behind the U.S. and all other legal systems comes from God, *not* from the consent of the governed; and consequently the U.S. Constitution opens with a false statement (the Preamble), which falsely makes the people sovereign, and falsely denies the sovereignty of God. Justice Scalia also, in tacit retrospect of the previous U.S. Presidential election, and of his personal role in its outcome, tactfully asserted that a nation's leaders shouldn't be chosen by democratic elections, but ought instead to be hereditary kings or else imposed by force in "unpredictable battle," and thus (presumably) chosen by The Almighty. Here are Scalia's shocking exact words on this: "It is easy to see the hand of the Almighty God behind rulers whose forebears, deep in the mists of history, were mythically anointed by God, or who at least obtained their thrones in awful and unpredictable battle whose outcome was determined by the Lord of Hosts; that is, the Lord of Armies. It is much more difficult to see the hand of God or of any higher moral authority behind the fools and rogues – as the losers would have it – whom we ourselves elect to do our own will." This contempt for "the fools and rogues – as the losers would have it – whom we ourselves elect to do our will" helps to explain the report, in the Cleveland *Plain Dealer,* that Scalia told a questioner, at the end of a March 19, 2003 local speech, that "it was 'a wonderful feeling'" to have led the Supreme Court's rejection of a Florida vote-recount – Scalia appears there to have seen himself as having been, on that momentous occasion, "the hand of God" that in "unpredictable battle" between the Bush and Gore forces, "mythically anointed" God's selected new king, for which this Supreme Court Justice understandably felt very proud – "a wonderful feeling."

What President Bush was doing in Iraq was theocratic – executing the "Law of God" – in this very same sense, but now on an international, Imperial, stage; and not merely on a national, and thus merely regal, one: namely, this Emperor was tearing down the post-WWII international democracy of the U.N., and imposing, instead, what he as God's chosen new King of Kings promulgated as the Christian "God's Law," over not just Iraq, but the entire world. He was thus now performing, on the international legal stage, the same starring theocratic role that he was playing on the domestic U.S. legal stage.

His supporting theocratic cast on the domestic stage featured a different troupe of performers, not names such as Donald Rumsfeld and Condoleezza Rice, but instead, the President's fundamentalist Christian Attorney General John Ashcroft, and the White House's many fundamentalist Christian judicial nominees. However, they were all – foreign and domestic – performing their respective roles from the same theocratic script, fully in accord with the views not just of George W. Bush, but of Rev. LaHaye and his CNP. President Bush reflected a large, longstanding, well organized, and exceptionally well financed, American cultural movement.

Justice Scalia, in his speech on January 25, 2002, urged precisely the kind of determined theocratic leadership that his friend Mr. Bush was now providing. Scalia said, "The reaction of people of faith to this tendency of democracy to obscure the divine authority behind government should not be resignation to it but resolution to combat it." G.W. Bush *was* combating it.

President Bush's breaking of (Man-made) international Law was therefore a crucial part of the *purpose* of this invasion, and was no mere happenstance feature of it, such as is commonly supposed. For tactical reasons, he needed to make the invasion *appear* to be in accord with international Law. He required Britain as part of a "coalition," in order to satisfy the masses of Americans, and to disguise the fact that he was manipulating events in this grand, international theocratic, Imperial, design, to bring all of mankind under the Christian "God's Law." But this "coalition" was just a tactic; in strategic reality, a historically important *principle* was now being *established* here, by means of the conquest of Iraq, to restore the world-order prior to not only the United Nations, but the League of Nations, all the way back to the Holy Roman Empire.

As has been mentioned, it was considered to be morally *acceptable* in that old era to become not only a king who ruled over one nation, but an emperor who by conquest ruled many nations. In the present Bush version, Christian America will rule the entire world. The existing international balance of powers is therefore repudiated in favor of the military imposition of a *single* global superpower, the U.S.A.: Christ's new vicar or regent for the entire world. This is the Bush Administration's strategic New World Order – the "National Security Strategy of the United States" *in actual practice.*

Consequently, for example, U.S. National Security Adviser, Condoleezza Rice, was reported by France's AFP, on June 26, to have "attacked French President Jacques Chirac's concept of a multipolar [or multilateral] world, dismissing it as a 'theory of rivalry' that had never promoted peace." This news story, datelined from London, and headlined, "Rice Attacks French Multipolar 'Evil,'" quoted comments she had made that day at the International Institute of Strategic Studies: "'Multipolarity is a theory of rivalry, of competing interests and, at its very worst, of competing values,' she said. ... 'Only the enemies of freedom would cheer these divisions.'" Her underlying assumption was that every nation should accept American rule, and that any nation opposing it is evil – an "enemy of freedom," as she had put it. To such a provincial and culturally blind mentality, it is simply inconceivable that submitting to the rule of any foreign nation will inevitably be viewed, in any such subordinate nation, to be inconsistent with the maintenance of its own freedom. And yet that's the case. In any nation, the rule by a foreign country must always be imposed; foreign rule is never accepted voluntarily. There is an important distinction between a nation's *voluntarily* joining a union (such as the E.U. or U.N.), in which it will have a vote; and its being *conquered*, so that the nation must simply submit to the will imposed by a more powerful country. The difference is between international democracy, and international dictatorship. However, to religious, self-righteous, people, such as Ms. Rice, who don't merely respect power, but who actually worship its very personification "The Almighty," that distinction cannot be accepted: only an evil person – an "enemy of freedom" – can stand in the opposition to oneself. This is the theocratic religious view.

The view that she was attacking, by contrast, is the modern view, and it asserts that the international order must be democratic, just as the national sphere ought to be. Ms. Rice, the daughter of an Alabama preacher, sometimes leads the White House in its frequent prayer services. Religious people such as she think only in terms of "good" versus "evil," not also in terms of actual competing interests, which they cannot understand at all. They don't understand a freely competitive, capitalist economy, much less democracy in the political sphere. They don't feel that they *have* to understand competing interests: they possess the *faith* – the closed-minded comfort of "knowing" what is right, and what is wrong – that *they* are "right," and their opponents are "wrong." Their mental world recognizes *no* competing interests, other than *simply* "good" and "bad." Their "Almighty God," they are firmly convinced, sees themselves as being good, and sees their enemies as being bad, and that is *all there is to it*. In their view, competing interests "never promoted peace." However, in the *real* world, the "peace" that they seek can be imposed only by armaments: it's the "peace" of the graveyard – never the true peace of mutually autonomous real *living* entities, cooperating and voluntarily working out their differences, in a commercial enterprise, or internationally in the U.N., or via other international bodies, to the mutual benefit of *all* participants. The self-righteous religious, worshipers of power, rely instead upon *imposed* order, by The Almighty, via conquest over those who are evil ("evil," that is, in *their* view). They are *sincere* in these convictions.

This is the goal of Mr. Bush's U.S.A.: defeating those who are "evil." It was, therefore, only natural that this President responded to the 9/11 attacks against the U.S. by speaking of an "axis of evil." He even refused to accept the fact that the 9/11 suicide terrorists were (*tragically*, in their particular cases) *courageous* people. These authentic enemies of America willingly gave up their lives for their horrible cause, yet he called them "cowards," because he possessed no desire – none at all – to *understand* the world from an *enemy's* standpoint. In order to defeat an enemy, understanding him can be crucially important.* However, this President was reacting from faith, *not* from reason. This was a reflection, actually, of his arrogance, his self-righteousness. His faith was totally top-down, and so he had no

---

* This is an incredibly important point. The 2003 documentary movie, *The Fog of War: Eleven Lessons from the Life of Robert S. McNamara*, by Errol Morris, interviews the former U.S. Defense Secretary, who served during the Cuban missile crisis and subsequently oversaw the build-up of the Vietnam War. Mr. McNamara frankly reviewed both his successes and his failures, and drew his life's conclusions looking back now with hindsight, at the ripe age of 85. His life's first "Lesson" is "Empathize with your enemy." He indicates there that, because an obscure State Department advisor to President John F. Kennedy personally knew the U.S.S.R.'s leader, Nikita Khrushchev, and was thus able to empathize with Mr. Khrushchev's political predicament in the Cuban Missile Crisis, President Kennedy was swayed away from the course he had been set on – a course that would almost certainly have led to a nuclear World War III. The result of this change was that the U.S. agreed not to invade Cuba again, in return for which Soviet nuclear missiles were removed from Cuba: it was a deal between two men that saved civilization.

doubt that he, as the leader of the world's sole superpower, was on top, and that anyone who challenged him had therefore to be morally inferior. He didn't even *need* to understand those people. He merely had to destroy them; they were *nothing* but objects to be destroyed.

Such a top-down mentality can *sometimes* be constructive in military organizations, but never in a president or other executive, because an effective executive must constantly listen and learn, and not merely act. In order to learn, he must welcome having his opinions and beliefs questioned by his subordinates. He welcomes being challenged by them, and he won't be at all hostile towards such give-and-take. This President, by contrast, is entirely focused upon expressing himself through action; he bans frank equalitarian verbal exchanges with anyone down below – even with his own advisers. (And, of course, he selects *only* advisers who agree with him anyway.) Equality is banned; hierarchy is total.

On CBS 60 Minutes, November 17, 2002, Bob Woodward managed to induce George W. Bush to explain the President's prohibiting his advisers to question his opinions. Mr. Bush said, "I am the commander, see? I do not need to explain why I do things. That's the interesting part of being the President. Maybe somebody [advising me] needs to explain to me why they say something, but I don't feel like I owe anybody an explanation."

This top-down mentality came from his birth. As a conservative aristocrat, he had been raised since infancy to feel, quite simply, entitled. After he grew to adulthood and found Christ, the combination of the power of "The Almighty," along with his own never-questioned sense of entitlement, emerged explosive. It became explosive not just in regards to Iraq, but generally throughout his Presidency, because he had now won the most powerful executive position on earth. His having won this position of supreme power was further *proof* to him of his God-given entitlement. In his view, anyone whose interests compete with his is therefore simply evil. Sometimes he won't *say* it, but he always *acts* this way.

Many liberals are thus dumbfounded by his actions. For example, it seems incredible to some people that George W. Bush genuinely expected that the waters would part for him in Iraq. But he apparently believed it. Resistance by any country was, it seems, perceived by him to be resistance against the will of God. He proceeded with full confidence, based upon deep faith, in accord with his Biblical beliefs.

Likewise, at the beginning of September 2003, the Administration was trying to induce other countries to assume the burdens of Iraq. Secretary of State Powell dismissed the objections expressed by many nations that the U.S. ought not to continue controlling the Iraqi operation if the operation's burdens were to become shared. Mr.

Powell said that this objection had no validity because all of the participating nations shared "the same values." His statement ignored a crucial fact: Even if everyone has identical values, they can't reasonably be assumed to have the same *interests*. Mr. Powell, like Mr. Bush and Ms. Rice, simply couldn't understand competing interests, other than merely "good" versus "evil." And, since their common assumption was that the U.S. is always "good," everyone *ought* to do the bidding of America.

Consequently, there's every indication that Mr. Bush's arrogance is sincere. Many liberals find this hard to believe. But the President's fellow conservatives, his followers, share similar religious faith in their being "on the right side." They therefore perceive their President's arrogance as simply a reflection of his "leadership"; it's his *right*. Their God is the Great Leader, and He is anything *but* humble. So, America's conservatives see no problem with Mr. Bush. However, people outside the United States, reasonably fear his arrogance, and have grown to hate it. They don't assume that Mr. Bush's interests are necessarily their interests. They think: "*Maybe* Americans elected him; *we, certainly,* didn't."

Unfortunately, Americans often aren't even permitted to know about this President's arrogance, or about its sweeping scope. For example, Don van Natta Jr. reported on the key June 26th speech by Ms. Rice in the next day's *New York Times*, under the headline, "Rice Urges European Union to Classify Hamas as Terrorist." No mention whatsoever was made there of Ms. Rice's comments that were the focus of AFP's report. The very subject of a multilateral versus a unilateral world went unmentioned. *NYT* readers were simply kept in the dark about that entire crucial matter. With such poor journalism, how is it even possible for the U.S. public to understand international events accurately? At best, it's *extremely* difficult. All that the major media presented most Americans, regarding the core unilateral-versus-multilateral international debate, was that "our side" wants unilateral.

The difference between the CFR and CNP visions of American international relations concerned precisely this issue: The CFR, Rockefeller-Morgan, group sought to graft American dominance onto capitalism, allowing multiple independent centers of power, in the U.S., Europe, and Japan, and perhaps elsewhere. Man-made international Law, and the United Nations as an institutional vehicle for imposing it, were acceptable to those secularist capitalists. They could work with it. By contrast, the feudalist Birchers and CNP are strictly American hegemonists, absolutists who hate that secular cooperative vision, and who wish to impose American Christian control over the entire world, resuscitating, in a modern, technologically enhanced, form, the Holy

Roman Empire of old, and so restoring, too, in effect, an enhanced form of international feudalism: corporate feudalism, otherwise known as *fascism*. The origins of this vision were ancient indeed.

The Holy Roman Empire, in the strictest sense of the phrase, actually refers only to a line of predominantly German Emperors, which started with Charlemagne, who was anointed by the Pope on Christmas day in the year 800. The aim at that time was to restore the Christian Emperorship that had begun with Constantine but then petered out. The first two German Reichs were actually two different stages of the Holy Roman Empire, and therefore when Adolf Hitler named his reign the "Third Reich," he was implicitly laying claim to his continuing the Holy Roman Empire. The First Reich was the first, the Catholic, "Holy Roman Empire." The Second Reich was the Hohenzollern, Protestant imperial, dynasty, after the schism. Hitler reverted to the original Christian aim of a universal and united empire. His new wrinkle on the idea was to define "God's People" as "pure-blooded" Christians ("Aryans") and to aim for them to run the world. All other people were to be either enslaved by them (like Slavs), or else exterminated (like Jews), resulting in not just Christian supremacy, but Christian *"racial"* supremacy. (It actually had nothing to do with "race" as a geneticist or any other scientist knows the term; it was a religious concept, of "a people" sharing a common "blood.")

However, even in Charlemagne's time, the basic goal was the same: to impose Christianity upon the entire world. Early in his career, Charlemagne as king set out to exterminate all non-Christians, or "pagans," in the Germany of his time. As the Frankish king, prior to being anointed Emperor, he offered his subjects the choice of either becoming Christians or else being executed. This elementary "incentive" system was naturally of immense assistance to the clergymen of his day, who were the evangelicals of the time: Catholic evangelicals, of course, not Protestant ones, but evangelicals just the same. In fact, it was largely because of gratitude for this King's services rendered to the Church, that the Pope *anointed* Charlemagne as the first "Holy Roman Emperor."

The description U.S. Supreme Court jurist Scalia gave of what he felt to be the right way for political leaders to win power – mythical anointment – was ideally exemplified by Charlemagne even at the very start of the Holy Roman Empire, and was also exemplified in almost every feudal culture, in all religions. In the most basic sense, the Holy Roman Empire can be considered to be Christian theocracy extended by force over many nations, rather than being *merely* national in scope. It is not just feudal: it is a grand *international type* of feudalism.

This neo-feudal thrust has its proponents at all levels of American society, including within academia. Dr. Paul Wolfowitz, though not a Christian himself (he is a Platonist, via his teacher and fellow former or secular Jew, Dr. Leo Strauss) is the dominant foreign-policy intellectual in the Bush Administration; and, as was mentioned, he's the man who in 1992 first theoretically formulated this Administration's goal of resuscitating the Holy Roman Empire with Washington as the new Rome. Michael Hirsh revealingly described him as follows, in a *Newsweek* article, June 23, 2003, titled "Neocons on The Line": "At the University of Chicago grad school, a haven for right-wing thinkers, Wolfowitz was smitten with the grandeur of great empires, says Charles Fairbanks, a fellow Chicago grad and friend. ... 'He had just been reading Livy's history of Rome. He was obviously somehow in love with political greatness. ... He talked for hours at a time about the ancient Romans, about what kind of men they were and what they achieved.'" Wolfowitz was now one of these *neo*-Roman elite, even if only as a power behind the new Bush Imperial throne. He was exactly the kind of man with whom King Bush sought to surround himself – the kind of man who would help this king become the Emperor of the entire world. When Rome ruled the world, there wasn't even a possibility of cooperative rule by democratic international institutions such as the United Nations; and Dr. Wolfowitz, like his friend Dr. Perle, and others, would be happy to see those secular institutions – now that they were formed after WWII – simply fade away. It was a grand enterprise in rolling back the historical clock.

Here is how the John Birch Society's William F. Jasper expressed this viewpoint in the Society's magazine, the *New American*, on April 3, 1995, concluding an article which argued that, "Global government under the UN would be this era's Black Death": "The human mind cannot even begin to conceive the enormity of the global slaughter that would certainly accompany the 'Plague of Power' issuing from a world government under any entity other than God Himself." That was the basic Bush viewpoint. It was also the Scalia viewpoint, and the LaHaye viewpoint. Political tact, however, prohibited the Bush Administration from saying it in so direct a fashion as that. Instead, they logically *implied* this viewpoint in many venues and on many occasions, such as in the NSSUS.

At www.fpif.org/commentary/2003/0307icc.html appears a commentary by liberal opponents of that view. Titled, "White House Hobbles International Criminal Court, World Security," it opens by asserting, "The current U.S. administration has a near-religious aversion to the new, permanent International Criminal Court." That statement would have been correct if only it did not include the word "near." Religious liberals don't understand what they are up against, because they're up against religion; they are up against something that's within themselves.*

---

*   A typical example is Chalmers Johnson, in his 2003 book, *The Sorrows of Empire: Militarism, Secrecy, and the End of the Republic*, which interprets the Bush Administration's aggressive unilateralist foreign policy as being a reflection of the Roman Empire, which started in 27 BC and extended until the Emperors themselves became Christian starting with Constantine. After that fusion of Church and State during the subsequent Holy Roman Empire, there emerged the universal theocratic Christian State led by such conquering "heroes" as Charlemagne, Frederick Barbarossa, Adolf Hitler, and George W. Bush. However, the liberal Mr. Johnson finds unappealing any such attribution of aggressive political tendencies to a religious cause. He therefore prefers to see Mr. Bush's aggression as reflecting the *pre*-Christian Roman Empire. Even though those emperors were *likewise* religious, they were not Christian, and Mr. Chalmers, coming himself from a Christian background, perhaps therefore finds *them* more convenient to cast as bad guys. In any event, he attributes Mr. Bush's militarism to that *non*-Christian source.

    One of the advantages to blaming the "neo-conservatives," instead of simply the conservatives, for causing American fascism, is that it conveniently covers up the common Christian origins of *all* forms of fascism in Christian-majority nations. Not only was Adolf Hitler Christian; but so, too, were Benito Mussolini, Francisco Franco, Juan Peron, and Augusto Pinochet. Mr. Johnson, like other liberal intellectuals, would much rather blame "pagan" sources for fascism. But unfortunately, this entirely avoids the important theocratic component of all forms of fascism, and it thereby prohibits truthful understanding of the very nature of fascism.

    Many neo-conservatives, furthermore, aren't Christians at all, but Jews. There is some debate about the extent to which the Jewish ones might be more concerned with supporting a Likud Israeli agenda, instead of representing Republican U.S. concerns. However, it's more likely that the Jewish neo-cons see no conflict between the two agendas, both of which have historically been similar, and both of which are equally fascistic. It seems quite natural, therefore, that such a Jewish neo-con as Mr. Wolfowitz, would, as an American, derive greater personal inspiration from the *pre*-Christian Roman emperors, than from the more overtly theocratic Christian ones. However, liberals such as Mr. Johnson would have no valid reason for inferring from this that Mr. Bush's foreign policy derives its inspiration from any Jewish or pre-Christian pagan models. Mr. Bush is neither Jewish nor pre-Christian pagan. Furthermore, the Birch/CNP and other fundamentalist Christians who placed this President in the White House are also not. Therefore, the *only* advantage to be gained by attributing Mr. Bush's foreign policies to specifically "neo" conservative inspirations – and thereby to the *pre*-Christian Roman model – is that one avoids the unpleasant task of understanding theocracy, and thus of understanding conservatism/fascism.

    Adolf Hitler, for example, was just as much of a fundamentalist as is G.W. Bush, though he tried to hide it from the largely secular German public, who would have considered it irrational and even unscientific. However, in his private notes in 1919, when he was first outlining what would become his theory behind the Holocaust, he credited "The Bible – Monumental History of Mankind." (See my *WHY the Holocaust Happened*.) This belief in the Bible's inerrancy as "History" not myth, is the basic belief of *all* fundamentalist Christians. Also like G.W. Bush, Hitler's early career was a flop. Here, in fact, is the description that Oliver James provided of Bush's transformation to *become* an active Christian, in the *Guardian,* on September 2nd, under the headline of "So, George, how do you feel about your mom and dad?":

    "As the alcoholic George Bush approached his 40th birthday in 1986, he had achieved nothing he could call his own. He was all too aware that none of his

The extremists have focus; the moderates have confusion. The progressives hardly yet even exist at all. If the moderates are like an unguided missile, the progressives are like a guided missile without yet an explosive charge. Without religion, what can supply the progressives' warhead? Maybe, someday, science? We're surely not there *yet*.

The focus extremists have comes from their faith, their religion. This focus was indicated in a Fall 2002 poll of American evangelical Christians by beliefnet (www.beliefnet.com/story/124/story_122447 .html), showing that fully 67% "disagree" with the statement, "U.S. should accept jurisdiction of new world court." Only 18% "agree"; 15% registered "neutral." That made sense: these people believe in the Law of God, *not* in the Law of Man. They're theocrats. So, the International Criminal Court cannot judge the world's leaders; *only* God can do that.

The international stakes in the invasion of Iraq are thus a choice between two diametrically opposed visions of Man's political future: conservative (totalitarian), versus progressive (democratic). The conservative, theocratic, vision is by far the clearer of the two, because it has a much longer history. And yet what that history says is not encouraging for the conservative who occupies this White House:

President Bush will fail. The Holy Roman Empire never succeeded at its grandiloquent aims. Even the President of the modern superpower won't be able to change reality. Only the casualties in his war are real. Everything else is mythology.

In fact, by late August of 2003, the U.S. was already pleading for help from the U.N. troops they had previously so maligned. On August 28th, Paul Reynolds of the BBC headlined "Why the US Needs the UN in Iraq," and astutely observed, "The presidential election next year is a powerful incentive for the Bush team to consider any proposal that prevents Iraq from becoming a determining campaign issue." George W. Bush, in other words, was now struggling to offload into other people's backyards the mess he had created in Iraq. On Sep-

---

educational and professional accomplishments would have occured [sic] without his father. He felt so low that he did not care if he lived or died. Taking a friend out for a flight in a Cessna aeroplane, it only became apparent he had not flown one before when they nearly crashed on take-off. Narrowly avoiding stalling a few times, they crash-landed and the friend breathed a sigh of relief – only for Bush to rev up the engine and take off again.

"Not long afterwards, staring at his vomit-spattered face in the mirror, this dangerously self-destructive man fell to his knees and implored God to help him and became a teetotalling fundamentalist Christian. David Frum, his speechwriter, described the change: 'Sigmund Freud imported the Latin pronoun id to describe the impulsive, carnal, unruly elements of the human personality. [In his youth] Bush's id seems to have been every bit as powerful and destructive as Clinton's id. But sometime in Bush's middle years, his id was captured, shackled and manacled, and locked away." G.W. Bush was convinced that The Almighty had transformed him, and he was grateful to The Lord and determined to return the favor.

tember 2nd, Reuters headlined "Pentagon May Have to Reduce U.S. Forces in Iraq," and opened, "The Bush administration may have to cut U.S. troops in Iraq by more than half to keep enough forces to face other threats, a congressional agency said on Tuesday in a report that fueled calls for more international help for peacekeeping in Iraq. The Congressional Budget Office said ... the Pentagon would be able to sustain an occupation force of 38,000 to 64,000 in Iraq long term, down from the existing 150,000 that a number of lawmakers said is not enough to confront the spiraling violence."

Here's how columnist James Carroll put the matter, that same day in the Boston *Globe*, under the head "Facing the Truth about Iraq":

"The war is lost. By most measures of what the Bush administration forecast for its adventure in Iraq, it is already a failure. The war was going to make the Middle East a more peaceful place. It was going to undercut terrorism. It was going to show the evil dictators of the world that American power is not to be resisted. It was going to improve the lives of ordinary Iraqis. It was going to stabilize oil markets. The American army was going to be greeted with flowers. None of that happened. The most radical elements of various fascist movements in the Arab world have been energized by the invasion of Iraq. The American occupation is a rallying point for terrorists. Instead of undermining extremism, Washington has sponsored its next phase. ... Moderates in every Arab society are more on the defensive than ever."

Mr. Carroll went on to express a perceptive viewpoint that drew upon his extensive knowledge of history: "As rekindled North Korean and Iranian nuclear programs prove, Washington's rhetoric of 'evil' is as self-defeating as it is self-delusional. No one could have predicted a year ago that the fall from the Bush high horse of American Empire would come so hard and so quickly. Where are the comparisons with Rome now? The rise and fall of imperial Washington took not hundreds of years, but a few hundred days."

And yet still, such news articles were then only just beginning to appear. The American public still remained way behind the curve. The nation's masses had been so deceived so thoroughly for so long by the Republican Administration and its Republican Congress, crucially assisted by what had served as little more than the Republican Party's press organs, which were euphemistically, and perhaps even pompously, called "America's news media," or simply "the U.S. press."

Therefore, Americans were ignorant of the disaster that was by then already at an advanced stage. A CNN/*USA Today* poll, on August 25th-26th, showed that still 57% "Approve" and only 41% "Disapprove," in response to the question, "Do you approve or disapprove of the way George W. Bush is handling the situation with Iraq?" Even more strikingly, 63% still answered "Worth Going to War," and only

35% chose "Not Worth Going to War," in response to the question, "All in all, do you think the situation in Iraq was worth going to war over, or not?" Much time would be required before Americans' delusions significantly wore off.

By contrast, Reuters, at around the same time (September 1st) was already headlining "Britons Want UK Forces Out of Iraq": a poll had shown that, "More than 60 percent of Britons believe their government should be withdrawing its troops from Iraq." A few days before that, Reuters headlined "Trust in Blair Takes Dive over Iraq Row," and reported, "Just 22 per cent of those polled by the Daily Telegraph said the government had been honest and trustworthy." In Britain, it didn't take an inordinate time for people to grow to learn that their government had been deceiving them all along, and that the Blair team had gotten all of them into some very deep trouble.

Americans, since they were inaccurately informed of what was going on, became instead simply embarrassed in front of the whole world. People outside the U.S. were far less impressed with American empire than were Americans who knew only American media reports. Consequently, on September 3rd, the German magazine, *Stern*, published an interview with an expatriate U.S. Hollywood star, in which the subject of his previous country came up, and he commented, "America is like a stupid puppy with large teeth. It can bite and hurt you. It's an aggressive country." He derided America's Republican Congress for renaming "French fries" as "freedom fries," and said, "these people in power expose themselves as idiots." He called America's popular and deeply trusted (because strongly religious) President, Mr. Bush, "one of the worst liars I've ever seen." And he said that although he occasionally brings his family to America on business, they always want to leave as soon as possible, because the nation has become for his children like "a broken toy." That was a view of the Holy American Empire many non-Americans could identify with, but it was oblique to most Americans, because of the country's fascist, rabidly nationalistic or "patriotic," press (America's *so-called* "press"). Americans weren't indoctrinated to despise their tyrant, but to admire him. It's the only way he could continue to remain as tyrant. After all, America is a "democracy." It's the land where fascism became refined.

Whether or not their tyrant's all-time-record high $200 million "re"-election war chest from his aristocratic pals will suffice to give him another four years as tyrant, only time will tell. On the same day as the publication of the *Stern* interview, an American network, CNN, telecast an interview with a different star, a famous singer, who, when asked about the war in Iraq, responded, "I think we should just trust this president in every decision that he makes and we should just support that, you know, and be faithful in what happens." Asked, then,

"Do you trust this president?" she replied simply, "Yes, I do." She represented the view of the broader American public: polls showed Mr. Bush remaining widely respected in the U.S.

Furthermore, just seven days later, the Gallup Organization headlined, "Six in 10 Americans Say United Nations Doing Poor Job: Highest negative rating for U.N. in Gallup polling history." In other words, all the propaganda by the President, with the cooperation of his compliant press, had profoundly affected American public opinion. Yet another poll from Gallup just the prior day, September 9th, confirmed this conclusion, from a different perspective: it bannered, "Public Little Concerned About Patriot Act: Wants civil liberties respected, but feels Bush administration has not gone 'too far' in restricting liberties." This poll showed that the percentage of Americans who were willing for the Government even to "violate your basic civil liberties," if need be, in order to prosecute the war against terrorism, had risen steadily from an already high half of the U.S. public in January of 2002, to over two-thirds in August the next year. Not only was this a trusting public; it was an increasingly scared public – frightened by the world outside (including by the U.N. itself), and *not* by their own tyrant. The American people seemed little inclined to free themselves from him, and more inclined to huddle around him, in fear of that outside world.

The Christian American Emperor had a grand plan to protect his "God's People" from "the Axis of Evil," a plan based on the very same fundamentalist Christian Apocalyptic thinking that had inspired his breaking the back of Man-made international Law via the invasion of Iraq. Central to this plan was President Bush's passionate commitment, ever since he first came into office, to scrap the disarmament treaties the U.S. had signed under prior presidents, and to institute a crash program modernizing and expanding America's nuclear deterrent. But the aim was no longer simply to *deter* potential attacks against the U.S., it's *pre-emptively to annihilate the attackers*, by employing new nuclear super-weapons. On December 7th, James Sterngold of the *San Francisco Chronicle* headlined "A New Era of Nuclear Weapons: Bush's Buildup Begins with Little Debate in Congress." He opened, "Congress, with only a limited debate, has given the Bush administration a green light for the biggest revitalization of the country's nuclear weapons program since the end of the Cold War, leaving many Democrats and even some hawkish Republicans seething." Congressional Republicans voted overwhelmingly to approve the program, but Sterngold quoted one such supporter as saying, "I happen to think they're out of bounds on this, ... and we have no idea what our policy is," while another objected, "We have more nuclear weapons now than we know what to do with," and yet a third said, "We don't need" these new and astronomically expensive weapons. Andrew Lichterman of the

Western States Legal Foundation noted, "There's no debate on this at all." His blistering study of the subject was aptly titled, "Missiles of Empire: America's 21st Century Global Legions," and can be found at www.wslfweb.org/space.htm. Nuclear weapons as a "defense" against terrorists are an insanity that extends old Cold War thinking, which is thoroughly inappropriate to such challenges as Al Qaeda. But no matter: Bush is a man of *faith*. And so, adding yet more trillions to the U.S. federal debt, our new Roman Legions are about to be supplied with *super*-WMD. After all, *only* "God's People" have the right to *any* WMD – to *all* WMD. A *monopoly* of nukes, to enforce a *monopoly* of good. *That* is the Holy American Empire.

Shortly after the new year, Nicholas Kristof of *The New York Times* commented upon Vice President Cheney's Christmas card. Under the banner "The God Gulf," on January 7, 2004, Mr. Kristof noted that the card was engraved, "If a sparrow cannot fall to the ground without His notice, is it probable that an empire can rise without His aid?" Kristof aptly observed, "It's hard not to see that as a boast that the U.S. has become the global superpower because God is on our side. And 'empire' suggests Iraq." At least the mentality shown was clear.

As the President's National Security Adviser (his long-term planner) told the Jan. 2004 *Readers Digest* (p. 131), "There is nothing I am worse at than long-term planning. ... I believe that serendipity or fate or divine intervention has led me." More of: *God* is in control here.

In the aftermath of the invasion of Iraq, Americans were left abandoned in confusion, as the tidy myths they were sold became punctured by the nation's major media. These media tried to escape their own responsibilities for the disaster, by turning against the President and his previously fawned-over Administration. Consequently, Joe Klein of *Time* lambasted these former media ikons on October 11, 2003, under the headline "Dick Cheney, Hard-Liner in Chief."

Mr. Klein said: "The President's rut reflects a gathering dysfunction in his Administration. The White House seems paralyzed, unable to stanch the political, diplomatic and actual bleeding over Iraq. There are turf wars everywhere. The CIA is at war with the White House; the Pentagon is at war with the State Department and the National Security Council (NSC); some elements of the uniformed military are furious with the civilian leadership of the Pentagon, partly for launching the attack against Iraq in the first place without enough allied support. The fault lines are largely between moderate diplomatic and military traditionalists and more aggressive neoconservatives and nationalists. ... The Administration's exposure of a covert CIA operative, Valerie Plame, was unprecedented, but at last week's Cabinet meeting, the President shrugged and said he didn't think the leaker would be caught. His apparent nonchalance is outrageous. Plame was integral to the CIA's effort to suss out the movement of weapons of mass destruction – ground zero in the [real] war on terror."

The next day, even the Republican Senator Richard Lugar was telling NBC's Meet the Press, "The president has to be president, over the vice president and over these secretaries," which was a limp way of saying that Mr. Bush finally had to take responsibility for the disaster that he had set into motion. On the same TV program, Senator Lugar stated that the $87 billion supplemental appropriation, mainly for Iraq, would need to be followed quickly by yet another special request of at least $50 billion more for that same purpose. $87 billion had low-balled the real costs America's taxpayers would have to pay to these Republican U.S. military contractors. (Months later, on January 21, 2004, Reuters headlined "Bush May Seek Billions for Iraq After Election." The story quoted various experts saying that the President's military request for 2004 was $40 billion to $100 billion short of the actual need for Iraq and Afghanistan.) Senator Lugar further predicted that American troops might have to occupy Iraq for as long as eight years in order to stabilize the country.

Of course, the United States could end its occupation much earlier – even right away. But unless America keeps over a hundred thousand troops there for many years, and efficiently spends vast sums on reconstruction, an Iraqi civil war will break out as we leave. And after we've left, we cannot re-invade; we'll have to do business with whomever wins that civil war. In fact, Amy Chua and Jed Rubenfeld, both of Yale, published a commentary in the *Washington Post* on January 4, 2004, titled "Ethnic Division in Iraq," which opined that rushed elections in Iraq "could very well produce renewed ethnic radicalism and violence; an illiberal, Islamist regime in which women are murdered ... for the crime of being raped," and "an anti-American government." This is the Hobson's choice that President Bush created by invading Iraq. Americans won't like it. And it will be even *worse* for Iraqis: the future of Iraq will almost certainly be a replay of what happened when Yugoslavia broke up, more fractious even than Beirut.

On October 20, 2003, the AP headlined "Ellsberg: Vietnam, Iraq Similar Conflicts," and reported that the one-time marine, and subsequent Pentagon analyst Daniel Ellsberg, who had leaked the Pentagon Papers to *The New York Times* in order to help bring an end to the Vietnam war, was now observing, "This war could go on forever, ... very like Vietnam." He asserted, "It was clear we were being lied into war again." On the same day, Reuters was headlining "Ex-Iraq Bank Head Says Cost Will Force U.S. Pullout." The story quoted Mr. Salah Shaikhly: "Once the U.S. Congress and public opinion realize the true cost of the burden of the Iraq campaigns for the U.S. taxpayer, they will force this and any future administration to quickly look for an honorable exit strategy," much like President Nixon had done in Vietnam. Mr. Shaikhly went on to observe, "Religious and fundamentalist groups seem to have the upper hand, while the democratic forces in Iraqi society are on the retreat." So, America's "honorable exit strategy" will depart Iraq – a land that was no terrorist threat *prior* to our invasion – leaving a new and *genuine* terrorist threat. Confirming this grim assessment the same day, Reuters also headlined "U.N. Report: U.S. War on Terror Radicalizes Arabs." According to the Arab Human Development Report 2003, Arabic regimes' "spurious justification for curbing freedoms on the pretext of fighting terrorism," under pressure from Washington, was fueling Arabic anti-Americanism.

The Iraq war story goes on, and its biggest issue remains yet to be resolved: Will America's tinhorn dictator win the legal immunity that has been at the core of his objectives in this war, and that he believes he deserves, by right, as God's agent reigning over the entire earth? That's the great question in this whole affair.

Making the world safe for ... theocracy

By DOUG SAUNDERS
Saturday, August 30, 2003 – (Toronto) *Globe and Mail*

The Iranian cab driver was taking me across one of the largest Persian cities when he confessed that he had become worried about his country's fate.

"Everywhere there is religion," he told me. "This is the most religious place anywhere. This should be the most modern country in the world, but the politicians want God to run everything."

His country, in his view, was hanging in the balance. The legislature, officially secular, was dominated by a circle of strict religious adherents who controlled the executive branch. In every speech, they invoked God's powers, and they were making determined efforts to bring religious authority into every branch of public life. Half the country's people seemed to support religious authoritarianism, while the other half seemed to hide in frightened silence.

The only thing surprising about this conversation was that it took place in Los Angeles, home to hundreds of thousands of expatriate Iranians, and the subject of my taxi driver's complaints was the United States.

The driver was asking a question that seems to hang on the world's lips: Does the United States have its own problem with fundamentalism, perhaps as serious as the one faced by the Islamic world? ...

This week, the world watched as many Americans rallied behind an Alabama judge who was thwarted in his efforts to assert a theocratic foundation for his country's laws by putting a statue of the Ten Commandments in his courthouse. His arguments sounded uncannily like those used by the Taliban, the Iranian mullahs and like-minded fundamentalists.

Already spooked by the religious faith of George W. Bush (who said in 2000 that his favourite political philosopher is Jesus Christ), foreigners couldn't help wonder what was going on. One of my colleagues, watching the throngs of Christian protesters outside the Alabama courthouse, suggested that this newspaper mark the 25th anniversary of the Iranian revolution with a series. Part 1: "The struggle for democracy in Iran." Part 2: "The struggle for theocracy in America." ...

Annan Challenges U.S. Doctrine of Preventive Action

Tue Sep 23, 2003
By Evelyn Leopold

UNITED NATIONS, N.Y. (Reuters) – U.N. Secretary General Kofi Annan warned President Bush Tuesday that his doctrine of pre-emptive military intervention posed a fundamental challenge to the United Nations and could lead to the law of the jungle.

In a speech shortly before Bush addressed the U.N. General Assembly, Annan took an unusually blunt swipe at the world's only superpower, delivering his strongest criticism to date on the doctrine of preventive war.

"My concern is that, if it were to be adopted, it could set precedents that resulted in a proliferation of the unilateral and lawless use of force, with or without credible justification," said Annan to sustained applause. He did not mention the United States by name. ...

According to Annan, sidestepping the United Nations in waging war against Iraq or elsewhere called into question the entire structure of collective action forged when the United Nations was created out of the ashes of World War II.

"Excellencies, we have come to a fork in the road," Annan said. "This may be a moment no less decisive than 1945 itself, when the United Nations was founded." ...

NOTE ON TONY BLAIR

The best example to demonstrate the confusion of political moderates is the moderate (or religious liberal) British Prime Minister, Tony Blair. And the best single source for understanding why Mr. Blair made the fatal commitment, on September 7, 2002, to support George W. Bush and to join in the invasion of Iraq, is eurolegal.org, which is the finest comprehensive website about politics, both in the U.S., and in the U.K. Of particular interest here is its page: www.eurolegal.org/useur/bbiraqwar.htm.

That web-page starts, appropriately, by quoting from the famous Fulton, Missouri speech, on March 5, 1946, by British Prime Minister Winston

S. Churchill, in which the phrase "the special relationship" between the U.S. and Britain was introduced, and which is even more famous for its having introduced the phrase "the Iron Curtain." Mr. Churchill said:

"Neither the sure prevention of war, nor the continuous rise of world organization will be gained without what I have called the fraternal association of the English-speaking peoples. This means a special relationship between the British Commonwealth and Empire and the United States. This is no time for generalities, and I will venture to be precise. Fraternal association requires not only the growing friendship and mutual understanding between our two vast but kindred systems of society, but the continuance of the intimate relationship between our military advisers, leading to common study of potential dangers, the similarity of weapons and manuals of instructions, and to the interchange of officers and cadets at technical colleges. ...

"There is, however, an important question we must ask ourselves. Would a special relationship between the United States and the British Commonwealth be inconsistent with our over-riding loyalties to the World Organization [the U.N.]? I reply that, on the contrary, it is probably the only means by which that organization will achieve its full stature and strength. ...

"Special associations between members of the United Nations which have no aggressive point against any other country, which harbor no design incompatible with the Charter of the United Nations, far from being harmful, are beneficial and, as I believe, indispensable."

Significantly, Mr. Churchill's concept of "the special relationship" was subordinated by him to "our over-riding loyalties to the World Organization," and to the two provisos of "no aggressive point against any other country" and of "no design incompatible with the Charter of the United Nations." Tony Blair, far less of an anti-fascist than was Mr. Churchill, became the first British Prime Minister faced with a U.S. President who didn't accept those "over-riding loyalties." The CNP had finally beaten the CFR. Churchill reflected the liberal wing of the CFR vision. However, there was no liberal wing of the CNP vision; there is no liberal form of fascism. But Mr. Blair, faced with a choice between Churchill and Bush, nonetheless opted for the fascist Bush. According to Stephen Mansfield's 2003 *The Faith of George W. Bush*, aides assert that at the key September 2002 meeting between Blair and Bush at Camp David, the two men in private turned to the Bible for inspiration and guidance, and prayed together, before facing the world's press on September 7th to announce their decision to invade. This was a repudiation of a European future for Britain, in favor of partnership with America: Tony Blair had decided to follow President Bush's lead in repudiating these "over-riding loyalties," and joined President Bush's campaign to destroy them.

Here's the context, the inducements and the motivations, behind that decision:

The extraordinary eurolegal website continues:

"Since World War II, Britain has enjoyed unique access to America's nuclear weapons technology. [Prime Minister Harold] Macmillan's 1961 decision to acquire Polaris [nuclear submarines] from the United States rather than to continue independent development of nuclear weapons has allowed Britain to maintain a[n] ... effective nuclear deterrent (at a lower cost). ...

"A secret treaty [was] signed in 1948 to provide for privileged sharing of signals intelligence between the US, the UK, Canada, Australia, and New Zealand. This Anglo-Saxon club and its worldwide surveillance network, code-named Echelon, makes the French suspicious. ... It ... gives the UK a substantial strategic advantage over other medium-sized powers, particularly in Europe.

"Britain shares intelligence with the US and other Commonwealth countries that it does not share with the EU. The regular meetings of Britain's Joint Intelligence Committee ('JIC') are attended by representatives of the CIA and of the Canadian and Australian intelligence agencies.

"Intelligence sharing has caused the UK difficulties with its European partners, notably about commercial espionage. ...

"However, the Special Relationship only works when Britain aligns its policies with those of the USA. Notably, it did not count for much when:

"(a) [President] Eisenhower refused support for the Anglo-French invasion at Suez (1956)

"(b) [President] Reagan (advised by the neoconservative [National Security Adviser Jean] Kirkpatrick) was less than enthusiastic about the Falklands War

"The 'Special Relationship' between the United Kingdom and the United States of America (and particularly Blair's interpretation of it) plays a major part in the French conviction that the UK's commitment to Europe is of doubtful value. ...

"In a BBC 'Panorama' programme shortly before the war, the correspondents came up with two revealing bits of information. The BBC's Chief Political Correspondent, Andrew Marr, suggested that the one question Blair hates to be asked is whether he attends the White House prayer meetings. Marr suggested that at least in part Blair's support for Bush was 'faith-based' and that Blair feared that any suggestion [of this] ... would be politically very damaging. ...

"When Blair informed a Committee of Parliament in the starkest possible terms that the UK would be prepared to act unilaterally with the United States and defy a UN Security Council veto, this despite a poll showing that 81% of British voters thought a UN resolution authorising the use of force was an essential prerequisite for UK intervention, the writing on the wall became clear, even for those who had hoped that pressure from within the Labour party might bring Blair to his senses. Blair had espoused the concept of the 'Special Relationship' to the fullest extent of Foreign Office dogma: the UK must always support a US war."

So, President Bush forced Tony Blair to choose, and the Prime Minister cast Britain's lot with America, not with Europe. Good bye, too, to Winston S. Churchill.

World War II was essentially a contest between democracies and fascisms. That battle was won by the democracies. But the ideological war itself is still being waged. And several of its participants have traded sides. For example, Germany, under the Social Democrats, promotes democracy. Britain, forced finally to choose, went with fascism. But the British people actually did not.

Chapter 6
What Can We Do?

Germans knew the Big Lie that had come from their neo-feudal imperialistic Fuehrer, Adolf Hitler. Didn't Americans recognize it coming from theirs, George Bush? But had the Germans recognized this might-makes-right lie while it was still coming from their leader? Of course not: they had to be defeated in a war before they would recognize the Big Lie that was being practiced *upon themselves*. And, as the Bush Administration (which certainly ought to know better) discovered only after the Iraq war began, the same is also true for today's Iraqis: only after Saddam was deposed did his people come really to understand fully that they had been deceived all along by a tyrant. Like with the Russians and Stalin, they knew that the man was brutal, but they were shocked to find that he had been little else. The tacky private paraphernalia of this former king now sold on the streets of Iraq as pornography.

Isn't there a better way to truth – a way better than its being forced upon a nation by defeat in a war? Perhaps. But unfortunately, mankind doesn't seem to have found it yet.

Gleiwitz should have taught the world a crucial lesson, but it did not. For a national leader to deceive his people into an invasion is the highest form of high treason, the gravest crime against them, as well as against the people and the nation that he is invading. It was the case then, and it is the case now; and it will always be the case. Conservatives within the nation of the deceived invaders do not believe it, but, to the contrary, consider this highest form of treason against themselves, and against their own nation, to be instead a form of high patriotism; thus, these people of faith become unwitting accessories to high treason; their minds are raped, just as is the nation that they invade. But the trick works every time.

Sadly, Hitler's Field Marshall, Hermann Goering, remains correct, when he was quoted in 1947 by Gustave Gilbert in *Nuremberg*

Diary (p. 279) as saying, "The people can always be brought to the bidding of the leaders. That is easy. All you have to do is tell them they are being attacked and denounce the pacifists for lack of patriotism." That, in a nutshell, describes what President George W. Bush did to his own American people.

Bush, consciously or not, was reading from the Nazi playbook. Perhaps it came naturally to him: his grandfather and great grandfather had been top American financiers for Hitler, from 1924 to 1942, when the U.S. Government put a stop to it by freezing their German assets. (Much has been written about this, though it's suppressed in the American mass-circulation media;* a web-search for the two-word phrase, with quotation-marks, "Prescott Bush" will bring up some sources. A good starter might be www.clamormagazine.org/features/issue14.3_feature.html, "Heir to the Holocaust," by Toby Rogers. The least that can confidently be said about this is that George W. Bush's grandfather and great grandfather were leading American fundraisers for the German Nazi Party, and subsequently for German military industry during the Third Reich.) Regardless, however, of any possible Nazi sympathies that might or might not have shaped George W. Bush, an aristocratic/oligarchical world-view was inculcated into him since birth. Political rule by force, including by means of mass deception and military invasion, held – and holds – no moral stench for these aristocrats.

This time around, America's CIA weren't able to swing a coup, as in 1968 Iraq, and so an extraordinarily bold and ruthless President Bush resorted to lies about Iraq, to frighten and hoodwink the American public into supporting an illegal invasion with U.S. troops. He was acting, thus, not just from the military, but from the propaganda portions of Hitler's playbook – the "Big Lie" part, which was associated

---

* To indicate how rigorously this information is excluded not just from the major media in the United States, but from the entire American culture, consider that moveon.org was widely condemned at the start of 2004, when 2 of 1,500+ proposed anti-Bush TV commercials that its members had submitted in the organization's online contest for its members to vote on, compared Bush to Hitler. This was a grass-roots organization; by that very nature, it ought to have permitted its membership to vote upon every commercial that was submitted. What conservatives were actually objecting to was that this organization *was* a grass-roots organization. But no matter, the mere fact that *two* of these commercials compared Bush to Hitler produced a furor from the American right wing, including from the Republican Party, and from conservative Jews, such as the Simon Wiesenthal Center, the Anti-Defamation League, and the American Jewish Congress. The far right-wing, Moonie, *Washington Times* headlined, on January 6, 2004, "Ads Compare Bush to Hitler," and the torrent of right-wing attacks, against the progressive moveon.org, generated from moveon.org not anger (which would have been appropriate), but apologies, even though *only* two of the 1,500 entries compared Bush to Hitler. Evidently, that was *two too many* for conservatives.

more with Propaganda Minister Joseph Goebbels than with Field Marshall Goering.

Perhaps the World Court that Mr. Bush loathes will someday try him.

It should do so, even if America's gutless media continue their capitulation to this tyrant, and even though America's hoodwinked public (and especially the audience of Fox "News") would probably therefore continue believing, at least for a while longer, in Our Great Leader. A guilty verdict might have salutary consequences, even if unenforceable. After all, the people of Iraq changed their minds about Saddam. (But who knows, maybe the taste they're now getting of George W. Bush's rule will make them prefer their previous tyrant.)

The single favorable outcome possible from this war might be that the World Court (meaning here the International Criminal Court) would achieve, by moral suasion over the entire planet, the one salutary thing that America's military achieved in Iraq by brute force: the public repudiation of a tyrant. The fact that Mr. Bush refuses to recognize this Court would be immaterial; the Court's prosecution of him would be no mere application of international Law; it would be, in true effect, the actual start of the system of international criminal Law, which has never yet existed. All that has existed so far is victor's "justice." The fascists think of that as "God's justice." Finally, it can be challenged. Thus, great history would be made here, merely by the process of this prosecution, even if it does not succeed.

Afterwards, people such as Rupert Murdoch (all 175 of whose newspapers editorially supported this illegal invasion and followed through with pro-invasion news reporting on it) can be tried for propagandizing war crimes and the internationally recognized "crime of aggression" (i.e., illegal invasion), upon the same grounds for which Herr Goebbels is now universally detested, and for which the leading Nazi industrialists were likewise imprisoned. In both the Nazi and the current case (though, fortunately, less catastrophically this time than was the situation then), a nation has been duped into perpetrating war crimes and aggression. International prosecution, even if unenforceable, will not only establish the principle that duping a nation is unacceptable, but it will also enable the duped people to recognize themselves as being, likewise, in their own distinctive way, victims of the dupers. Americans, for example, are going to be paying hundreds of billions of dollars, and international shame, for this conquest, and for the reconstruction that must follow. America's children yet unborn are already in hock to pay this tyrant's tax give-aways to the rich; now, those infants will be paying also for the military occupation of America's hostile 51st state. It is not only the thousands of war-dead and injured who have suffered from the actions of those dupers. At the very least, there can be political accountability, which should go beyond the perpetrators being merely voted out of office. After all, these are high crimes of State.

And these crimes had their essential collaborators. As regards the propaganda for the war, the position of *The New York Times* was unique, and would be especially problematical under international Law. This newspaper's propaganda function for aggression and invasion was far more sophisticated than that of the leading German media under Hitler. Editorially, the paper wasn't pro-war, and is one of the most liberal in the nation, but the *Times*'s editorial positions are not what shapes the news reporting in the American "news" media; the *Times*'s reporting does, and that's generally slanted very conservative. On the Iraq issue, the slant went extremely to the Right, as media critic Jim Naureckas noted in his April 2003 "When 'Doves' Lie," at www .fair.org/extra/0304/nyt-doves.html. The paper's liberal editorial positions permit the *Times* to enjoy good sales among New York City's liberal educated middle class, which is the paper's prime market. These liberals will buy the paper because an editorial slant is so obvious; this, after all, is any editorial's purpose: to *exhibit* opinion or "slant." (Furthermore, almost all of the pittance that the Times contributes to politics goes to Democrats.) However, the paper's conservatively slanted news reporting goes generally unrecognized. The liberal readers, to the extent that they notice this slant at all, might even naïvely mistake it as reflecting the paper's "unbiased reporting," because it runs contrary to the paper's editorials. But the *Times*'s powerful though generally unrecognized "news" slant constitutes the institution's actual, and immense, influence and political clout.

Sometimes, this slant is even blatant, like a sledgehammer blow. The "news" reporting of *Times* journalist Judith Miller has provided many such examples, which, because of their blatancy, are now being widely discussed within the news trade. However, in other instances, the slant is more subtle, yet no less powerful. A good example of such a story was the one published by *Times* reporter Elaine Sciolino on July 29th, which was datelined from Paris the prior day, and headlined, "Estranged Allies: France and Germany Consider Possible Roles in Postwar Iraq." This report was sub-titled, "Opponents of the war weigh the idea of sending troops." The story's central subject was the U.S./European friction concerning President Bush's thrust for, in effect, a Holy American Empire ruling the entire world, including Europe. No indication was presented at the top of this story, nor anywhere else in it, to show that it was "Opinion," "Analysis," or anything like that; it was paraded as sufficiently non-analytical to pass as being straight news. However, the piece was potently slanted throughout in favor of the Holy American Empire.

For example, Ms. Sciolino wrote: "Complicating any rapproche-
ment with the United States is Mr. Chirac's clinging to his vision of a
'multipolar' world in which the United States does not dominate. 'We
can no longer accept the simple law of the strongest,' he said in a
prepared statement during a visit to Malaysia last week. The official
Elysée Palace interpreter gave Mr. Chirac's words an even more
ominous meaning in English, saying, 'We can no longer agree to have
the law of the strongest, the law of the jungle,' although Mr. Chirac did
not use that actual phrase."

The reporter's unquestioning implicit acceptance of might-
makes-right (or, as President Bush might have chosen to phrase this
idea: "the Almighty determines what is right") is important, as is her
implicit acceptance of the United States as representing this might and
right. *The New York Times*, after all, is the newspaper that can hire
any reporter it wants. And quite evidently, Ms. Sciolino's expressed
might-makes-right nationalistic attitude is attractive to *Times* management; they chose, and choose, her. However, this authoritarian
nationalist hegemonic attitude, expressed even (and especially) in a
"liberal" newspaper, helped to make "respectable" – and so to produce
– America's invasion against Iraq.

Ms. Sciolino's application of such loaded and prejudicial (hostile) terms to refer to the anti-hegemonic Mr. Chirac as "complicating,"
and "clinging," were clear violations of professional journalistic ethics,
even if the general news-reading public knows nothing about such
matters.* Ms. Sciolino's fascist slant, just as any slant, would meet

----

*   Imagine if her slant were the contrary: that, "Complicating any rapproche-
ment with France is Mr. Bush's clinging to his vision of a 'unipolar' world in which the
United States dominates. 'We insist upon the simple law of the strongest,' he said, in a
phrase that had ominous meaning." Americans would immediately have recognized the
bias there. Perhaps such a reporter would have been condemned as a "liberal." She
would certainly have been unprofessional, but not more so than she actually is as a
hegemonic nationalist. Why should fascists receive special privilege? She fell back upon
cultural narrow-mindedness to protect her. Her burying as an assumption, instead of
her stating honestly and overtly as being her opinion, the idea that to deny the might-
makes-right principle is something that is "ominous," which comes from someone who
is "complicating" and "clinging," is also a violation of yet another core professional
journalistic standard: honesty. If she were to have stated the might-makes-right
viewpoint overtly as being her viewpoint, in her "news report," it would at least have
been honest. She didn't do that, because it would have revealed, even to the casual
reader, that she was editorializing in her "news reporting."

    At www.cjr.org/year/93/2/iraqgate.asp appears "Iraqgate: The Big One That
(Almost) Got Away: Who Chased It – and Who Didn't," by Russ W. Baker. It tells how
The New York Times, and especially Elaine Sciolino, helped to cover up the senior
George H.W. Bush's secret key role in arming Saddam Hussein throughout the 1980's.
Under the heading "Don't Follow Me, I'm Lost," Baker says that "Particularly The New
York Times ... simply muddled matters" on this huge story whose press leadership
went instead to other, less respected, media. "One television producer who has

democratic journalistic standards if expressed in an editorial, but the *Times*'s management knows that having the honesty to state those views as representing the institution's accepted opinion would be suicidal for the paper. Its market is liberal, not fascist. The newspaper's editorials thus explicitly condemn those very same views that this "news" story implicitly expressed. Hypocrisy protects the institution, the newspaper's ownership and management.

The *Times* even went so far as to run an article by Sarah Lyall on September 25th, "The BBC Loses a Bit of Its Luster," insinuating that the BBC had inaccurately criticized the Blair Government's "dossier" on Iraqi WMD, and insinuating that the credibility of the BBC had been shattered and that that of Rupert Murdoch's newspapers had been enhanced on the Iraqi WMD matter. This article was a stunning example of grossly misleading "reporting" by false implication. It employed quotations by anti-BBC Labour and Conservative Party hacks to make its non-existent "case" for the Blair Government's, and Rupert Murdoch's, anti-BBC campaign.

However, there is, regardless, an important question as to whether the International Criminal Court ought to go after the propagandists, or instead ought to pursue charges against only their leader. Certainly, the ICC will have no credibility whatsoever if it fails to prosecute the leader, who was President Bush. At least at the start, he alone should be the target.

Harry S. Truman said it best: "The buck stops here." The present chapter, an extended editorial itself, endorses President Truman's

---

followed Iraqgate observed [of Elaine Sciolino's veiled wording in her reports, that it] 'makes The New York Times responsible for gross public apathy'" regarding the entire Iraqgate story. Baker said that "many reporters from other newspapers criticize" the *Times*'s "coverage of Iraqgate, and much of its coverage in general, for a bias toward authority, an unwillingness to challenge power." This is a charge that has been leveled against the *Times* for decades, by those journalistic observers who have been sufficiently astute to see past the paper's liberal editorials, and to recognize its dangerously rightwing news slant.

John W. McCormack, the Democratic Speaker of the U.S. House of Representatives, had headed a congressional investigation into a scheme that the Morgan bank and associated American aristocrats ran in the 1930's for a coup to overthrow President Franklin D. Roosevelt and to install a fascist U.S. dictator who would be modeled upon Italy's Benito Mussolini. Jules Archer, in his 1973 book about that aborted scheme, *The Plot to Seize the White House* (p. 190), quoted Mr. McCormack as being enraged at the cover-up by *The New York Times* of his committee's findings, and as having told Mr. Archer, "The Times is the most slanting newspaper in the world. I would not expect anything else from them. They brainwash the people." Journalist Heywood Broun was quoted there as having said that "the face of *The New York Times* is black with Morgan shoepolish." The far-right thrust in today's U.S. comes from an alliance between theocratic fundamentalist Christians and oligopolistic corporations, and G.W. Bush now leads it. The *Times* follows. But so, too, does the rest of the U.S. major media.

view: On Iraq, the Buck stopped with George W. Bush. He was the criminal-in-chief.

Furthermore, this repudiation of international law has gone hand-in-hand with the Bush gang's earlier having ridden roughshod over democratic Law even within their own country. The vast majority of American constitutional-law scholars, including many Republicans and even some supporters of President Bush, hold that the five partisan Republican judges on the U.S. Supreme Court, who effectively appointed Mr. Bush, on December 9th and 12th, 2000, to become the next U.S. President, were acting unconstitutionally, and that their decision in this matter was baldly unconstitutional on several clear and important grounds. However, after 9/11 and Mr. Bush's subsequent (thus far) two wars, this man became a very popular President, and his American mandate to rule emerged secure. But the U.S. President is also, in a very real sense, uniquely the President of the entire world. And, as Australia's Margo Kingston, on September 22, 2002, said in her introduction to Bush's just-released fascistic National Security Strategy of the United States, which was being published that day in the *Sydney Morning Herald:* "Now we know. The Americans have spelt it out in black and white. There will be a world government, but not one even pretending to be comprised of representatives of its nation states through the United Nations. The United States will rule, and not according to painstakingly developed international law and norms, but by what is in its interests. In declaring itself dictator of the world, the United States will have no accountability to non-United States citizens. It will bomb who it likes when it likes, and change regimes when and as it sees fit, it will not be subject to investigations for war crimes, for torture, or for breaches of fundamental human rights."

Is that *really* to become the future of the world?

It could be so, but it doesn't have to be. That's why the stakes here are unimaginably high.

And the Bush Administration is still continuing to play the version of the imperial game that comes from the Nazi rule-book. Wayne Madsen, of *CounterPunch* newsletter, well summarized the post-Iraq-war Hitlerite game in a column on May 9th (www. counterpunch.org/madsen05092003.html) titled, "When Lying Pays Off." He observed:

"America's manipulative neo-conservatives, who support unending aggression against any country that does not succumb to United States political, economic, and military control and who, themselves, seized power in Washington through electoral malfeasance, are taking a page from Nazi Germany's leaders in their quest for world domination. It is no coincidence that the neo-cons are worried about comparisons between their policies and those of Hitler. Ed Gernon, the Canadian executive producer of the upcoming CBS miniseries, 'Hitler: The Rise of Evil,' was fired when he suggested similarities between the methods used by both Hitler and Bush to wipe away civil liberties by playing on popular fear. The Nazi-like campaign against Gernon was launched by the New York Post and TV Guide, both owned by proto-fascist Rupert Murdoch's News Corporation.

"After being caught lying about Iraq's weapons of mass destruction to prove their flimsy case that Iraq was a world class threat, the neo-cons now are planting fabricated documents in the rubble of Iraqi intelligence and secret police facilities. Through a media laundering process, 'discovered' documents are handed over to right-wing outlets owned by such slash and burn media moguls as Murdoch, Conrad Black, and Sun Myung Moon.

"We are now being fed information that captured Iraqi intelligence documents 'prove' that France assisted escaping members of Saddam Hussein's government by handing them French passports in Syria. This follows repeated allegations that other 'documents' proved French (and Russian and German) intelligence cooperation with Iraq's intelligence service before the war. [The French Ambassador, on May 15th, issued a detailed letter of protest, with full documentation, that all of this, and other 'false information,' had been leaked to a trusting American press by 'anonymous administration officials,' in full knowledge that it was fabricated.] Syria has been accused of accepting Iraq's phony weapons of mass destruction. Iran is accused of helping Al Qaeda (its most bitter enemy). Hitler used false evidence and phony rhetoric to justify his invasions of Danzig, Austria, Czechoslovakia, and Poland. American ambassadors in New Zealand, Norway, Turkey, Greece, Canada, Mexico, Barbados, Jamaica, Brazil, Belgium, Chile, and Luxembourg have acted like Nazi German Foreign Minister Joachim Von Ribbentrop's bellicose ambassadors in bullying nations that failed to support the U.S. war on Iraq. France is being faced with being kicked out of NATO military planning meetings, Germany with a loss of U.S. military bases, Belgium with the loss of NATO's headquarters, and Canada, Chile, and Mexico with trade sanctions.

"There are lies, damned lies, and Ahmed Chalabi [the Bush-anointed Iraqi President-in-waiting]. The leader of the Iraqi National Congress, stooge of the neo-cons, and a convicted bank embezzler is now aiming his wrath at Jordan. Chalabi, who bilked the American taxpayer out of millions of dollars from State Department and CIA budgets in order to fight his self-styled struggle against Saddam from the restaurants of London's Mayfair District and the clothiers of Savile Row, now claims that recently 'found' documents implicate Jordan's Royal Family in Saddam's spider's web. Of course, it was a Jordanian court that found Chalabi guilty of stealing $300 million from the country's Petra Bank and which sentenced him to over 20 years at hard labor. [He escaped.] It is surprising that it took this Gollum-like sycophantic creature so long to accuse the Jordanians of being in bed with Saddam. Of course, Chalabi will not admit that while he was a math professor at the American University of Beirut during the 1970s, he served as an agent for the Shah of Iran's feared SAVAK secret police. So much for Chalabi's 'democratic' credentials. ..."

A "MEMORANDUM FOR: The President" was sent by a group of outraged senior CIA veterans to the White House on May 1st, protesting the Administration's "cooking intelligence to the recipe of high policy." It can be found via a web-search for the phrase "intelligence officers challenge Bush" (keeping the quotation marks). This memo alleged that Defense Secretary Donald Rumsfeld and his assistant Paul Wolfowitz had engaged Mr. Chalabi to fabricate and falsify intelligence information so as to deceive the U.S. Congress into authorizing President Bush to invade Iraq. In any case, the brazenness of this President's abuse of the democratic process within his own country has been total. And the American "news" media's participation in it has been an authentic news scandal all its own. The *Washington Post*'s media commentator, Howard Kurtz, in a May 25, 2003, article titled, "Intra-Times Battle Over Iraqi Weapons," published an internal e-mail from Judith Miller of *The New York Times* that he had managed to obtain, in which she revealed to a fellow *Times* reporter that Ahmed Chalabi "has provided most of the front page exclusives on WMD to our paper." (Mr. Chalabi confirmed this on the Charlie Rose Show a few weeks later, on June 10th.) That explains a lot, doesn't it? Yet the *Times*'s Assistant Managing Editor for Foreign News, when questioned by Mr. Kurtz about this, said he saw nothing improper. And similarly, when Daniel Forbes of GVNews.net questioned top *Times* executives about Judith Miller's affiliation with the far-right-wing Bush-Administration-connected Middle East Forum, they saw no problem in that, either. And even when the *Times* ran its lead story September 29th, acknowledging the falsity of all of Mr. Chalabi's WMD information, there was no mention that the *Times* had actually served as the vehicle through which these lies had been spread to the public. This story was headlined "Agency Belittles Information Given by Iraqi Defectors: Exile Group Got Millions: Pentagon Intelligence Review Says Debriefings Provided Little of Any Value." Judith Miller's name wasn't so much as mentioned in the article, nor did it say *anything* about the crucial and special role the *Times* had played in this matter.

The future does not have to be just continued repetitions of the past, rule by deceit and brute force, either domestically or internationally. The conservatives need not always win. Public mindsets can change. A national culture can be improved. But it requires guts, from the few decent people who have ended up in positions of high authority, and this means above all, who are on the International Criminal Court. As Ms. Kingston of the *Sydney Morning Herald* said, George Bush isn't only the dictator of the United States, but he seeks to make himself also the dictator of the world. However, the people of the world have not granted him such legitimacy, even if the people of the Unites States have (which remains in doubt until November 2004).

And what good has resulted, to *anyone*, from this invasion of Iraq? Who, really, is benefiting from it? Are the Americans? Are the Iraqis? Saddam Hussein was a horrible leader, of course (and so are some others), but does this necessarily mean that a foreign invader who conquers him cannot possibly be thereby committing aggression and war crimes against the Iraqi people? And what good would such a precedent of international immunity for Mr. Bush be, to anyone except himself? By contrast, the victims of this (as of any) conquest of an alien culture are numerous, even if they're often obscure.

We usually don't even know the Iraqi victims' individual names. But sometimes, these voiceless people are given voice.

After the war, when Mr. Bush's lies were beginning to sink him, even the American press occasionally let these victims speak. For example, on August 1st, the *Washington Post* ran a story under the banner "For an Iraqi Family, 'No Other Choice': Father and Brother Are Forced by Villagers to Execute Suspected U.S. Informant." Reporting from the town of Thuluya, this account told of a young man named Sabah Kerbul, who was led out of his house by his father and brother, who shot him several times until he died. The father said that his son hadn't *really* been an informer for the Americans. However, the villagers were convinced otherwise, and insisted that if his family failed to execute Sabah, then the entire family would be executed by the enraged townspeople. An American commander was asked why this alleged informer had received no U.S. protection. The commander replied, "We're not providing any kind of protection at the local level." So, American troops were out to kill their Iraqi opponents, but offered no protection to cooperating Iraqi informants. This was yet another reason why America's war for Iraqi hearts and minds didn't go very well. There was so much hatred of the occupying troops, that the occupiers wouldn't dare to protect their own informants.

from: www.iraq-today.com/news/archive/00039.html

Crime and punishment:
From a coroner's point of view,

Baghdad is as deadly as ever

By Sarmad S. Ali. Date posted: 25.08.2003.

BAGHDAD – Everyday, women mill about crying outside the courtyard of Baghdad's Institute of Forensic Medicine at Bab al Muadam Square, so overcome with grief that they are unable to stand. The men stand grim and silent, the sleepless nights showing on their faces. But behind the doors, the day is just beginning as the daily toll of postwar Iraq's crime wave gets counted.

Coroners have to work overtime these days to keep up with the stream of bodies that comes through everyday. Five coroners distributed along the five benches of the morgue are barely able to keep up. More than ten corpses lie around in the room as if they were in an abattoir, with chairs for students to study the place and the events. About 10 autopsies a day are completed here as partially decomposed bodies pile up on autopsy tables and along the office floors awaiting final approval for burial. From the outside, the smell of the room is enough to make one retch; inside the stench is simply overwhelming.

"Neither during the war nor during the previous two wars has this happened," said Dr. Qais Hassan Salman, a specialist in forensic medicine at the Institute. "The number of dead is absolutely unbelievable, and I'm just speaking of Baghdad alone. God knows what's happening elsewhere." ...

"Most of the dead that come here are young males, but sometimes whole families are killed – such as in the al-Suleikh incident two weeks ago, when a generator blew up near an American patrol and the Americans opened fire at random," Salman says. A family of four was killed in the incident. ...

Even Americans are victims of this President. On November 1st, Ed Blanche of London's International Institute for Strategic Studies headlined in Beirut's *Daily Star*, "Burying the Hatchet: US, Israel See Sunni-Shiite Alliance Emerging." He opened by observing that, "For years, the idea of an Islamic alliance between Sunni and Shiite extremists has been a nightmare scenario for Western intelligence agencies." This nightmare was coming true: Shiite Iran and Hizbullah joined hands with Sunni Al Qaeda, Hamas and Islamic Jihad. The reason: "US President George W. Bush's 'war against terrorism' is increasingly perceived in the Muslim world as a new Judeo-Christian crusade against Islam and its people." Mr. Blanche concluded, "It is ironic that the US invasion of Iraq may be the instrument that pushes Sunni and Shiite together."

Where is accountability? Who is responsible for this?

The Bush Administration's war against the United Nations should not be taken lightly; these people mean business. As has been mentioned, this Administration's roots lie in the John Birch Society, and in many other theocratic fundamentalist organizations, which have long favored "God's Law" over Man-made international Law, and which have therefore been hostile toward organizations, such as the United Nations, that seek to promote international democracy. This hostility to Man-made international Law was exhibited not only at the start of G.W. Bush's Presidential Administration, but especially in the lead-up to their invasion of Iraq. In fact, upon the outbreak of that invasion, the neo-conservative Richard Perle, the chairman of President Bush's Defense Advisory Board at the Pentagon, exulted, on March 22, 2003, in the conservative British magazine the *Spectator:* "Saddam Hussein's reign of terror is about to end. He will go quickly, but not alone: in a parting irony he will take the United Nations down with him." This prime instigator of the invasion of Iraq had, along with Misters Rumsfeld and Wolfowitz, unsuccessfully tried to persuade the Clinton Administration to invade Iraq in 1998. Now magnanimously continuing his triumphal tirade against the U.N. and against the Man-made international Law it represents, Mr. Perle granted that, "The 'good works' part will survive, the low-risk peace-keeping bureaucracies will remain, the looming chatterbox on the Hudson will continue to bleat. What will die in Iraq is the fantasy of the United Nations as the foundation of a new world order." (Mr. Wolfowitz said essentially the same thing more tactfully on American TV networks, April 6th.) And Mr. Perle bid the U.N. good riddance: "As we sift the debris of the war to liberate Iraq, it will be important to preserve, the better to understand, the intellectual wreckage of the liberal conceit of safety through international law administered by international institutions." Presumably, he would rather rely *instead* upon a higher "safety": force, otherwise known as coercion (ergo, "The Almighty").

Along the same lines, John R. Bolton, subsequently Colin Powell's Undersecretary of State, had told the House International Relations Committee, on July 7, 2000, "Support for the International Criminal Court is based largely on emotional appeals ... unsupported by any meaningful evidence." On February 3, 1994, Mr. Bolton told the Global Structures Convocation that if the U.N. building in New York "lost ten stories, it wouldn't make any difference," and that the United Nations is so useless that, actually, "There is no such thing as the United Nations." He wrote in the *Washington Times* on October 24, 1998, that most Republicans oppose the U.N. and prefer terminating U.S. financial contributions to it, and that, "even if the General Assembly vote is lost [to the U.S., because of this termination], we retain our Security Council seat and veto, which are far more important."

These Bushites reek of their hatred towards Man-made international Law. Such are the people that Mr. Bush selected to manage

U.S. foreign policy. Less political than their master, they speak this hatred boldly, which the politician cannot.

On August 14, 2003, shortly before the United Nations headquarters in Baghdad was destroyed by a massive car-bomb, *The New York Times* led with the headline, "U.S. Abandons Idea of Bigger U.N. Role in Iraq Occupation – Seeks Aid by More Allies – Bush Aides Reject Conditions Set by France and India for Sending Peacekeepers."

The car-bombing of the U.N. compound occurred on August 19th. Numerous U.N. personnel were killed and injured in this terrible explosion. Everyone now recognized that the U.S. was failing to provide security in Iraq. Suddenly, there were increasing calls for U.N. troops to replace the Americans, in order to lay the foundations to reestablish peace in that now-lawless country.

Mr. Perle naturally reacted with vigor against this suggestion, telling *Le Figaro* and AFP on August 28th, "The United Nations system is not adapted to deal with the new threats, like international terrorism." As if that slap in the face to the U.N. weren't sufficient, he went on to say, "The administration of Iraq by the UN is a bad idea. Where has the UN succeeded in administering the territories where it has been placed in charge?" One might reasonably have answered his question by saying: just about everywhere, much better than the Bush Administration has done.

On the same day, however, an admission by the U.S. Deputy Secretary of State Richard Armitage was published, acknowledging that some sort of multinational force under U.N. leadership was being considered even within the Bush Administration, so long as an "American would be the U.N. commander." The U.S. now wanted other nations to take over the burden it had created, but still aimed to remain in control of Iraq, though clearly there was no control at all, but merely chaos inside that country. Only with immense difficulty could Bush's America accept that it was *not* God's anointed agent.

This arrogant and deeply anti-democratic aversion to the United Nations was, however, well noticed abroad, by perceptive commentators on world events. The Bush Administration's hostility toward the U.N. was already a matter of grave concern to many knowledgeable observers well *before* the invasion, but the conservative American news media offered such commentators short shrift, if any at all.

A good example of someone who foresaw, and understood, prior to the invasion, what was about to happen, was Anthony Westell, the former Ottawa bureau chief of the Toronto *Globe and Mail*, and a past associate at the Carnegie Endowment for International Peace. Shortly after Misters Bush and Blair held their historic joint press conference on September 7, 2002, effectively announcing their intention to invade Iraq, Mr. Westell published in the *Globe and Mail* on September 21st an op-ed titled "Another League of Nations," containing the following profound, even prophetic, analysis:

"President George W. Bush has made it clear beyond reasonable doubt that he is going to make war on Iraq, with or without the support of the United Nations. If the Security Council, despite the public reluctance of its leading members, passes the authorizing resolution Mr. Bush demands, it will be seen as a mere American puppet; if it refuses, Mr. Bush will contemptuously brush it aside. In either case, it will be clear for all to see that the United Nations is without power or influence when U.S. interests are involved – and that's most of the time in most of the world. It may survive as an international welfare agency, but not as an organization to keep the peace.

"That's roughly what happened to the League of Nations. Under the idealistic leadership of [Democratic] U.S. president Woodrow Wilson, the League grew out of the First World War with the idea that it could prevent future wars. But when the conservative [Republican] congress refused to sign the treaty of membership, the League, which was established in 1920, became a mere talk shop that could do nothing to block the road that led to the Second World War.

"Attempting to correct that mistake, [Democratic] president Franklin D. Roosevelt, after the Second World War, led the United States into the United Nations."

President Roosevelt, in fact, even named it the "United Nations" after having first prepared his country psychologically to join the new organization by his having long referred to the Allied powers, who had just then won the War, as "the United Nations." President Roosevelt recognized that the Republicans would wreck the international peace-keeping organization if they could, just as they had wrecked its predecessor the League of Nations. Mr. Roosevelt's skillful maneuvering managed to win the support of an almost unanimous Senate to join a democratic world community under a Law made by Man, instead of under the pre-existing Law of The Almighty (otherwise known as the law of force).

FDR recognized that the law of force had produced both World Wars. He knew that he had to overcome America's native deep-seated fascist inclinations, before he could set the entire world onto the new course, toward a more peaceful world, which we were on until George W. Bush became President and tried to re-impose the Law of The Almighty.

The reason Republicans and other conservatives are opposed to Man-made international Law is that they have a higher loyalty: to the Law of The Almighty, the law of force – the law whose guiding principle is: the more *powerful* combatant *should* win, since The Almighty Himself has already *made* that choice for reasons that *only* He knows, or ever *can* know. The ethical system of religion is based upon this *faith*. These people have faith that God should choose who wins and loses; and this necessarily means: Man should *not* make that critically important choice; science (modernity) is *rejected*.

However, this time around, the international legal organization, the U.N., unlike was the case with the League of Nations, is already an established fact. The International Criminal Court, on the other hand, must somehow become part of such an organization if the whole institutional scheme is to function effectively as a democratic international political organization, and the ICC *doesn't* yet securely exist. The ICC is therefore an essential part of the system of Man-made international Law. If the ICC is aborted, the U.N. will have no criminal court, and no functioning criminal law. The U.N. will be impotent, exactly the kind of organization that Richard Perle and other Bushites have said that they want it to be. That is what is actually at issue now. And in the final analysis, it's what the invasion of Iraq was most importantly about.

War critics astonished as US hawk admits invasion was illegal

Oliver Burkeman and Julian Borger in Washington
The Guardian, Thursday, November 20, 2003

International lawyers and anti-war campaigners reacted with astonishment yesterday after the influential Pentagon hawk Richard Perle conceded that the invasion of Iraq had been illegal.

In a startling break with official White House and Downing Street lines, Mr Perle told an audience in London: "I think in this case international law stood in the way of doing the right thing." ...

French intransigence, he added, meant there had been "no practical mechanism consistent with the rules of the UN for dealing with Saddam Hussein." ...

"They're just not interested in international law, are they?" said Linda Hugl, a spokeswoman for the Campaign for Nuclear Disarmament, which launched a high court challenge to the war's legality last year. "It's only when the law suits them that they want to use it." ...

As we said earlier, what's crucial here is not that Mr. Bush be seized and convicted, but merely that the prosecutorial process proceed against him. History and common sense both tell us that the victor in any international war will always assert that there's no higher power – except "The Almighty" – who can judge the victor, and that he consequently stands above all (merely Man-made) international laws. In this regard, Mr. Bush is no different from any emperor or imperial aspirant throughout the past; he's clearly a throwback. But one would *expect* a threat to the world's future to *be* a throwback.

Consequently, the basic question now is: is this new International Criminal Court (ICC) no different, actually, from all of previous human history; or will it break with the past, and stand up in the name of humanity, to resist even a successful tyrant? Or, if not, then will the private Belgian Iraq-war prosecution case that was launched on May 14th against the American General Tommy Franks boost a step up to his boss, Mr. Rumsfeld; and, finally, to the tyrant himself, President Bush? Unfortunately, the Belgian Parliament, on August 1st, caved to Bush Administration threats, and immunized Mr. Bush and his agents. But another private group, including Swiss Parliamentarian Christian Grobet, earlier, on May 1st, also filed charges, in a case directly against Misters Bush and Blair, before a Swiss court, on behalf of 19 Iraqi war victims. However, the defendants in that court case will be immune from prosecution until they leave office. And on May 15th, Heinrich Comes and thirteen other lawyers in Cologne announced that they would sue Misters Bush and Blair in a German court. Furthermore, on May 23rd, the Athens Bar Association announced that it was going to file suit against British officials, including Prime Minister Blair, in the ICC, to whose jurisdiction Britain's Blair had signed, but America's President Bush had not.

The ideal tribunal to try Mr. Bush is clearly the ICC, or criminal "World Court." This Court was established by the Rome Statute in July 1998, and was officially opened, ironically, right before the invasion of Iraq, on March 11, 2003, by a ceremony that was boycotted by the United States. The U.S. had been the only country in the world to campaign actively against the creation of this Court. The American Government was now putting pressure upon the European Union, and upon many individual countries, to sign agreements immunizing Americans from ICC prosecution. On May 2nd, Albania became the 32nd weak, small, country to sign such an agreement (no major country did so), and U.S. Secretary of State Colin Powell said that this action by the Albanian Government demonstrated "the closeness of the relationship that we enjoy, a relationship that will grow even closer in the months and years ahead." Amnesty International issued a press release five days later urging that, "No one, regardless of their nationality, should have impunity for the worst crimes known to humanity." However, it's doubtful, in any event, that the World Court could simply be strong-armed into honoring the claimed immunity of any country, even if every nation were to sign pledges to immunize Americans.

In fact, during March and early April, the U.S. was maneuvering to have Saddam Hussein tried by the World Court as a war criminal, but on April 4th, George Fletcher of Columbia University published a commentary at www.findlaw.com, "War-Crimes Proceedings in Iraq?" noting that, "Ironically, ... Iraq could, in theory, invoke the ICC to charge the United States for war crimes committed on their territory in the current campaign – but the U.S. could not invoke the ICC to charge Iraq with war crimes committed in the past on Iraq's own territory." The Bush Administration did a quick double-take; it was clear that America's refusal to sign the Rome document would fail to protect Mr. Bush, and that he would be on dangerous territory staying within a million miles of the ICC. So, on April 8th, David Rennie of the *Telegraph* headlined, "We Will Handle Trials, Say Americans," and led with, "The United States has the 'sovereign right' to prosecute Iraqi leaders for war crimes in its own courts, and will not hand Saddam Hussein or his henchmen to any international tribunal, senior American officials said yesterday." Mr. Bush thus gave up on his audacious effort to use the very Court that he was trying to cripple. The report continued, "In a move likely to alarm Downing Street, senior Pentagon and State Department officials summoned reporters to hear a pre-emptive rejection of any role for the International Criminal Court." The Bush Administration, now understanding its vulnerability, was arguing that the ICC had no role to play in the Iraq war at all, on the bogus grounds that the Hussein regime, like the Bush regime, had refused to sign the Rome document. Mr. Bush was hardly more of a friend to either international law or the victims of Saddam Hussein than was Mr. Hussein himself.

In fact, President Bush was outright callous to Saddam's victims. On May 14th, Human Rights Watch issued a press release headlined, "Iraq: U.S. Unresponsive on Mass Graves." It reported that, "The U.S. Government has not acted on important information about mass graves in Iraq. The result is desperate families trying to dig up the site themselves – disturbing the evidence for forensic experts." In September, HRW issued a report, "Ensuring Justice for Iraq: Evidence Preservation and Fair Trials." It observed: "To date, the United States and its coalition partners have failed to take concrete steps to ensure that those responsible for serious past crimes are brought to justice in fair trials before impartial and independent courts. After taking control of Iraq, coalition forces failed to secure mass gravesites and substantial evidence was destroyed. ... There is an urgent need to collect and safeguard evidence that will be vital to the conduct of future trials." However, the evidence-destruction just continued, and a September 14th *Newsday* story, "Glimpse of a Massacre," quoted one frustrated researcher at the "chaotic excavation" of a mass gravesite in the Iraqi town of Muhawil as saying, "For all the endless talk by the Bush administration about Saddam's horrendous crimes, if they were really serious about prosecuting these people they would have forensic experts here today." President Bush, the self-claimed "liberator" of Iraq, was, it seems, of at best a split mind about helping Saddam's victims. An Emperor doesn't bother himself much about such matters; those are just the *little* people.

President Bush has been so obsessed with exemption from international Law that on July 1, 2003, his Administration declared ineligible for military aid almost 50 countries which, unlike Albania, had refused to sign to U.S. immunity from the ICC. This military aid ban included even Colombia, the recipient of $98 million in military aid from the United States the previous year in order to fight terrorists and drug traffickers. Mr. Bush subordinated *all* foreign-policy goals to that of U.S. international immunity. On July 5th, the *Washington Post* editorialized about this, saying that, "During his last visit to Europe, President Bush promised new U.S. allies in the eastern half of the continent that they would not be forced to choose between their allegiances to the United States and to the European Union. Yet now the White House is insisting on just such a choice. This week U.S. military aid to nine European countries, including six incoming members of NATO, was suspended because of their failure to conclude agreements exempting Americans from the jurisdiction of the International Criminal Court. ... That they have not met Washington's demand for a court exemption is due only to their status as incoming members of the EU, which has adopted a policy against such accords." President Bush had lied again, this time in order to win nations' (nominal) support for invading Iraq. He had promised these nations, such as Bulgaria, Lithuania, and Slovakia that if they would join his "coalition" against Iraq, he wouldn't demand that they violate the EU requirement against exempting the U.S., or any other government, from ICC jurisdiction. And now he had broken that promise, too. Those are just the *little* countries.

Even America's relations with larger nations, such as France and Germany, have been sacrificed on this policy ground that is so holy to this fanatical would-be Emperor, Mr. Bush. Even the interests of the American people have been sacrificed for that "higher" purpose.

In fact, Mr. Bush's extremism has been too much not only for liberals, but for some of Mr. Bush's fellow conservatives, to stomach. Thus, Lawrence Korb, a CFR official who had served as Assistant Secretary of Defense in the Reagan Administration, published an op-ed in *The New York Times* on July 30th, headlined, "The Pentagon's Eastern Obsession: Closing bases in Germany doesn't make sense." He noted that the Bush Administration's planned spiteful relocation of

America's European military bases to Romania, Poland, and Bulgaria, removing them from their long-established sites in Germany, will increase Pentagon costs enormously, while it will diminish the morale of U.S. servicemen based in Europe, by separating those soldiers from their families. All of this is to be done in order to retaliate against Germany, for Germany's having opposed the American invasion of Iraq. And once it is done, the increased costs will go on year after year. All of the massive investment that America has sunk into the bases in Germany will go to waste. There's simply no other superpower who needs those existing facilities. Mr. Korb concluded by condemning "the Bush administration cutting off its nose to spite its face." That "face" is *America*.

And the damage to the American people just kept on getting worse. Even after the March 18th international Pew poll headlined "America's Image Further Erodes," and then the June 3rd Pew poll bannered "World's View of U.S. Sours After Iraq War," and then the June 16th BBC report titled "Poll Suggests World Hostile to US," the bottom had still not yet been reached. On September 3rd, the AP headlined from Brussels "Poll: European Support for U.S. Fading." This story reported, "President Bush's standing has just about evaporated in Germany where his approval rating is 16 percent – down from 36 percent in 2002." One of the two sponsors of the new poll was the German Marshall Fund of the United States, which concluded that, "The Germany that never sought to choose between Europe and the United States has now expressed an unambiguous preference for Europe." This poll reported that America's image was *continuing* to plunge in almost every European country. The outlook for both U.S. brands and American tourism is grim.

The "Business Outlook" column in *Business Week*, on December 1st, confirmed this as it headlined "Is the Dollar in the Danger Zone?" It presented a chart showing steady drops each month from May through the latest (September) in "Net Purchases of U.S. Securities by Foreigners." In May, these "net purchases" had amounted to $110 billion. By September, they were $5 billion. And the value of the dollar hit new record lows.

The American people will be suffering hugely from this invasion during the years and decades to come, all unnecessary losses: in the value of brands, in the value of the dollar, in surging recruitments to Al Qaeda and other anti-American groups and organizations, in needless drains upon the American military, in sinking U.S. military morale, and in countless other ways.

On August 18th, two stories appeared whose very juxtaposition highlighted the perversity of this invasion of Iraq. CBS News headlined, "'Qaeda' Tape Urges Iraqi Attacks," and opened, "The latest purported audiotape from al Qaeda urges Muslims to fight American troops in Iraq." At the same time the Boston *Globe* headlined, "US Shifting Focus, Agents from Kabul to Baghdad," and the *Globe*'s reporter Bryan Bender opened with: "As the hunt for Saddam Hussein grows more urgent and the guerrilla war in Iraq shows little sign of abating, the Bush administration is continuing to shift highly specialized intelligence officers from the hunt for Al Qaeda leader Osama bin Laden in Afghanistan to the Iraq crisis. ... The recent moves ... follow the transfer of hundreds of elite commandos from Afghanistan duty to service in Iraq." Meanwhile, *Time* magazine reported, "Al-Qaeda and the Taliban are still very much alive in Afghanistan, and are right now in the midst of what appears to be a spectacular comeback. Over the past week, more than 100 Afghanis have been killed in clashes between large Taliban formations and government forces." Three weeks later, on September 8th, *Newsweek* observed, "For more than a year, Afghanistan has been sinking deeper into poverty, chaos and despair while the White House focuses on Iraq. Al Qaeda and the Taliban have not wasted the chance to regroup." Three days later, the AP reported that Taliban rebels had blocked a car carrying four workers from the Danish Committee for Aid to Afghan Refugees, "ordered them to get out of the car and then tied their hands," and "then opened fire with AK-47 rifles." This was "raising fears in the aid community that vital reconstruction work is becoming too risky to carry out." Opium production, which the Taliban had stamped out, was soaring, and Afghanistan was now the world's leading source of heroin. Al Qaeda's base country was virtually abandoned for the invasion and occupation of Iraq.

On August 15th, CBS News correspondent David Martin reported on "The High Cost of War," from the standpoint of America's troops whose misfortune was to be sent into this needless invasion. Mr. Martin visited the Army's Walter Reed Medical Center in Washington. "'This hospital is overloaded with orthopedics because of things like this; because they're so many amputees coming back from war,' said David Pettigrew. [He] lost his right leg when his armored vehicle was hit by a rocket propelled grenade. 'I woke up and I could look down and see. 'Wow, look, there's my left leg and my right leg went AWOL.' ... The leg is gone but not the pain." These people's lives will never be the same. Though the Pentagon is reluctant to report the precise numbers, thousands of U.S. troops have become casualties inside Iraq. And thousands of Iraqis and of other Moslems have become suicide bombers or terrorists due to this invasion.

On August 21st, the Minneapolis *Star Tribune* headlined, "Andover Marine Admits He Shot Himself." A 20-year-old was so opposed to this war, and "despondent about an impending long-term overseas military assignment" there, that he put a bullet into his left shoulder to avoid being sent.

The Baltimore *Sun,* on October 26th, bannered "After Iraq, The Guilt of Killing Tears a Life Apart: 'A very different man' returns from the battlefield." This story, by Scott Calvert, described Pfc. Tyrone Roper, a star killer on the battlefield, who had become one of 478 soldiers returned home to the U.S. for psychiatric reasons. Now, the 27-year-old married man and father of two was on the run, location unknown, sending e-mails to the *Sun,* saying that he was wracked with guilt and nightmares, for his participation in this war.

On November 5th, the *Guardian* headlined "Appeal for Draft Board Volunteers Revives Memories of Vietnam Era," and opened, "The Pentagon has begun recruiting for local draft boards." Three days later, the *Seattle Post-Intelligencer* bannered "Talk of a Draft Grows Despite Denials by White House." Then the Pentagon stopped its advertisements for draft-board workers, because Mr. Bush was seeking re-election.

The Chicago *Tribune,* on December 26th, headlined "Troop Suicides Raise Red Flag: Since the Iraq conflict began, 20 GIs have taken their own lives in the theater. Military and outside experts, alarmed by the high number, hope to find out why." Three days later, the *Washington Post* bannered "Army Stops Many Soldiers From Quitting: Orders Extend Enlistments to Curtail Troop Shortages." Men who had been due to retire from the military were seeing their retirements cancelled. "On their Army paychecks, the expiration date of their military service is now listed sometime after 2030." This was actually a stopgap measure, until the election passes and the draft is re-instituted. Meanwhile, the lawns of millions of heavily indoctrinated Americans continued to display signs saying "SUPPORT OUR TROOPS," meaning: *don't* bring them home; prolong their pointless sacrifices, waste yet more blood.

The President is desperate to delay restoring the draft until after he is "re-" elected. Just as with the fiscal mess that George W. Bush created by means of his enormous upper-bracket tax cuts, his only concern now is to postpone news of the coming disaster until November 2, 2004. *Then* he can restore the draft.

All for *what?*

One man made the decision to do this: George W. Bush.

What kind of treason is it when a President of the United States deceives his country into such an invasion? How many victims does this man have? Where do we start counting?

Obviously, the world already lost this war at the moment the needless conflict started. But did Mr. Bush actually win it? Did he win his war against Man-made international Law, for which Iraqis and Americans are both suffering? That question is still to be decided.

Mr. Bush's invasion was not only a crime against the people of Iraq. It was truly a crime against the entire world, including against the American people.

But in any event, right after the invasion, it had seemed clear that there would be no justice imposed upon this tyrant by the U.S. public, despite his having deceived the country into invading, wrecked the nation's economy with his tax-cut hand-outs to the rich, and tolerated (and, actually, encouraged) CEO and Wall Street corruption and cronyism (such as Cheney Halliburton-Iraq no-bid contracts). The American people would not (except perhaps by not voting for him) hold him responsible for the huge economic drag of that corruption, or of this war, much less for his lies that had caused this war and its potentially deepening economic drag on the nation, and that had turned the country into an international outlaw. Thus, on May 17th, the *Washington Post* headlined, "No Political Fallout for Bush on Weapons," and reported that, "President Bush appears to be in no political danger from the failure to find chemical, biological and nuclear weapons in Iraq," notwithstanding the fact that "disarming Saddam Hussein of his 'weapons of mass destruction' was the main justification the Bush administration used both at home and abroad for attacking Iraq." A Republican Senator was quoted there as saying, "Our constituents like a victory, and at this point it's a victory." And that's the point here: this has been the *old* way, always based upon the common private conviction that might makes right, known more publicly as the basic religious belief that, "The Almighty determines what is right."

On August 13, 2003, America's largest newspaper, *USA Today*, headlined on the internet, "Why Bush, GOP Can Block All Inquiries." The printed newsstand version of the story employed a longer and more informative headline: "Bush Unscathed by Investigations. Here's Why: Special counsels are a thing of the past, and GOP-controlled Congress has stifled partisan inquiries." Throughout the article, criticisms of the President were likewise described as purely "partisan" – a word that appeared there five times. Impeachment was described as always only a "partisan" matter, never an authentic redress against actual treason or other "high crimes and misdemeanors" as stated in the U.S. Constitution. The reporter, Susan Page, simply assumed that, because the impeachment proceedings against Mr. Bush's Democratic predecessor, Bill Clinton, had been "partisan," it's a good thing that the country this time "has a president" with "more breathing room."

In a nation that's cursed with a press like this, how likely is it that the thousands of U.S. troops who are fighting, killing, and dying, in a war they increasingly recognize to be criminal, will ever have the satisfaction of seeing their country hold accountable the President who's responsible for this crime against themselves, against American taxpayers, against the people of Iraq, and against the entire world?

This lying Bush Administration invaded Iraq upon the pretext that this invasion was going to help defeat the international terrorism that had caused the 9/11 attacks. But the invasion was instead a huge gift to Al Qaeda and to other anti-American terrorist organizations. On August 31st, the *Los Angeles Times* headlined "Iraqis' Rage at Boiling Point," and quoted one Iraqi as asserting, "America considers itself the superpower of the world, but here it is powerless to keep any semblance of order." Another said, "In Iraq now, yesterday was always better than today, and tomorrow will be even worse." Yet another bitterly observed, "We can't walk our streets even in daylight. I had to come here with my daughter so she could apply for a job. This never happened under the previous regime. ... Nothing works. No electricity. No water. Our food ration is nothing. We want our share of the oil money!"

On October 15th, Reuters headlined "Iraq War Swells Al Qaeda's Ranks, Report Says." Citing the just-released authoritative annual report of London's International Institute for Strategic Studies, the story noted that this invasion "galvanized the Islamic militant group's will." President Bush allegedly invaded Iraq in order to weaken terrorism, but the result was the exact reverse: by choosing a wrong target, he strengthened terrorism and spurred it on.

He also spurred on the Islamic fundamentalism that *feeds* such terrorism. His unprovoked invasion of Iraq, and his widely perceived hostility towards Islam, were behind the story bannered October 24th on the front page of *The New York Times:* "Syria, Long Ruthlessly Secular, Sees Fervent Islamic Resurgence." This article said, "The widespread sense that the faith is being singled out for attack by Washington has invigorated" Islamic fundamentalists. Even the most secular of governments in the Moslem world could now be toppled by them, just as Osama bin Laden has been aiming. President Bush hugely advanced Al Qaeda's long-term goals. Is he, in fact, a lying traitor to America, and to all victims of terrorism?

So let's now see who in high authority authentically deserves to be there. One person who early answered this question for herself is Swiss Foreign Minister Micheline Calmy-Rey, who on March 31st placed on her official website an information-gathering section for prospective indictments concerning the invasion of Iraq. However, some other offices of the Swiss Government did not join her endeavor, and remain committed to the past, and not yet to the future.

Success in inducing the International Criminal Court to bring formal charges against President Bush concerning his invasion of Iraq is anything but assured. But if complicit Republicans in the U.S. Congress and press have the power to prevent this tyrant from being impeached and removed from office, then at least the conviction of him and his henchmen by an international (or even just by a foreign) court he belittles, might help. It would publicly shame him, and might bring an end to his despotic reign (if U.S. voters fail to do so), and would thus free the American people from the fascists who are America's curse, and who have now become the world's curse.

* * *

"To put it bluntly, if Bush has taken Congress and the nation into war based on bogus information, he is cooked. Manipulation or deliberate misuse of national security intelligence data, if proven, could be 'a high crime' under the Constitution's impeachment clause. It would also be a violation of federal criminal law, including the broad federal anti-conspiracy statute, which renders it a felony 'to defraud the United States, or any agency thereof in any manner or for any purpose.'" **Former Nixon White House Counsel John Dean, June 6, 2003, at http://writ.news.findlaw.com/dean/20030 606.html**.

* * *

On Monday, December 15th, John McCarthy of *Florida Today* headlined "Senators Were Told Iraqi Weapons Could Hit U.S.: Nelson said claim made during classified briefing." This stunner opened: "U.S. Senator Bill Nelson said Monday the Bush administration last year told him and other senators that Iraq not only had weapons of mass destruction, but they had the means to deliver them to East Coast cities. Nelson ... said about 75 senators got that news during a classified briefing before last October's congressional vote authorizing the use of force to remove Saddam Hussein from power."*

---

* In an impeachment hearing, this testimony would be of central importance to demonstrate that the President had perpetrated the "high crime" of having, with forethought and planning, deceived the U.S. Congress into authorizing him to invade Iraq. This evidence powerfully reinforces the smoking gun that was set forth in Chapter 2. An additional key item of evidence is that which was first revealed to the public at cbsnews.com and on "60 Minutes" on January 10 and 11, 2004, to the effect that, even when he first came into office, President Bush was determined to invade Iraq, and that WMD had nothing to do with this intention. The allegation was made there, by former Treasury Secretary Paul O'Neill, and supposedly by other but unnamed members of the National Security Council, that during the first two meetings of the NSC in late January

Though President Bush did commit numerous impeachable offenses (and one of several bills of particulars for his impeachment can be seen at http://votetoimpeach.org/articles_rc.htm), the Republicans in Congress are unlikely to permit his impeachment; and such a purely domestic approach would, in any event, probably fail to free the American people from their tyrant. International help is needed.

After all, who ended up saving the German people from the continuation of the disasters by their tyrant, Adolf Hitler? Not the Germans themselves, but outsiders – foreigners (who then included the United States itself, under more liberal Democratic Presidents). Who ended up saving the Yugoslavian peoples from the continuation of the disasters by their tyrant, Slobodan Milosevic? Also foreigners (again including a Democratic-led America). Who ended up saving the Iraqi people from the continuation of the disasters by their tyrant, Saddam Hussein? Likewise foreigners, though this time in blatant violation of international law – and, ironically, the violator, the United States, had itself largely installed and maintained that particular tyrant. And who might be able to save the American people from the continuation of the disasters by their own tyrant, George W. Bush? Perhaps only foreigners – only the international community, only the United Nations, only the International Criminal Court. Mr. Bush has, indeed, been waging war against what could turn out to be the only thing that will save the American people from himself.

The problem is severe. Chris Floyd has shown *how* severe. He's one of the world's greatest investigative journalists, and he writes for the *St. Petersburg Times* in Russia. Mr. Floyd has exposed the U.S. Republican Party corporate and theocratic Christian network that's attempting to rig U.S. elections by means of the mandated installation throughout the U.S. of electronic voting machines, which leave no "paper trail" or reliable record of any sort, and whose accuracy can therefore never be checked or verified.

from: www.sptimes.ru/archive/times/904/opinion/o_10419.htm
The *St. Petersburg* [Russia] *Times*, September 23, 2003

Opinion: Chris Floyd's Global Eye

Vanishing Act

and early February 2001, the assumption went unquestioned "that Saddam Hussein was a bad person and that he needed to go," and, "Day one, these things were laid and sealed." President Bush's deceit on this was the most heinous "high crime" that has ever been committed by any President in U.S. history, and if the Republicans in Congress continue to block its prosecution, then the Republican Party is complicit in it.

It's a shell game, with money, companies and corporate brands switching in a blur of buy-outs and bogus fronts. It's a sinkhole, where mobbed-up operators, paid-off public servants, crazed Christian fascists, CIA shadow-jobbers, war-pimping arms dealers – and presidential family members – lie down together in the slime. It's a hacker's dream, with pork-funded, half-finished, secretly-programmed computer systems installed without basic security standards by politically-partisan private firms, and protected by law from public scrutiny.

It's how the United States, the "world's greatest democracy," casts its votes. And it's why George W. Bush will almost certainly be the next president of the United States – no matter what the ***people*** of the United States might want.

The American vote-count is controlled by three major corporate players – Diebold, ES&S, and Sequoia – with a fourth, Science Applications International Corporation (SAIC), coming on strong. These companies – all of them hardwired into the Bushist Party power grid – have been given billions of dollars by the Bush Regime to complete a sweeping computerization of voting machines nationwide by the 2004 election. These glitch-riddled systems – many using "touch-screen" technology that leaves no paper trail at all – are almost laughably open to manipulation, according to corporate whistleblowers and computer scientists at Stanford, John Hopkins and other universities.

The technology had a trial run in the 2002 mid-term elections. In Georgia, serviced by new Diebold systems, a popular Democratic governor and senator were both unseated in what the media called "amazing" upsets, with results showing vote swings of up to 16 percent from the last pre-ballot polls. In computerized Minnesota, former vice president Walter Mondale – a replacement for popular incumbent Paul Wellstone, who died in a plane crash days before the vote – was also defeated in a large last-second vote swing. Convenient "glitches" in Florida saw an untold number of votes intended for the Democratic candidate registering instead for Governor Jeb "L'il Brother" Bush. A Florida Democrat who lost a similarly "glitched" local election went to court to have the computers examined – but the case was thrown out by a judge who ruled that the innards of America's voting machines are the "trade secrets" of the private companies who make them.

Who's behind these private companies? It's hard to tell: the corporate lines – even the bloodlines – of these "competitors" are so intricately mixed. For example, at Diebold – whose corporate chief, Wally O'Dell, a top Bush fundraiser, has publicly committed himself to "delivering" his home state's votes to Bush next year – the election division is run by Bob Urosevich. Bob's brother, Todd, is a top executive at "rival" ES&S. The brothers were originally staked in the vote-count business by Howard Ahmanson, a member of the Council for National Policy, a right-wing "steering group" stacked with Bushist faithful.

Ahmanson is also one of the bagmen behind the extremist "Christian Reconstructionist" movement [headed by R.J. Rushdoony], which openly advocates a theocratic takeover of American democracy, placing the entire society under the "dominion" of "Christ the King." This "dominion" includes the death penalty for homosexuals, exclusion of citizenship for non-Christians, stoning of sinners and – we kid you not – slavery, "one of the most beneficent of Biblical laws."

Ahmanson also has major holdings in ES&S, whose former CEO is Republican Senator Chuck Hagel of Nebraska. When Hagel ran for office, his own company counted the votes; needless to say, his initial victory was reported as "an amazing upset." Hagel still has a million-dollar stake in the parent company of ES&S. In Florida, Jeb Bush's first choice for a running mate in his 1998 gubernatorial race was ES&S lobbyist Sandra Mortham, who made a mint installing the machines that counted Jeb's votes.

Sequoia also has a colorful history, most recently in Louisiana, where it was the center of a massive corruption case that sent top state officials to jail for bribery, most of it funneled through Mob-connected front firms. Sequoia executives were also indicted, but escaped trial after giving immunized testimony against state officials. The UK-owned company's corporate parent is private equity firm Madison Dearborn – a partner of the Carlyle Group, where George Bush I makes millions trolling the world for war pork, privatizations and sweetheart deals with government insiders.

Meanwhile, the shadowy defense contractor SAIC has jumped into the vote-counting game, both directly and through spin-offs by its top brass, including Admiral Bill Owens – former military aide to Dick Cheney and Carlyle honcho Frank Carlucci – and ex-CIA chief Robert Gates. SAIC's history of fraud charges and security lapses in its electronic systems hasn't prevented it from becoming one of the largest contractors for the Pentagon and the CIA – and will doubtless pose little obstacle to its entrance into election engineering.

The mad rush to install unverifiable computer voting is driven by the Help America Vote Act, signed by Bush last year. The chief lobbying group pushing for HAVA was a consortium of arms dealers – those disinterested corporate citizens – including Northop-Grumman and Lockheed-Martin. The bill also mandates that all states adopt the computerized "ineligible voter purge" system which Jeb used to eliminate 91,000 ***eligible*** black voters from the Florida rolls in 2000. The Republican-run private company that accomplished this electoral miracle, ChoicePoint, is bagging the lion's share of the new Bush-ordered purge contracts.

The unelected Bush Regime now controls the government, the military, the judiciary – and the machinery of democracy itself. Absent some unlikely great awakening by the co-opted dullards of the corporate media, next November the last shreds of a genuine American republic will disappear – at the push of a button.

Furthermore, even if Mr. Bush *does* get voted out of office, or even becomes domestically impeached and removed from office, that alone won't overcome his war against secular international Law. His war is more important than the fate of just one man, or even than just one country. His war against the ICC can still be decisively defeated *only* by action of the ICC. Mr. Bush is no mere garden variety domestic tyrant; he's a threat to Man-made international Law, which is thus challenged to assert its authority, if it has any.

Moreover, if the new world of international law is really authentically *new*, then this time around, the blessed act of freeing a deceived people from their tyrant won't require them to be militarily defeated, as in the past, but will demand only their tyrant's international shaming; prosecution for his war crimes. It's like a "truth commission" imposed from the outside, by a body representing international opinion, rather than domestic opinion. Without that official declaration of international condemnation, by a court representing mankind itself, there might be no change, even if Mr. Bush does become forced out of office by domestic American politics. If force is no longer to be the only ultimate law, then there must, in any event, finally be introduced this voice of international Law that stands *beyond* force. Once this is introduced in practice, the International Criminal Court will be a reality, and not merely more of the same under a new name.

The ICC has the potential to succeed, but its time-window available to establish its authority will be brief, because President Bush has laid down the gauntlet to it immediately at its start, and only if the Court accepts that challenge, and prosecutes him, will the Court be able to achieve the necessary international credibility to succeed.

The advantage that the Court has is its ability to apply precedents from existing national courts; in effect, to create international law by its own decisions. However, if the Court fails to do that, and instead makes the foolish and unwarranted choice to wait until crucial legal crimes such as "aggression" become statutorily defined specifically for this Court, then its window of opportunity will close, and the Court will have committed suicide by passivity. This Court will have to be as aggressive in asserting its prerogatives as is the Bush Administration, or else it will quickly die. Unlike any national or other merely local court, it cannot rely upon a police force for establishing its credibility by the application of might; it must rely instead totally upon its moral authority, without reliance upon power. It is truly *post*-religious. Therefore, if it effectively fails to assert its moral authority, it will have none; it is nothing at all, and President Bush will, by the Court's inaction, have succeeded in re-establishing the Holy Roman Empire, with Washington as the new Rome, thus setting human political development back by more than a century.

Would a satisfactory substitute, instead of prosecuting Mr. Bush, be the ICC's prosecuting the British Prime Minister, Tony Blair? (This question applies irrespective of whether he's still in office at the time.) That would be punishing Mr. Blair for his having signed onto the Court's authority, and would be rewarding Mr. Bush for his having not done so and for his systematic campaign of war against that Court. Tony Blair is not at war against the United Nations and the ICC, so prosecuting him will do nothing to oppose George W. Bush's war against (Man-made) international Law, and assertion of (supposedly Christian God-made) divine Law – Bush's Holy American Empire.

It is only President Bush's United States that's demanding immunity from democratic international Law. And it is chiefly the United States that has violated international democracy in this invasion of Iraq. Moreover, the first decision that the ICC would have to make on any claim regarding this war would be to rule on whether or not the invasion itself was illegal. The Court, in the first case it takes up against Mr. Bush, would have to make that determination before it could proceed to any other issues concerning the war. Whether or not this invasion was illegal will powerfully affect any further judgments to be made concerning it. Only then can claims by the war's victims be appropriately judged. At that time, both the civilian and the military victims can have their cases presented against Mr. Bush.

For example, on August 5th, James W. Crawley of the San Diego *Union Tribune*, revealed, under the headline, "Officials Confirm Dropping Firebombs on Iraqi Troops: Results are 'remarkably similar' to using napalm," that: "American jets killed Iraqi troops with firebombs – similar to the controversial napalm used in the Vietnam War – in March and April as Marines battled toward Baghdad. ... The explosions created massive fireballs. ... 'We napalmed ... [bridge] approaches,' said Col. Randolph Alles in a recent interview. ... 'They were Iraqi soldiers there. It's no great way to die.'" At the war's start, the *Sydney Morning Herald* first raised this firebombing matter in a report by Lindsey Murdoch dated March 22nd, and headlined "'Dead Bodies Are Everywhere.'" It said that an unnamed "US officer told the Herald" American forces were entering Iraq "supported by US Navy aircraft which dropped 40,000 pounds of explosives and napalm" on Iraqi troops. "But a navy spokesman in Washington, Lieutenant Commander Danny Hernandez, denied that napalm – which was banned by a United Nations convention in 1980 – was used." The clear implication is that U.S. military brass were nervous about whether or not their use of a chemical agent indistinguishable from napalm might get them into trouble. Was this in accord with the laws of warfare? In an international democracy, only an International Criminal Court can make such a determination. During the Vietnam war, the ICC didn't exist. But now, it does.

Or does it, really? That is what's at stake.

And then, too, there's the issue of depleted uranium, which was used profusely in this invasion, and which might raise even *greater* questions of possible war crimes.

US forces' use of depleted uranium weapons is 'illegal'

By Neil Mackay, Investigations Editor
The Sunday Herald (Glasgow, Scotland), March 30, 2003

BRITISH and American coalition forces are using depleted uranium (DU) shells in the war against Iraq and deliberately flouting a United Nations resolution which classifies the munitions as illegal weapons of mass destruction.

DU contaminates land, causes ill-health and cancers among the soldiers using the weapons, the armies they target and civilians, leading to birth defects in children.

Professor Doug Rokke, ex-director of the Pentagon's depleted uranium project – a former professor of environmental science at Jacksonville University and onetime US army colonel who was tasked by the US department of defence with the post-first Gulf war depleted uranium desert clean-up – said use of DU was a 'war crime'.

Rokke said: 'There is a moral point to be made here. This war was about Iraq possessing illegal weapons of mass destruction – yet we are using weapons of mass destruction ourselves.' He added: 'Such double-standards are repellent.'

The latest use of DU in the current conflict came on Friday when an American A10 tankbuster plane fired a DU shell, killing one British soldier and injuring three others in a 'friendly fire' incident.

According to a August 2002 report by the UN subcommission, laws which are breached by the use of DU shells include: the Universal Declaration of Human Rights; the Charter of the United Nations; the Genocide Convention; the Convention Against Torture; the four Geneva Conventions of 1949; the Conventional Weapons Convention of 1980; and the Hague Conventions of 1899 and 1907, which expressly forbid employing 'poison or poisoned weapons' and 'arms, projectiles or materials calculated to cause unnecessary suffering'. All of these laws are designed to spare civilians from unwarranted suffering in armed conflicts.

DU has been blamed for the effects of Gulf war syndrome – typified by chronic muscle and joint pain, fatigue and memory loss – among 200,000 US soldiers after the 1991 conflict.

It is also cited as the most likely cause of the 'increased number of birth deformities and cancer in Iraq' following the first Gulf war.

'Cancer appears to have increased between seven and 10 times and deformities between four and six times,' according to the UN subcommission.

...

Should such issues continue to be dealt with in the old might-makes-right way, or should they be decided instead by *Man*-made international Law – the new, post-WWII, U.N. path? If the ICC does not act on these issues, it will thereby be answering this question, by default, in favor of might-makes-right, and will, in effect, be thereby committing suicide.

How much credibility, and how much moral legitimacy, will an international criminal court have if, by its inaction, it effectively immunizes one country or a group of countries? None, because unequal justice is no justice at all, and everyone knows this.

Furthermore, there's something important that conservatives especially don't understand: if one nation is to stand above international Law, then every nation will have contempt for international Law, because justice that is unequal is fake "justice" and will have no moral authority whatsoever. That's why *any* "Holy Empire" is intrinsically evil.

A world driven by science rather than by religion can never accept the right of one people to *rule over* another. The only "empire" that's acceptable to a modern and forward-looking mentality is mutually voluntary, never one that is imposed by force. It is therefore no actual *empire* at all, and the members have chosen to join only because it benefits everyone who joins it. That, for example, is the reason why countries join the United Nations. Membership in the U.N. is not obligatory; it's entirely voluntary. This is why virtually no one even thinks to *call* the United Nations an "empire"; it's the *antithesis* of empire, though it is obviously global, and obviously also political. For example, among the countries that have, for various reasons, not (as yet) chosen to join the United Nations, are Switzerland, Nauru, Aruba, and Kyrgyzstan. Switzerland even contributes more money, per capita, to the U.N. than does the United States. Yet, still, the Swiss do not wish to join. Monaco chose for almost forty years not to belong to the U.N., but finally changed its mind and joined in 1993. Nobody ever *forces* any nation to join the United Nations. That's why it is truly *not* an empire.

As was said earlier, George W. Bush is the Christian Osama bin Laden, and both are united in their respective imperial wars against international democracy. Their common war pits a Christian global theocratic vision against an Islamic global theocratic vision, but both sides stand *united as one* in their global theocratic vision; both sides are enemies of democracy; and if the democrats of the world will not unite against *both* sides of that shared vision, then this century will be a very dark one indeed. Many people don't understand what is at stake, nor what the invasion of Iraq is really about.

Man's theocratic past is warring against Man's democratic future, and Mr. Bush has chosen Iraq as his main battlefield to swipe the scepter of rule out of the hands of the heirs of Thomas Jefferson and of America's other great Founders, and to restore it once again to the heirs of the Emperor Charlemagne. Actually, the original vision goes even back to the first Christian Emperor, Constantine. U.S. President Bush is looking to undo not only the progress of the past more-than-fifty years, but the progress of the American nation itself, reverting to the governmental system that the American Revolution had battled to defeat. America's Founders didn't give their blood in order to establish a global American dictatorship, but rather to *free* the American people from such foreign tyrants as this.

If the conclusion here seems odd, then perhaps that is only because raw honesty about politics is odd. But what better place is there to break such a taboo than in journalism? Thus, it's appropriate to break that taboo here and now. George W. Bush, in the Twenty First Century, is nothing else than an international war criminal. Practically, and morally, he ought to be treated like one.

Among the dangers of failing to do so would be a further deterioration of the global economy. As *Business Week* reported, on June 2, 2003, under the heading of "A World of Hurt: The G-8's Challenge": "There are signs that the rancor over Iraq is spilling over into the economic arena. Rather than pulling together to rev up the global economy, the U.S. and its industrialized allies look increasingly to be going their own way." CNN headlined, on June 1st, from the G-8 Conference at Evian, France, "Iraq War Shadow Over G-8," and noted, "The G-8 summit is about personal chemistry" – and this was an acidic chemistry, as the aspiring Emperor Bush sought to dictate to what he viewed to be his recalcitrant vassal kings: German Chancellor Helmut Schroeder, and French President Jacques Chirac. The structure of international law and commerce that was set up at the end of World War II is collapsing on account of resentments created by Mr. Bush's scheme to establish his Holy American Empire. Countries that cannot retaliate militarily can still find economic ways to express their hurts. Needless economic conflicts like these mean needless economic damages, and needless retaliations.

This can even reach into the military sphere: on September 2nd, the Belgian Prime Minister announced that a final agreement had been reached by four NATO nations – Belgium, Luxembourg, France, and Germany – to establish in Belgium the headquarters for a new European military alliance without the United States; this means that NATO's days are numbered. Mr. Bush alone is to blame for this.

Opening remarks of Zbigniew Brzezinski, the former U.S. National Security Adviser and current Counselor and Trustee for the Center for Strategic and International Studies, given at the conference "New American Strategies for Security and Peace," in Washington, D.C., October 28, 2003:

Ladies and gentlemen, forty years ago almost to the day an important Presidential emissary was sent abroad by a beleaguered President of the United States. The United States was facing the prospect of nuclear war. These were the days of the Cuban Missile Crisis.

Several emissaries went to our principal allies. One of them was a tough-minded former Secretary of State, Dean Acheson whose mission was to brief [French] President [Charles] De Gaulle and to solicit French support in what could be a nuclear war involving not just the United States and the Soviet Union but the entire NATO Alliance and the Warsaw Pact.

The former Secretary of State briefed the French President and then said to him at the end of the briefing, I would now like to show you the evidence, the photographs that we have of Soviet missiles armed with nuclear weapons. The French President responded by saying, I do not wish to see the photographs. The word of the President of the United States is good enough for me. Please tell him that France stands with America.

Would any foreign leader today react the same way to an American emissary who would go abroad and say that country X is armed with weapons of mass destruction which threaten the United States? There's food for thought in that question. ...

Better by far is to re-assert the edifice, so painstakingly constructed after World War II, of decidedly Man-made international Law. U.S. President Bush is its sorest test ever. For the world to fail this test would be dangerous and needless folly, capping this needless and tragic war.

Although America's great Founders tried to defeat the ancient theocratic system, they actually only just started; they won their battle, but not this bigger ideological war.

If that war of America's founding is a game, the game goes on. More than two centuries later, the ball is now across the Atlantic, in Europe's court, finally now in mankind's Court, the International Criminal Court in the Hague. Will they pick it up and run with it, or will they simply defer to the self-assigned American Christian Emperor of the world, and just hand this ball, of Man's future, back to this tyrant, to destroy?

The International Criminal Court represents international democracy, and all of us are citizens of the world.

Or are we? If we have a voice in this matter, where will it be heard? Is final redress really only to God, to pray? Or, if to Man, then where, and how? We all have a stake in Man's future. But do we have a *voice* in it, as well? Where, then, can our voice be heard?

The public information office of the ICC can be reached at pio@icc-cpi.int.

NOTE: Regarding U.S. Iraqi Policy Looking Forward

I sent this e-mail to U.S. presidential candidate Howard Dean on September 1, 2003:

Subject: Your assertion that U.S. troops should stay in Iraq.
Dear Gov./Dr. Dean:

In your interview with Fred Hiatt concerning the Iraq war, appearing in the *Washington Post* on August 25th, you said, "Now that we're there, we're stuck," and "We have no choice" but to keep U.S. troops there until "we get a democracy in Iraq."

That comment is much like one's having said of Vietnam, during the Vietnam War, "Now that we're there, we're stuck," and so we have to stay until we win. I hope that you will agree that this thinking was wrong then, and that, upon further reflection, you recognize that it's wrong now.

The sooner we get out, the less disastrous it will be that we got in.

The best that we can now *realistically* hope for from this invasion is for whatever government that emerges in Iraq to respond favorably to a conditional offer from us of reconstruction assistance, an offer that's made *conditional* upon Iraq's government's waging, essentially, a war against the extremist/terrorist fundamentalist Islamic groups now pouring into Iraq, groups that constitute a genuine, major, and enduring, threat to U.S. security. The fundamentalists inside Iraq are also receiving help from some outside Islamic countries, and the U.S. should provide help to any Iraqi government that seeks to defeat those fundamentalists. We might possess resources sufficient to win that way, but not the existing way (i.e., not by means of our troops occupying Iraq).

We cannot choose Iraq's government, but we can offer *incentives* to whatever government ends up in that country. Only *we* can provide such huge cash, and are tragically obliged to by Bush's invasion.

We should offer very generous financial assistance indeed to any such government, but *ONLY IF* they vigorously attack supporters of Al Qaeda there. It's our only constructive way forward.

The U.S. is legally obliged, *as* the invader, to offer this aid, but *ONLY if* the Iraqi government suppresses anti-U.S. terrorism. If Iraq's government complies with this American need, then the perhaps hundreds of billions of dollars that America will be obliged to provide to Iraq will be purchasing improvements for *both* the Iraqi and the American peoples. This will cost far less than continued military occupation, and will be vastly more effective toward serving both American and Iraqi interests.

It is the most that can now be salvaged from the catastrophic mess that Bush got us into.

As long as we will be trying instead to *impose* in Iraq a government that's acceptable to us, the result will be essentially what we had in Vietnam when we were insisting upon propping up there a government that was acceptable to us: it will make our self-imposed disaster there even worse.

Your statement to Fred Hiatt was ill considered and ought to be retracted. Similarly, our troops inside Iraq should be soon extracted.

Wielding the stick will inevitably fail, where offering the carrot *might* succeed. But in any case, it's the *best* way out.

Sincerely,
Eric Zuesse

I received no reply.

Unfortunately, it's not enough merely to recognize when something was done that ought *not* to have been done. A leader needs to go beyond that, and frequently has to make decisions as to how best to extricate the organization – or, in this case, country – that he leads, from *existing* bad situations. That is certainly the case here.

There are no *good* options for the United States in Iraq. Instead, the real question – for the best interests of both the U.S. and Iraqi people – is: What is the *least bad* option?

That question, and that challenge, will be one of the great tests of the American President going forward.

George W. Bush has gotten the United States (and the entire world) into a very big mess. Dealing with the many problems that the worst president in U.S. history has created will test not merely the ICC and the world. It will very much – and most especially – test the United States itself.

Army War College Study Blasts U.S. War on Terrorism

By Will Dunham, Mon., Jan. 12, 2004

WASHINGTON, (Reuters) – The Iraq invasion was "an unnecessary preventive war of choice" that has robbed resources and attention from the more critical fight against al Qaeda in a hopeless U.S. quest for absolute security, according to a study recently published by the U.S. Army War College. [It's at: www.carlisle.army.mil/ssi/pubs/2003/bounding/bounding.htm.]

The 56-page document written by Jeffrey Record, a veteran defense expert who serves as a visiting research professor at the Strategic Studies Institute of the Army War College, represents a blistering assessment of what President Bush calls the U.S. global war on terrorism.

Pentagon officials on Monday said Record was entitled to his opinion, but reiterated Bush's view that Iraq is the "central front" in the war on terrorism. ...

FROM THAT STUDY: *"The global war on terrorism as currently defined and waged is dangerously indiscriminate, ... strategically unfocused, promises much more than it can deliver, and threatens to dissipate U.S. military and other resources. ... The United States may be able to defeat, even destroy, al-Qaeda, but it cannot rid the world of terrorism, much less evil."*

APPENDIX

A Plea From Iraq: The Weblog of an Iraqi

http://riverbendblog.blogspot.com/2003_08_01_riverbendblog_archive.html

Baghdad Burning

... I'll meet you 'round the bend my friend, where hearts can heal and souls can mend. ...

Sunday, August 24, 2003

Will Work for Food...

Over 65% of the Iraqi population is unemployed. The reason for this is because Bremer made some horrible decisions. The first major decision he made was to dissolve the Iraqi army. That may make sense in Washington, but here, we were left speechless. Now there are over 400,000 trained, armed men with families that need to be fed. Where are they supposed to go? What are they supposed to do for a living? I don't know. They certainly don't know.

They roam the streets looking for work, looking for an answer. You can see perplexity and anger in their stance, their walk, their whole demeanor. Their eyes shift from face to face, looking for a clue. Who is to answer for this mess? Who do you think?

Bremer also dissolved the Ministry of Information and the Ministry of Defense. No matter what the excuses, these ministries were full of ordinary people with ordinary jobs--accountants, janitors, secretaries, engineers, journalists, technicians, operators ... these people are now jobless. Companies have been asked to 'cut down' their staff. It no longer has anything to do with politics. The company my uncle works in as an engineer was asked by the CPA to get rid of 680 of the 1,500+ employees--engineers, designers, contractors, mechanics, technicians and the administration were all involved.

Other companies, firms, bureaus, factories and shops shut down as a result of the looting and damage done in the post-war chaos--thousands of other workers lost their jobs. Where to go? What to do?

It isn't any easier for employed people ... the standard $50 being given out in various ministries and hospitals is not nearly enough to support a single person, let alone a family. But at least it is work. At least it is a reason to wake up every morning and accomplish something.

Someone asked why the thousands of Iraqi men roaming the streets don't go out and get work. For weeks, after the occupation, men would line up daily by the thousands outside of the 'Alwiyah Club' filling out papers, begging for work. But there is no work. Men were reluctant to apply to the Iraqi police force because they weren't given weapons! The Iraqi police were expected to roam and guard the hellish cities without weapons ... to stop looters, abductors, and murderers with the sheer force of an application to their warped sense of morality.

The story of how I lost my job isn't unique. It has actually become very common--despondently, depressingly, unbearably common:

I'm a computer science graduate. Before the war, I was working in an Iraqi database/software company located in Baghdad as a programmer/ network administrator (yes, yes ... a geek). Every day, I would climb three flights of stairs, enter the little office I shared with one female colleague and two males, start up my PC and spend hours staring at little numbers and letters rolling across the screen. It was tedious, it was back-breaking, it was geeky and it was ... wonderful.

When I needed a break, I'd go visit my favorite sites on the internet, bother my colleagues or rant about 'impossible bosses' and 'improbable deadlines'.

I loved my job--I was *good* at my job. I came and went to work on my own. At 8 am I'd walk in lugging a backpack filled with enough CDs, floppies, notebooks, chewed-on pens, paperclips and screwdrivers to make Bill Gates proud. I made as much money as my two male colleagues and got an equal amount of respect from the manager (that was because he was clueless when it came to any type of programming and anyone who could do it was worthy of respect ... a girl, no less--you get the picture).

What I'm trying to say is that no matter *what* anyone heard, females in Iraq were a lot better off than females in other parts of the Arab world (and some parts of the Western world--we had equal salaries!). We made up over 50% of the working force. We were doctors, lawyers, nurses, teachers, professors, deans, architects, programmers, and more. We came and went as we pleased. We wore what we wanted (within the restrictions of a conservative society).

During the first week of June, I heard my company was back in business. It took several hours, seemingly thousands of family meetings, but I finally convinced everyone that it was necessary for my **sanity** to go back to work. They agreed that I would visit the company (with my two male bodyguards) and ask them if they had any work I could possibly take home and submit later on, or through the internet.

One fine day in mid-June, I packed my big bag of geeky wonders, put on my long skirt and shirt, tied back my hair and left the house with a mixture of anticipation and apprehension.

We had to park the car about 100 meters away from the door of the company because the major road in front of it was cracked and broken with the weight of the American tanks as they entered Baghdad. I half-ran, half-plodded up to the door of the company, my heart throbbing in anticipation of seeing friends, colleagues, secretaries ... just generally something familiar again in the strange new nightmare we were living.

The moment I walked through the door, I noticed it. Everything looked shabbier somehow--sadder. The maroon carpet lining the hallways was dingy, scuffed and spoke of the burden of a thousand rushing feet. The windows we had so diligently taped prior to the war were cracked in some places and broken in others ... dirty all over. The lights were shattered, desks overturned, doors kicked in, and clocks torn from the walls.

I stood a moment, hesitantly, in the door. There were strange new faces--fewer of the old ones. Everyone was standing around, looking at everyone else. The faces were sad and lethargic and exhausted. And I was one of the only females. I weaved through the strange mess and made my way upstairs, pausing for a moment on the second floor where management was located, to listen to the rising male voices. The director had died of a stroke during the second week of the war and suddenly, we had our own little 'power vacuum'. At least 20 different men thought they were qualified to be boss. Some thought they qualified because of experience, some because of rank and some because they were being backed by differing political parties (SCIRI, Al-Daawa, INC).

I continued upstairs, chilled to the bone, in spite of the muggy heat of the building which hadn't seen electricity for at least 2 months. My little room wasn't much better off than the rest of the building. The desks were gone, papers all over the place ... but A. was there! I couldn't believe it--a familiar, welcoming face. He looked at me for a moment, without really seeing me, then his eyes opened wide and disbelief took over the initial vague expression. He congratulated me on being alive, asked about my family and told me that he wasn't coming back after today. Things had changed. I should go home and stay safe. He was quitting--going to find work abroad. Nothing to do here anymore. I told him about my plan to work at home and submit projects ... he shook his head sadly.

I stood staring at the mess for a few moments longer, trying to sort out the mess in my head, my heart being torn to pieces. My cousin and E. were downstairs waiting for me--there was nothing more to do, except ask how I could maybe help? A. and I left the room and started making our way downstairs. We paused on the second floor and stopped to talk to one of the former department directors. I asked him when they thought things would be functioning, he wouldn't look at me. His eyes stayed glued to A.'s face as he told him that females weren't welcome right now--especially females who 'couldn't be protected'. He finally turned to me and told me, in so many words, to go home because 'they' refused to be responsible for what might happen to me.

Ok. Fine. Your loss. I turned my back, walked down the stairs and went to find E. and my cousin. Suddenly, the faces didn't look strange--they were the same faces as before, mostly, but there was a hostility I couldn't believe. What was I doing here? E. and the cousin were looking grim. I must have been looking broken, because they rushed me out of the first place I had ever worked and to the car. I cried bitterly all the way home--cried for my job, cried for my future and cried for the torn streets, damaged buildings and crumbling people.

I'm one of the lucky ones. I'm not important. I'm not vital. Over a month ago, a prominent electrical engineer (one of the smartest females in the country) named Henna Aziz was assassinated in front of her family--two daughters and her husband. She was threatened by some fundamentalists from Badir's Army and told to stay at home because she was a woman, she shouldn't be in charge. She refused--the country needed her expertise to get things functioning--she was brilliant. She would not and could not stay at home. They came to her house one evening: men with machine-guns, broke in and opened fire. She lost her life--she wasn't the first, she won't be the last.

Saturday, August 23, 2003

We've Only Just Begun...

Females can no longer leave their homes alone. Each time I go out, E. and either a father, uncle or cousin has to accompany me. It feels like we've gone back 50 years ever since the beginning of the occupation. A woman, or girl, out alone, risks anything from insults to abduction. An outing has to be arranged at least an hour beforehand. I state that I need to buy something or have to visit someone. Two males have to be procured (preferably large) and 'safety arrangements' must be made in this total state of lawlessness. And always the question: "But do you have to go out and buy it? Can't I get it for you?" No you can't, because the kilo of eggplant I absolutely have to select with my own hands is just an excuse to see the light of day and walk down a street. The situation is incredibly frustrating to females who work or go to college.

Before the war, around 50% of the college students were females, and over 50% of the working force was composed of women. Not so anymore. We are seeing an increase of fundamentalism in Iraq which is terrifying. ...

Thursday, January 15, 2004

Shari'a and Family Law...

On Wednesday our darling Iraqi Puppet Council decided [it was actually decided behind closed doors December 29th, and was only made public January 14th] that secular Iraqi family law would no longer be secular--it is now going to be according to Islamic Shari'a. ...

The news has barely been covered by Western or even Arab media and Iraqi media certainly aren't covering it. ... This latest decision is going to be catastrophic for females--we're going backwards. ...

Under the Iraqi constitution, men and women are equal. Under our past secular family law (which has been in practice since the '50s) women had unalterable divorce, marriage, inheritance, custody, and alimony rights. All of this is going to change. ... Women are outraged...

I usually ignore the emails I receive telling me to 'embrace' my new-found freedom and be happy that the circumstances of all Iraqi women are going to 'improve drastically' from what we had before. They quote Bush (which in itself speaks volumes) saying things about how repressed the Iraqi women were and how, now, they are going to be able to live free lives.

The people who write those emails often lob Iraq together with Saudi Arabia, Iran and Afghanistan and I shake my head at their ignorance. ... But I'm telling everyone now--if I get any more emails about how free and liberated the Iraqi women are *now* thanks to America, they can expect a very nasty answer.

REFERENCES/SOURCES

All of the sources in this book are cited in the text at the place where they are being used. The characteristic manner of citation here is by means of a quotation (which may be a headline), and its date, and the name of the news-medium where it first appeared. (Sometimes, a fourth item is included: the author's name.) Those three items employed together in a web-search will normally bring up the source. (Of course, it's important to place each of the items between quotation-marks for this search. Where a given quotation is long, you might want to use instead the briefest unusual succession of words that are in that quote, or two or three such sub-quotations.) Occasionally, a specific web-address is cited. However, since those often have only a brief life-span, the three-item citation is more commonly employed here.

Another advantage of citing sources in this manner is that for the reader, a news-headline and/or other quotation from a news report will typically have more immediacy, and will always be closer to the facts that are being reported, than will any mere paraphrase, such as writers more traditionally employ. Furthermore, the traditional approach of paraphrasing sources introduces a needless additional basis for inaccuracy: paraphrases can distort/misrepresent sources.

Now with the advent of the Internet, this writer believes that it is irresponsible to continue using the old academic citation-method, which relies instead upon the reader's having access to a first-rate, typically academic, physical library. That method is grossly inconsiderate to most readers, and needlessly inconvenient to all readers. Unlike traditional books, the sole purpose here is to serve the reader. Virtually every fact that is presented in this work can be accessed more readily via the internet than via a physical library. This book, thus, is designed for readers in the current computer age.

My aim has been to facilitate the reader's learning more about anything that interests him here. By providing the search-string to get to any source immediately, this computer-age referencing system gives readers access to other documents that have mentioned that source. The traditional system of documentation should, I think, no longer be generally used; it is inferior in every practical respect; it is archaic.

INDEX